WOMEN IN THE RĀMKATHĀS

WOMEN IN THE RĀMKATHĀS
Silent Voices and Untold Stories

Atreyi Biswas

GYAN

ISBN : 978-81-2121-312-7
Price : ₹ 625

First Published 2015

Published by

Gyan Publishing House
5, Ansari Road, Darya Ganj
New Delhi-110002
Mob: 9811692060
E-mail: books@gyanbooks.com
Website : www.gyanbooks.com

Laser Typesetting : Abhishek Mandal, Delhi
Printed at : G. Print Process, Delhi

Cataloging in Publication Data—DK
Courtesy: D.K. Agencies (P) Ltd. <docinfo@dkagencies.com>

Biswas, Atreyi, author.
Women in the Ramkathas : silent voices and untold stories / Atreyi Biswas.
pages cm
Includes bibliographical references and index.
ISBN 9788121213127

1. Valmiki. Ramayanòa. 2. Indic literature—History and criticism. 3. Sita (Hindu deity) in literature. 4. Women in literature. 5. Women—India—Social conditions. I. Title.

BL1139.27.B57 2015 DDC 294.5922046 23

Dedicated to the three lovely women of my family,
Mahua, Anu and Noyona

Contents

Acknowledgements

During my long academic career of over fifty years, part of which I had the good fortune of consulting collections of several valuable printed sources on Indian epic literature, history and culture at the British Library, including India Office Library and Records, and the library of the School of Oriental and African Studies, London in the early sixties while working on my first publication, *The Hunas in Ancient India* (1976). This was followed by my other useful book, *Famines in Ancient India* (2000) for which I was consulting various types of documents on relevant topics at the libraries of India International Centre, Central Secretariat Library, Archaeological Survey of India, National Museum, New Delhi and the Indian Institute of Advanced Study, Shimla. It was during this period, the idea of working on the status of women in Indian society, as originally depicted in the two epics, especially on Sita, as presented in different variants of the story of Rama, *Rāmāyanas* or *Rāmakathās* developed.

Right from the beginning of literature search followed by the actual search for the texts, I had to take the help of several individuals and libraries as these were not available in one library or institution. I am grateful to Dr Anil Tyagi, a former student and colleague of mine for lending me several volumes of different variants of the *Rāmāyana* from his personal collection. Ms. Charanjeet Singh of Central Secretariat Library who sometimes, went out of her way to locate a book or to make extensive search of library catalogues and bibliographies to meet my demands. There are also some extremely valuable collection of back volumes of journals on Indian history and culture at the Indian Institute of Advanced Study, Shimla which

I had the good fortune of consulting while I was at the Institute for a short duration in 2012. I am thankful to the staff of the Institute for extending their whole hearted support for making my stay there very fruitful and enjoyable. I am indeed highly indebted to the staff of the India International Centre Library for their continuous help on so many occasions, such as, in locating a book or some journal article, from the stack or borrowing a title through inter-library loan facilities from some other libraries. I would also like to acknowledge the love and kind help extended by Manju Khanna and Usha Kataria for extending help in Romanization of Sanskrit words, checking bibliographical references and much more. They were always ready and made themselves readily available to discuss with me some of my problems, at a very short notice. I deeply acknowledge my debt to Sudha Menon whose skilled editorial eye spotted a number of inefficiencies in the original version of the typescript which I hope, I have managed to eliminate. Last but not the least, I would like to express my gratitude to my husband, Subhas for his untiring support and encouragement throughout my entire academic career and life.

Atreyi Biswas

Preface

The *Rāmāyana* is a venerated religious text of the Hindus, which was communicated orally over a long period and then composed in literary forms by elite scholars and imaginative poets, and was sung in various forms by folk-musicians. The *Rāmāyana* can be comprehended purely as a book of religious studies, paying due respect to its mythological characters. Religion can be studied in various forms—its ceremonial observances, symbols, philosophy and myth. Even interpreting a particular religious text falls under its purview. Orthodox religious studies are primarily committed for the purpose of spiritual benefit; and theological discussions are one of the many such activities. To study religion as a discipline, a scholar would not have any liability other than to provide a logical analysis of all the matters in question, more in their scientific and sociological contexts. The study of religions may or may not be confined to any specific religion and its relevant practices and rituals but a complex, multi-disciplinary, objective explanation of contemporary society related to time and space notions only. Such academic study would necessarily deal with the topic 'religion' in its pluralistic arrangements. For the 'study of religions', academics are to focus on society, in its historical context, and seek to combine neutrality with the originality of both the scholars and believers because it looks at religions as historically rooted with magnetically changing relations. A scholar distinguishes his task from that of the incidents of miracles, theology and philosophy.

The job of a historian is to give more judicious analyses, including all the aspects and their inter-relationships, as presented in the text.

A historian endeavours to bring back to life the subsequent stages of development of society, which has created the background for the evolution of a particular religion and its relevant texts. Every religious text is studied in a wide-ranging formation of society. These texts are interpreted and reinterpreted, according to changed concepts, beliefs and principles. Modification of religions was closely related to the degree to which man advances rationally and increases his knowledge (Waardenburg, J., 1973:29). His concepts follow his vision. The role of thought in shaping the culture of a society must be properly understood. Although the established mode of production provides the basis of a culture, religious ideas also play a prominent role in the overall social transition process.

Society, with its developing and changing subsistence economy, and the resultant political remodelling, has a parallel evolution of religious ideas and conceptions. The fundamental idea is that religion is a socio-economic phenomenon. Thoughts are both products and producers of cultures. When the culturally acquired idea and principles of a society fail to answer the growing material or intellectual demands of a sizable section of its members adequately, an objective state, necessītāting the exploration and approval of ideas and ideals are created (Chattopadhyaya, D.P., 1992:11). Historians work within a conceptual framework, which determines the subject matter and sheds light on the sphere of history in question. A historian is concerned with some facts, based on some evidences when dealing with the socio-cultural developmental process of continuity by bringing in missing links. She/He handles a large amount of material dealing with rituals, symbols, rites, philosophical interpretations, ideas and myths. The epic *Rāmāyana* formed the most crucial chronicle, carrying images of society. We need to study it in depth, to dig into the layers of myth and discover reality. It provides a veritable depository of events, views, ideals, customs, codes and variations from traditions as well as the consequences of these bones of contention on various stages of social development, broadly changing according to the age/region/caste bifurcations of the author. It has been instrumental in producing an orthodox role model for successive age groups.

The *Rāmāyana* presents an unarguable definition of *dharma.* The core story of the *Rāmāyana* is based on mythological characters, who are the sustainers of *dharma*. These two concepts—mythology and *dharma*—need some clarification in the very beginning. In the mythology of *Rāmāyana*, there are benevolent characters, who were the protectors of *dharma*, and evil characters, who were bent upon disrupting *dharma.* Myths express many different things to different people, depending on the text. It can be a 'false belief' too. In the nineteenth century, the meaning of the word 'myth' was 'fable' or 'fiction'. Now 'myth' meant a 'true story' and a story that is a most precious possession because it is hallowed, exemplary and meaningful (Eliad, M., 1959:68). To a historian of religion, this means "sacred tradition, ancient reports and an exemplary model." The 'actors' of a myth are considered to be supernatural beings. Theologians and performers of religious rituals justify pursuing the examples of mythological heroes because they are the manifestations of a sacred power. For a believer, myth reveals the nature of the divine. Notionally, a mythical hero is believed to be an agent through whom the sacredness is manifested, to be an object of worship. On the other hand, a historian's approach would be to reject these myth-based stories and characters as historical truth or reality. For them 'myth' represents an obscure recollection of brilliant achievements of the early kings; in literary works, myths are nothing but the allegorical interpretations of some natural phenomenon. The truth of myth is not the truth of reason but the truth of faith. This is what one may call the prevailing value of 'myth'.

Rituals, rites and symbols are important information for understanding the history of religion. A theologian concentrates on this aspect of study. A historian utilises these data to understand the ideas and values of the society under survey. The philosophy of religion is the most important aspect in this field of study. Philosophy verifies the survival of religion. It explains the truth behind the religion, with the object of presenting a critical reflection. It clarifies that religion is not only a fantasy or an emotional temptation but also answers to the most severe analysis of reason. Religion is still the main theme. The transcendental self-experience in life and its theoretical criterion can be assessed critically with its philosophical explanation. This falls under the purview of theosophical studies and forms an important part of it. The first and foremost thing to reckon with is that, in our present study, we are not going to focus 'religion in the abstract' but will concentrate on the people, who follow the religion. Our approach is to critically evaluate historical data and to examine logical inconsistencies, if any, in the religious traditions of the Hindus. In this project, an attempt has been made to analyse and identify major historical developments and fundamental problems, which explicitly and implicitly, focus on socio-religious criteria that supervised gender relations and reveal the state of consequences it had specially on women.

Rama, the mythological hero of our text and upholder of *dharma*, was elevated to Godhood in the process of its evolution. From a heroic character of its earlier phase, he was converted to an *avatāra*, or incarnation of God, himself. He was projected as the guardian of *dharma*. Broadly, 'religion' can be termed as equivalent to the Sanskrit '*dharma*'. Whenever a notion is translated into a foreign language, we have a problem of not being able to translate adequately the conceptual acumen that exists in that language. *Dharma* is one of those Sanskrit words that eludes all attempts at an accurate rendering in English or any other tongue. Etymologically, the word *dharma* is derived from the root *dhr*, meaning 'to uphold', 'to sustain', which indicates that *dharma* is that which 'upholds and sustain' (Kane, P.V., 1930:1). But the established meaning in a particular era differed according to its context. In Vedic texts, *dharma* signifies 'religious rituals' (*Ṛgveda* I. 87.1; *Ait.Br.* xi.9.17). In the Upanisadic literature, three types of '*dharma*' are referred to, (a) rituals *(yajña)*, (b) study of the scriptures (*adhyayana*) and (c) austerities (*tapas*) (*Chh.Up.* ii.33.1). Gradually, it came to mean the prevalent religious-ethical duties and conduct in a society of a particular period. The rational basis of *dharma* is often in harmony with the supple interpretations of the various scriptures. Sometimes, the *dharma* of a particular social class contradicts the *dharma* of another social group or sect. There is, therefore, no hard and fast rule of defining *dharma*. And to translate

'Hindu *dharma*' as 'Hindu religion' will bring more ambiguity than clarification. We prefer to use *'dharma'* throughout the text.

Similarly, the Western conception of 'God' as the source of religion is not appropriate in the Hindu context. Usually, the Sanskrit terminology *Brahman*, or *Īśvara*, are used for the word God. The Western God definitely has a male profile. In Hindu mythology, the concept of *Brahman* is a neuter gender, and the male form, *Īśvara*, has a feminine consort, *Īśvaraī*—an equally important concept, sometimes, ideologically, even more important. Without the associated female phenomenon, the male idea of *Īśvara* becomes inactive and redundant. Therefore, we reject the idea of using 'God' as a substitute of *Brahman, Īśvara* or *Īśvaraī*. *Brahman* and *Īśvara* (including the feminine form, *Īśvaraī*) are not considered to be the source of *dharma*, as 'God' is in Western thought. *Dharma* originated from 'power' (or *Śakti*) and, historically, *dharma* has been used to express 'power'. To the people of antiquity, power originates from that Super-human Being. And even if power is not explicitly ascribed a name, the idea behind the term 'power' forms the basis of religion. The world and its processes are merely a display of the invisible, eternally sustained, motivating 'power'. Vedic poets called it *Ṛta,* the Law of the Universe, identical with the moral law. In the primitive world, the king is the power-bearer and, indeed, is in one of the oldest 'image' of 'God' as the power incorporated in a living emblem. It is very likely that earlier kings were passively strong individuals but their efficacy as power-bearers was conjectured from elsewhere. A king represented the good and beneficial power of God in general. But primitive people experienced the terrifying and devastating power of the world as well. Dismay, trepidation, vagueness and obscurity gave shape to the concept of the demon. The demonic figure emerges from extremely assorted exposures—the confused mass of unknown land, the isolation of the mountainous regions, the forests outside human settlements—all these experiences of nature contributed to the creation of demonic forms. The volatility of nature and its cosmological simplifications such as floods or droughts were metamorphosed into demons and witches. Sometimes, the people of antiquity fostered partial or unconfirmed beliefs in far-fetched tales about far-flung lands. The idea of myth-making is real enough in war time—when enemies are portrayed in the darkest colour. All myths are not the results of ignorance, enmity or hero-worship. Poetry and folklore and art too have supplemented mythology, as myths find a permanent place in the emotional and spiritual lives of the community. God represented the sensible and ethical side of human society and infinite mysterious aspects of life whereas the antitheses of God are the demons and the devils. In mythological concepts, good always triumphs over evil. Deities are aligned with traditional concepts of light, preservation of universal order and the welfare of humanity whereas their rivals are represented as demons and devils, planning to encroach on the place of God.

Evaluation of Sources

To study the status of women, one must consider the myths related with women in the *Rāmakathā*. The most glaring myth is that the role of gender—male and female—is determined by nature rather than by the society. In the ancient world, it was largely believed that gender roles are biologically decided and thus unchangeable. These theories justified a widespread male dominance system. Women had a tacit part to play, namely, motherhood and homemaking—tasks relegated to humbleness and roles considered not worth reporting. Men controlled their destinies. Women were placed to serve as witnesses. Their weaknesses—physical, mental and moral—were highlighted. In reality, the history of women is the history of their ongoing activity in the perimeter of male boundaries of morality. Undoubtedly, men have historically been both—the main initiators and the practitioners of writing. Most of the written material resources, in the form of scriptures, literary compositions or even epigraphs of ancient times were by male composers. Kum Kum Roy (1999a:3–4) observes that there was an undeviating endeavour to make women invisible in history so that their contribution is met by boundless silence. Women are viewed as passive receptacles with their 'status' or 'positions' changing, to reflect the state of the world around them. Men have also decided the definitions of notions such as good, evil, sanity, insanity and, of course, masculinity and femininity. Leela Dube (1986: a: Intro. 1) categorically criticises by saying, "incomplete and one sided understanding is distorted understanding. By ignoring women as social actors, who contribute to continuity and change in society, the social sciences have seriously impaired their understanding of the total social reality." She recommends, "On the whole, there is a strong advocacy for the need to look into women's lives, attend to the arenas in which women function, and to emphasise women's perceptions and subjective experiences." We must accept these specific parameters when interpreting feminine characters in classical literary texts that also reflect a feminist standpoint. This would likely be considered a more balanced approach to any literary criticism.

Textual evidences, which are the depository of our trust in the evaluation of an earlier historical period, were authored and controlled by brahminical scribal groups, who were invariably men. The male elite of the brahminical society controlled speech (*vāc*) by confining access to and possession of the Sanskrit language to those who were pure, refined and enlightened. This formula excluded women, in general, from having the right to master the pure form of *vāc*, or true language. Goldman S, (2000b:57–83) examines this obsession of the male elite, who dominate the social code by controlling the women and prohibiting them access to the language. *Vāc* is given the entity of a feminine deity. Just like women were controlled socially to avert impurity, *vāc* was kept away from women to keep it free from corruption. This attitude of the brahminical elite explains why the *Rāmakathās* were written and composed only by men. As a result, women remained on the fringes, and outside the domain of both the written and the oral texts. Women did not occupy a central role in these male-dominated texts. They rarely took a leading role, and if and when they did, their weaknesses were highlighted by the male authors. Women's contributions were under-estimated and they were given insignificant roles in literary episodes. The involvement of women was made inconsequential even if it bore a significant impact on the basics of the story. The women of the *Rāmakathās* show the existence of formidable female power, from encompassing informal influence on the throne to active participation in socio-political life; yet, women were presented as dependent wives and passive receptacles of the prescribed norms. Without any formal education, the women of those times were hardly in a position to write their own stories or give their own interpretations of any event. The stories were perceptions of men writers. Male writers conceptualised and described women characters in their own language, with their own convictions. Women's sensitivity, impression, passion and sentiments were never dealt with and explained rationally by the scribes. They assumed men to be the principal actors and women only as inactive repositories. This continued till we reach the era when texts materialised from a different social milieu, presented a significant deviation from the paramount tradition, and the images of the feminine were re-cast.

An attempt has been made to assess woman's questioning of the traditions and values, wherever there are glimpses of these in the literary texts. These are of considerable significance in defining the role of women. There is no autobiographical writing that could be called as personal narrative or the memoirs of a women writer at that time. There is hardly any record of a woman poetess except the one Bengali retelling in Chandrawati's *Rāmāyana* and the other in Telugu named *Mollā Rāmāyana*. Old traditions, as reflected in folksongs and village tales, may provide us with some material to fill up the gaps because many of these were composed by the village women.

The *Rāmakathā* tradition usually follows the written text and overlooks the oral traditions, which not only preceded it but continued later in various forms—folktales, folk music, dramatic performances, in puppetries, paintings and cultural elaborations—not only in far-flung areas of the Indian subcontinent but also outside the region. The story was originally formulated as part of oral history and only in a subsequent period did it take a literary, or written, format. The Indian tradition of oral presentation or recital of tales in the epics and other sacred texts dates back to the time of *Ṛgveda*. In the later Vedic texts—the *Brāhmaṇas* and the *Upaniṣadas*, recital-setting, involving oral elaboration of a sacred text by story-telling, took an important role.

A popular backdrop was the lengthy *yajña* that continued for days or months and was sponsored mainly by the royalty. During the recess in ritual processes, it was conventional for priests and their patrons to pass the time by discussing questions of metaphysical inferences, emerging out of sacrificial methodology, or by listening to the narrations or tales prevailed or as told by others. This tradition became known as the '*kathā*' tradition and was a popular part of lengthy *yajñas*. This continued till the oral literary format, or the story telling tradition, was crystallised gradually into written form such as the epics and the *Purāna*s. *Sūta*s were a special class of story-tellers whose reference is available in Valmiki's *Rāmāyana* itself. The *sūta*s, or bards, in this case, were the two sons of Rama—Lava and Kusa. The *Rāmāyana* story, in its unwritten form, remains prevalent even at present in some parts of rural India. The continuity of the oral version of the *Rāmāyana* is referred to in the Jain version of the *Rāmāyana*, the *Paumacariyam*. This book was composed by Vimala Suri in the first half of the first century AD. It tells us that King Bimbisara, a contemporary of Gautama Buddha, listened to 'this Rama story in its oral form'. The Buddhist work *Kalpanāmaṇdī Tīkā*, written by Kumaralata, was a work of the second century AD. This also refers the 'oral recitation' of *Rāmakathā*. It can, thus, be concluded that the tradition of story-telling was part of our cultural heritage and has been popular from hoary past till this date in some parts of India.

There is ample evidence to prove that Valmiki's *Rāmāyana* was a popular story around the beginning of Christian era. In the *Mahāvibhāsa*, a commentary on *Jñānaprasthāna* of Katyayiniputra, there is a passage that says in the *Rāmāyana*, there are 12,000 *Śloka*s and these refer to two topics—the abduction of Sita by Ravana and the rescue of Sita by Rama and their return to Ayodhya. The *Mahāvibhāsa*, composed, perhaps, during the reign of King Kaniska, is the earliest record that mentions the *Rāmāyana* as a complete written work. The famous Buddhist poet Asvaghosa was well acquainted with Valmiki's *Rāmāyana. Sūtrālankāra* is deemed to be a work of Asvaghosa. This was translated into Chinese by Kumarajiva in 400 AD. In Asvaghosa's composition *Buddhacarita*, the author seems to be well acquainted with the story of *Rāmāyana*. Asvaghosa was a contemporary of Kaniska. Later, Kumaralata's *Kalpanāmaṇdī Tīkā* (second century AD) refers to the public recitation of the *Rāmāyana*. Similarly, Bhasa (second century AD) in his *Pratimā Nāṭaka* and *Abhiṣek Nāṭaka* has used the theme of the *Rāmāyana*. It is clear that Valmiki's *Rāmāyana,* as a complete work, was well established by the beginning of the Christian era.

Macdonell (1919:X.575) believes that the *Rāmāyana* was composed in the middle of the fourth century BC. It attained its present form, including the *Bālakaṇḍa* and *Uttarakāṇḍa*, by the end of the second century BC. Keith (1915:318–28) also places the composition of the original portion of the *Rāmāyana* during the fourth century BC. Winternitz (1927:450) thinks that it was originally composed in the third century BC and its present form was achieved by the second century AD. Bulcke (1962) suggest a date towards the end of the fourth century BC as the beginning, and may have been completed by the second century AD.

According to the tradition, the original version was composed in one go by Valmiki. He identified himself as an actor in this tragedy. He figures in the *Bālakāṇḍa* of the *Rāmāyana*, receiving inspiration to narrate the epic, and then in the *Uttarakāṇḍa* as providing shelter to Sita, when she was abandoned by Rāma. He brings up the two sons of Sita—Lava and Kusa, composes a poem on the lively episodes of their lives and teaches them to sing it during Rama's *Aśvamedha yajña*. Whether Valmiki was a contemporary of Rama or not, he was undoubtedly an ancient *ṛṣi*, well-recorded in *Taittirīya Prātiñākhya* and in the *Vājasaneyī Saṁhitā*. He was well-respected as *rsi* in the *Mahābhārata* by Vyasa, who sometimes quotes his verses from the *Rāmāyana*. Brocklington (1984:9–11) made a detailed study of the *Rāmāyana*, dealing with question of its historicity.

Valmiki's *Rāmāyana*, as available to us now, however, differs from the original poems of Valmiki. The present version is divided into seven *kāṇḍa*s, or books, each comprising between 66 and 116 *sarga*s, or chapters. The idea of Valmiki as the author of the first *sarga-baddha-kāvya* may be untenable. The *Rāmāyana* was not divided into *sarga*s but into *adhyāyas* till the beginning of the seventh century AD. Bhavabhuti, in his *Uttararāmacarita*, quotes amply from

Valmiki's *Rāmāyana* directly, and these quotations can be actually found in *Bālakāṇḍa*; these, however, refer to *adhyāyas* and not *sargas*. There are many variations and similarities of old and new ideas in the present version of the *Rāmāyana.* Critical analyses of the gist and the narrative style of presentation allow us to be assured of several successive stages of its creation. The original *Rāmāyana* was composed basically in simple style. Whenever there is evidence of new ideas or *ślokas* with long meters and complex *alankāras*, one can accept these as later interpolations (Brocklington, 1984:46*)*. The *Bālakaṇḍa* and *Uttarakāṇḍa* were not part of the original *Rāmāyana*. The original book comprised the II to VI *kāṇḍas* only, and has undergone alterations and additions over the centuries. The present version of the *Rāmāyana* may be grouped under three basic recensions—southern, eastern and north-western recensions. These are owing to the long time-span over which the epic has been 'kept alive'. Besides, as pointed out earlier, the epic remained in the folk-tale motif for a very long time, and was transmitted through recitation by bards (*sūtas*). Naturally, with the passage of time, there will be deviations in linguistic, aesthetic as well as content. In the course of its growth, the *Rāmāyana* transformed from a heroic narrative to a literary epic—a predecessor to its recognition as an *ādikāvya*. The change from the poetry of adventure to the poetry of emotion is marked by much greater use of *alankāras* such as *rūpaka, svabhāvokti* and the lyrical description of nature. The northern recension presents, in almost all aspects, a more refined version than any of the southern versions. There seems to be little difference between the north-western and north-eastern recensions, with regard to style. The original Valmiki's *Rāmāyana* comprised 6,000 verses; it increased to 12,000 verses and, finally, to 24,000 verses, through continuous interpolations of the epic.

To give a precise date to the events as recorded in Valmiki's *Rāmāyana* is a very difficult task. Its narrative cannot be treated as authentic history without adequate cross-checking the sources. The historicity of the characters, events or even the narrator is a matter of academic debate. Some of the names, as they occur in the *Rāmāyana*, may be traced back even to the *Vedas*. *Ṛgveda* (X.60.4) and

Atharvaveda (XIX.39.9) refer to a king named Iksvaku although not in much detail. It only reveals that there was a king named Iksvaku; however, his relationship with Rama's dynasty is nowhere indicated. The earliest reference of Janaka occurs in *Taittirīya Brāhmaṇa* (III.10.9). Janaka Vaideha is named also in *Śatapatha Brāhmaṇa* (11.3.1.2–4) and in *Jaiminīya Brāhmaṇa*(I.19) as having some philosophical discussions with Yajnavalkya and of presenting him with one hundred cows. Janaka was a respected philosopher king, whose is referred to again and again in literary documents such as *Brhadāraṇyaka Upaniṣada* (II.1.1) and *Kauśitakī Brāhmaṇa* (4.1). Dasaratha's name occurs only once in the *Ṛgveda* (I.126.4), in connection with *dānastuti*, where along with other kings, he was also mentioned as donating 40 brown horses. Rama-Dasarathi does not seem to be a character of common knowledge. Rama-Margaveya is referred to in *Aitareya Brāhmaṇa* (vii.27.34); Rama-Aupatsvini in *ūatapatha Brāhmaṇa* (iv.6.1.7); and Rama-Kratujateya in *Jaiminīya Brāhmaṇa* (iii.7.3.2). One can only deduce from these references that Rama was a common name used by the Vedic Aryans but none of them has any link with the *Rāmāyana* story. *Sītā* is, of course, mentioned in the *Vedas*, but only as part of agricultural processing. In the oldest portion of the *Ṛgveda*—II to VII *maṇḍala*s—agriculture is not featured as a prominent mode of occupation of the Vedic Aryans. The X *maṇḍala,* which is considered to be of later origin, shows agricultural activities gaining prominence. Once Aryans began settling down, deviating from their occupation of herdsmen and warrior tribes, they became more and more engaged in agricultural activities. *Sītā*, in the *Ṛgveda*, is primarily connected with the process of furrowing the land. The *Yajurveda Saṁhitā* mentions that for preparing the field for the *Aśvamedha yajña*, they use to make *sītās* (lines) with the help of a plough (*Kaṭhaka Saṁhitā*, 20.3; *Maitrāyani Saṁhitā*, iii.2.4–5; *Taittirīya Saṁhitā*, v.2.5.5, etc.). Similarly, *ūatapatha Brāhmaṇa* refers to drawing *sītās* (lines) for the purpose of preparing a tract for the *srāddha* ceremony. These references do not have any connection with the Sita of the *Rāmāyana*, except that the Sita of the epic is also closely linked with the earth because she was found when King Janaka was furrowing a field; finally, at the end of the story, she is assimilated in the earth. The *Taittirīya*

Brāhmaṇa of *Kṛṣna Yajurveda* (ii.3.10) does have a character called Sita Savitri, who gets some prominence. She is the daughter of Prajapati, and was enamoured of King Soma, who in fact was in love with Sītā's sister Sraddha. However, she is in no way connected with the Sita of the *Rāmāyana.* It is justifiable to deduce that the Sita of the *Rāmāyana* was not a known character in the Vedic period.

With the growth of agricultural activities in the Vedic period, Sita became a *kṛṣi-devī*, or agricultural goddess. In the *Atharvaveda*, many *mantras* were composed to pacify and please gods to get the best return in agricultural activities, and *sītā* is referred to a few times (for example, AV.iii.17.4), where it is said, "May Indra accept *sītā;* Pusan secure her and may she remain filled with water and produce us crops every year," etc. The *Taittirīya Āraṇyaka* says that Sita was worshipped during the time of *pitṛmedha yajña.* Till the time of composition of *Gṛhyasūtras*, *sītā* was mentioned time and again with regard to agricultural process and these have no connection to the Sita of the *Rāmāyana*, wife of Rama. It can be emphatically concluded, therefore, that during the Vedic period, the story of Rama, as known to us through Valmiki's *Rāmāyana*, did not gain much popularity. It cannot be suggested either that the events of the *Rāmāyana* happened during Vedic times. Besides, neither Panini's *Aṣṭādhyāyī* nor Patanjali's *Mahābhāṣya* mentions any character of the *Rāmāyana.* So the story of the *Rāmāyana* did not gain much popularity till 100 BC.

Valmiki's *Rāmāyana* is not a historical chronicle. Its characters and events cannot be given a precise structure of period within the ancient Indian historical calendar. Neither did the composers treat the story as if it were based on historical fact with a chronological sequence of events. For them, the Rama lore rose above its historicity and became metaphorical. It reflects, however, the society of the specific eras when it was composed and recomposed, and how the people of that contemporary period adopted it. There is room for the possibility that there is a substance of historical or semi-historical situational truth around which the epic was composed. The social environment of the *Rāmāyana* was gentle, restrained and more in accordance with later Vedic notions and *brahmanic* ideals. A study of the *Rāmāyana* shows that during the age as reflected in the epic, the Vedic gods were popular. The pronounced religious activities show that big *yajña*s such as *Aśvamedha* and *Pitṛmedha* were performed by the *Rāmāyana* characters. *Munis* and *ṛṣis* are recorded as spending their lives in forest hermitages, *āñramas* and *gurukulas*. They were engaged in *yajña*s and other religious rites as were prevalent in later Vedic society. *Kṣatriya* kings were quite accomplished in religious and philosophical pursuits—Janaka and *brāhmin ṛṣis* such as Parañurāma were accomplished warriors. Monarchy had, of course, taken roots but it was still in its infancy. They were called *rājan* not *gopa* or *viśapati* as in the *Ṛgvedic* style. *Viśa* of the *Ṛgvedic* times have settled down in *janapadas*. Except for a few cities such as Ayodhya, Mithila, Kiskindha and Lanka, there were not many *mahājanapadas*. The conditions were more akin to the pre-Buddhist period.

The economy was relatively underdeveloped. There is no clear evidence of the use of coins. There is only one clear reference to *niṣka,* which originally was a gold chest ornament but was later used to signify money, in the context of Bharata receiving presents from his grandfather, who gifted him elephants, blankets, hides, two thousand *niṣka*s and 600 horses (*VRM.*, II.64.17–18). In the Buddhist era (c. 600 BC), *mahājanapadas* emerged in prominence as big trading cities, connected with cross-country trading routes. In the *Rāmāyana*, there are only a few references to vibrant trading activities and only a few times are merchants, *vaṇij* or *naigama* mentioned in the *Ayodhyākāṇḍa*. Guilds (*śreṇis)* and their leaders *(śreṇimukhya*), which suggest a developed pattern of economy, only emerged later during the Buddhist period.

There was distinct hate towards the non-Aryans, who were called *asuras, daityas* or *rākṣasas*; these were used as derogatory terms. The *Rāmāyana* can possibly be looked upon as an allegorical representation of the Aryan's first attempt to conquer South India. *Vānaras, niṣādas, asuras* and *rākṣasas* were most probably mythologised tribal groups. *Rākṣasas, daityas* and *asuras* were classified as the destroyers of *yajñas*. They terrorised *brāhmin* ascetics, and even their physical features were depicted with loathsome exaggerations. We make an attempt to understand the text within its contextual references. Kingdoms within the Gangetic plains faced a stubborn and intense resistance to their advance towards the South by various tribal settlements of the *rākṣasas, daityas* and *asuras*. However, there were a few other friendly non-Aryan tribes such as *nisādas, śabaras, vānaras, nāgas, yakṣas*, and *gandharvas,* who extended their friendly hand to North Indian invaders. These races were the original inhabitants of India, subsequently converted into good or evil spirits when they either collaborated with or were hostile to the Aryans. The hostility of the *Rākṣasas* to ascetics was clearly portrayed in later mythology. They were hated and feared because of their opposition to the Aryan penetration of the South. But Ravana, King of Lanka, was claimed to be an intelligent and sensible enough personality; a man of immense physical strength, a devout worshipper of Brahma and Siva, a strong warrior, who carved out a large kingdom for himself. He was certainly a challenge to the North Indian King Rama and, thus, a contender who deserved to be uprooted. In later mythology, *rākṣasas, daityas, asuras* became more or less synonyms; in reality though, they were distinctively separate. Whereas *daityas* and *asuras* were brother Aryans, most probably the forefathers of the Zends of Persia, who worshipped Mitra, Varuna, Nasatya, all *Ṛgvedic* gods, the *rākṣasas* were, on the other hand, aborigines of India. *Asuras* were also known as *daityas*. In Vedic mythology, *asuras or daityas* were the sons of Diti, co-wife of Aditi, who herself was the mother of the Adityas, who were *deva* worshippers. Ambiguity towards *vānaras* runs through all the stages of the epic. Sometimes, they were respected as humans and, at times, were mocked as monkeys. The term *vānara*—derived from the word *vana*, that is, forest—means forest-dweller. Sugriva and Hanuman were alluded to have knowledge of the *Vedas* and grammar (*VRM*, IV.6.4. I.3.1–2). Tara mourns Bali as *āryaputra* (*VRM*, IV.19.7).

The *Rāmāyana* reproduces the story of inter-group antagonism of the Aryan tribes and their conflict with non-Aryans in the process of expansion and command over the vast Gangetic delta and the southern states. The settings of these conflicts were historical, based on which different episodes of the *Rāmāyana* were imagined and created. This essentially belonged to that period of the Indian history when sacrifice was a distinctive feature of Aryan worship and Aryan women performed Vedic rites. This was the period in our history when *brahmins* and *kṣatriyas* used to consume non-vegetarian food, that is, animal food, and when Buddhism was not that commonly practiced. Jacobi (1893:139) considers that the core of the story must be before 500 BC, probably between fifth and sixth centuries BC. However, the historicity of the events and characters of the *Rāmāyana* continue to be under the scanner. Even with our present-day knowledge resources, we cannot accept these without reflecting some doubts.

A completely different analysis can be applied to the *Rāmāyana*. The technique of treating the *Rāmāyana* as an allegory, and contemplating each of its characters as symbolic of some spiritual or sentimental state, is not new. The metaphysical interpretation of the whole episode can well be argued on the basis of *Chhāndogya Upaniṣada* (I.2.1–14). Tendencies (*prakṛti*) of the human mind have both good and evil aspects. An invariable collision plays in the human mind. Evil nature (*prakṛti*) displaces good tendencies. A great battle ensues in human mind in which 'the good' takes revenge and, ultimately, eliminates 'the evil'. This philosophical conception was later mythologized as King Rama, representing the 'good tendencies' of the human mind and 'the evil' *prakṛti* of the human being were represented by *rākṣasas* and *asuras*. Brocklington (1984:12) observed that "such transformational interpretations are more readily applicable to the developed stages of the Epic than to its origin."

Men maintained certain assumptions about women—they are fragile as well as wild and a menace to society, if not restrained. In spite of these distorted images of women, she was worshipped as mother throughout the ages. As a consequence of domestication of plants and the introduction of agriculture, men traced a mystical fellowship between women and vegetation. The primitive man's transition from hunting and fishing to the settled stage of agriculturalist defined afresh the role of women. Women were closely associated with cultivation and men were primarily occupied with hunting, grazing their herds and aggressively struggling to acquire more land area. The fertility of the earth was equated with feminine productivity.

Women became responsible for the 'abundance' (or failure) of harvest for they knew the riddle of nature. Woman as mother was always compared with the all-nourishing-earth. Life is to be born of mother-earth. We need to understand how, in the earlier period of Indian history, the non-elitist, underprivileged groups—men and women—perceived their reality. Nevertheless, given the times and the space they occupied and the forces against which they had to express themselves, women's questioning of established traditions is meaningful.

Another issue that needs an explanation is the moral dilemma, projected from time to time, during the growth of this epic story. Valmiki's *Rāmāyana* has been interpreted and reinterpreted in different ways down the centuries. Reinterpretation was required as a result of the complexity created within the theme as well as the characters and their roles. New questions were raised by writers of different generations from different cultural backgrounds. The epic is full of episodes that present conflicting situations, resulting in moral conflicts. Morality, as a cherished treasure in public and private life, acquired an overrated importance. Evasiveness and ambiguity in *dharma* are perhaps the main source for such ethical polarity. Rama faces a behavioural dilemma when he exiled his pregnant wife just because of a foolish person's comment about her, knowing pretty well that she was innocent. Here his obligations towards his people and towards his wife were contradictory, and he faced a moral confusion. Similar is the story of Rama killing Bali from behind with an arrow when there was no direct hostility between the two. Rama faced another dilemma—to maintain the war ethics or to find a reliable friend like Sugriva in the game of political stratagem. These dilemmas were dealt with by the composers' own imaginative presentations, differently at different ages. Such presentations of the epic heroes of contentious ethical idiosyncrasies became the subject matter of scrutiny and sustained discussions in our conventional world. This was the reason that constant attempts were being made by critics and historians to find some logical solution in a customary sense of these narratives, added by retelling, modifying, restructuring and reconstructing the stories again and again. These stories reproduced the changing ethos of the community over the ages in an attempt to find a solution to these dilemmas from their own perspectives. The height of the story is attained when the *Rāmakathā* tradition employed a novel devotional device and Rama was adopted in the *Vaiṣṇava bhakti* movement. He was elevated to a position of an incarnation of Visnu, thus absolving him of all his misdeeds.

Valmiki's *Rāmāyana* contributed the core story. Its text should not be taken as fixed by any criterion. The present *Rāmāyana* stands as a well-installed synthesised manual. If one dissects its constituent parts, signs of many novel factors that got interwoven into its composition during the last two millennia can be found. There are endless versions of it, according to people's perception and different views of life. The *Rāmāyana* has been transmuted into a dynamic pan-Indian tradition, with new ideas and compositions incorporated in it. When, how, why and by whom these re-adaptations and re-creations took place needs a thorough investigation. We need to explain why variant renderings were composed and how much these variant versions retained the original narratives of Valmiki. Later re-adaptations were inducted to satisfy the sectional ethos of a particular part of Indian society. The period and its moral, ethical and cultural ideologies influenced its remoulding. Numerous questions have been raised within the tradition of the *Rāmakathā* about the standard of kingship, social covenant, codes of conduct, divines and demons, family relationships and gender expositions. Several elitist poets of different generations have expressed their views on many of these issues by creating new literary works, based on the stories of the *Rāmāyana*. As a result, new and variant explanations or interpretations are available on the episodes with the purpose of clarifying ambiguities.

Soon the Rama story went beyond the confines of Valmiki's *Rāmāyana*. Even the pali *Jātaka*, such as *Daśaratha Jātaka*, describes the Rama story through a Buddhist angle. Kautilya in his *Arthaśāstra* warns that no king should follow the example of Ravana and Duryodhana, which would lead one to ruin. This shows that Kautilya was well-acquainted with both the epics. *Rāmopakhyāna* occurs as a part of the *Mahābhārata*. It is, in general, closer to the northern recension of Valmiki's *Rāmāyana*. Certain divergences are, however, worth noting. Valmiki's *Rāmāyana* presents Rama as an exemplary but basically human figure, unlike some of the brief references of *Rāmakathā* in the *Āraṇyakaparvan* of the *Mahābhārata* that glorify him as an *avatāra*. The diversity of versions in the *Rāmakathā* tradition increased with the adaptation of the story in the *Vaiṣṇava* trend. In the original sections of Valmiki's *Rāmāyana* (that is, the secon to the sixth *maṇḍala*s), we have a human and natural account of Dasaratha's family. In *Bālakaṇḍa* and *Uttarakāṇḍa*, an interpolated section of the epic, Rama has been treated as an *avatāra* of Visnu. The development of the narrative and its transformation from an originally heroic epic into a Vaisnavite work happened only around second century A.D. The most important trend in the process of the development of tradition is the reinterpretation of the *Rāmakathā* in the light of *bhakti* (devotion) movement. As a result, Rama, the king with heroic qualities, was transformed into a full-fledged divinity.

Epic tradition continued in *Purāṇic* literature such as *Vāyu, Viṣṇu* and *Matsya Purāṇas* though in most of the *Purāṇas*, the Rama story is relatively brief. *Adhyātma Rāmāyana* is a part of the *Brahmāṇḍa Purāṇa*. It provided a significant dimension of theology of Rama. It presents the story of Rama from a philosophical standpoint, combining the ideas of *Advaita Vedānta*—Rama as a personification of *Brahman* (the Ultimate Reality) with the belief in Rama's grace. This theologically motivated ideology can also be found in *Adbhuta Rāmāyana.* In the *Purāṇic* tradition, much of the substance relating to the *Rāmakathā* is based on Valmiki's *Rāmāyana.* There are a number of divergent views and evidence of the dependence on Kalidasa and Bhavabhuti. In the *Uttarakāṇḍa* of the *Padma Purāṇa*, Rama is listed as an *avatāra* (V.269–71). *Agni Purāṇa* begins with an account of the *avatāras* of Visnu, devoting most space to Rama and summarising the *Rāmāyana* in seven chapters (5–11). *Bhāgavata Purāṇa*, although mainly concentrating on Kṛṣna, includes a fairly comprehensive treatment of the solar dynasty of Rama. The popularity of Rama story's influenced classical literature as well. Kalidas's *Raghuvamśa* (fourth century AD) was based on the Rama episode and he makes Dasarathi Rama an incarnation of Visnu. Similarly,

Bhatti's *Rāvanavadha* (or *Bhattīkāvya*) was a summary of the *Rāmāyana*. Bhavabhuti, of the early 8th century AD, wrote *Mahāvīracarita* and *Uttararāmacarita*, based on the Rama theme. These classical literary works were composed on the basis of Valmiki's *Rāmāyana*; however, these contain many divergences, which reflect their contemporary social attitudes and values. *Yogavaśiṣtha* (also known as *Maharāmāyana, Ārṣarāmāyana* and *Jñānvaśiṣtha*), accepted as an original work of Valmiki, was presented in the form of a dialogue between Valmiki and King Aristanemi and reproduces Vasistha's instructions to Rama. Its central theme is drawn from the *Bālakāṇḍa* and it retells the main incidents of the *Rāmāyana* in summary. The idea of Rama as an incarnation of Visnu spread far and wide; the most revealing development is that the opponents conquered by Rama attained eternal bliss. Emphasis is now given to the all-embracing grace *(kṛpā)* of Rama; he was absolved from all the misdeeds recorded in the earlier versions of Valmiki's *Rāmāyana*, in which he was only an exemplary human being.

The popularity of the Rama story in North India is reflected in the temple panels and sculptures beginning from the Gupta period. In sixth century AD, Varahamihira formulated the rules of making Rama's images. This proves that Rama worship was widely prevalent from this period onwards. At Paunar (Maharashtra), we find many *Rāmāyana* panels of the Gupta period. The stone panel of c. 400 AD shows an episode of *Uttarakāṇḍa*, wherein Ravana is shown shaking the Kailasa mountain. From Bhitargaon (Kanpur district, UP), interesting panels are available representing *Rāmāyana* episodes. The Dasavatara temple (c. 600 AD) at Deogarh (Jhansi) is embellished with many scenes from Rama story (Zaheer, M., 1981; fig. 74, 75). Similar trends are visible in Bihar. The plinth of the Aphsad temple (c. seventh century AD) is decorated with stuccos showing various *Rāmāyana* scenes (Ganguly, K.K., 1983:31–36). The terracotas from Chausa (c. eighth century AD), now preserved in Patna museum, depict Rama and Laksmana with their *vānara* army. An eighth century temple at Paharpur (Rajshahi, Bangladesh) depicts Rama sculptures, proving that even in Bengal Rama worship had penetrated deeply. Farther, in the east, Assam became imbibed with the flavour of Rama *bhakti* as early as 600 A.D. Dibi plates of Bhaskarvarman refer to Rama legends (Sircar, D.C. 1953:287). Orissa has a rich legacy of Rama legends. In the Ranigumpha temple of Udaigiri near Bhuvanesvar, there is a panel showing Rama chasing the golden deer. The Varahi temple of Chaurasi (Puri district), built in ninth century AD, presents many *Rāmāyana* scenes such as the killing of Bali, the abduction of Sita and the construction of the *setu* (bridge). In Madhya Pradesh, the earliest reference of Rama as an epic hero occurs as early as fourth century AD in the Eran pillar inscription of Samudra Gupta. A colossal statue of Hanuman has been traced near the western group of the Khajuraho temple, belonging to tenth century A.D. The Gwalior *praśasti* of Mihirabhoja refers to the episode of the rescue of Sita.

In South Indian art, the Rama story was reflected as early as third century AD. Representation of the *Daśaratha Jātaka* on a Nagarjunikonda stone panel (dated third century AD) points to the popularity of the legend in Andhra Pradesh. The earliest representation of the *Rāmāyana* scenes in Karnataka has been found in the Badami caves of early seventh century AD. (Sundararajan, K.V., 1981:72) Mahalingesvara temple in Karnataka has a large frieze embellished with *Rāmāyana* panels dealing with the events of *Āraṇyaka, Kiṣkindhā, Sundarakāṇḍa* and *Yuddhakāṇḍa*, which go back to tenth century AD. Jogeswari caves of Ellora (cave numbers 14 and 16, Maharashtra), depict Ravana shaking Kailash (Sundararajan, 1981:122,137,193). Similarly, Panhale Kaji caves in Dapoli, Ratnagiri, Maharashtra, contain many *Rāmāyana* scenes on its ceiling (Deshpande, M.N., 1981). The popularity of the Rama legend in Gujarat can be gauged from the sculptures and the temples found in the state. In Bardia, situated south of Dwarka, there are two shrines, one dedicated to Rama and the other to Lakshmana, dated 12th century AD. In short, it is absolutely clear that with the popularity of the *bhakti* movement from second century AD onwards, Rama worship also became very popular throughout India. As mentioned, Rama was worshipped as an incarnation of Visnu. Although Rama received veneration as an *avatāra* during the Gupta and early mediaeval period (fourth to tenth centuries AD), the cult worship of Rama, on the model of the 'cult worship' of Kṛṣna, had a late beginning. It was only in 13th century AD that Madhavacarya and Hemadri composed manuals giving the modes and procedures of Rama worship (Bhandarkar, R.G. 1928, reprint 1969:47). Ramananda (13th c. AD) laid a strong foundation for the devotional worship of Rama, and his followers are known as *Rāmāyets*. From his time onwards, the cult worship of Rama gained a regular feature within the Vaisnava sect. The *Bhakti* movement gave preference to local regional languages, reflecting its concern with making the teachings accessible to the widest possible audience, irrespective of caste or class. *Rāmāyana* stories affected a convenient media for approaching a socially divergent milieu. It transgressed metaphysical concepts.

With the advent of Muslim rule in India, the traditional presentation of *Rāmāyana* stories in Sanskrit literature became infrequent; instead, the story was accepted and improved by regional poets. The oral exposition of the *Rāmakathā* tradition gained acceptability during Islamic rule. These *Vaiṣṇava* storytellers were often wandering *sādhus,* who voiced their religious feelings through *bhajanas, kīrtanas* and *kathās*. The audience belonged to all strata of society, setting up a spiritually egalitarian background. Almost in every regional language, we find the adopted *Rāmakathā*—although their versions differ from each other—related to local ethos. None of them is an exact translation of the Sanskrit composition of Valmiki. The core story continued more or less the same but diverse clarifications were incorporated, to satisfy many perspectives on the main plot or to withhold their own concept of ideal and morality. We must note the lost approval of the story too. For the upper castes, Rama was '*maryādāpuruṣottama'*, an *avatāra* of Vishnu, etc. But for a non-Brahmin composer, Rama's act of killing the ascetic Sambuka, an *anārya*, could not be accepted without criticism. Another basic conception in the *'bhakti'* movement is that here is a devotee who acknowledges absolute confidence in the deity. *Prasāda* (grace) emanates from deity to devotee largely unmediated. Hence, there is not much need for an institutional arrangement such as a ceremonial observance and the priests as such. The epic story of Rama could be related to an open audience. Rama worship was now rescued from *brāhmin* or elite control. It must have caught up with the imagination of the regional poets and we find vernacular verses of *Rāmāyana* in almost every language of India.

The most well-known *Rāmakathā*, adopted in Hindi, was a composition of Tulsidas (16th century AD) known as *Rāmacarita Mānas*. Rama is presented in Tulsi's *Mānas* as an incarnation of Visnu, preserver of Earth, as well as the personification of the 'ultimate reality', the *Brahman* of the *Upaniṣadic* concepts. Tulsi successfully integrated the *Advaita* and *Vaiṣṇava* systems. Tulsi introduced striking deviation from the Valmiki *Rāmāyana* by the introduction of an 'illusory' Sita (*pratibimba* of Sita), who alone suffers the indignity of abduction and imprisonment in Ravana's household whereas the 'real' Sita, Rama's inviolable *Śakti*, or feminine energy, remains safely concealed in the element of fire (*Mānas*, 3.24.1–5). For Tulsi's *Rāmacarita Mānas* is not just a simple story of a *ksatriya* king. It has an abstruse, enigmatic and subtle meaning. Listener or reader should possess great wisdom to understand the *Mānas* in depth. The book is full of many allusions, which refer to Valmiki's *Rāmāyana* or *Purāṇa* stories, without providing the details of their context. Tulsi takes it for granted that these preceding traditions are well-known to the audience.

The first vernacular *Rāmāyana* in Tamil, *Īrāmvatāram*, was composed in 11th century AD by a poet named Kamba (or Kampan), and depicts Rama as the earthly incarnation of Visnu. Sita acquired the attributes of the goddess Laksmi, the divine consort of Visnu. Her inviolability was such a matter of concern that the poet had to frame a device of having her abductor scoop up the plot of earth she stood upon, lest the touch of his hands debase her.

The Telugu *Rāmāyana* was composed by Budharaja. Contemporary Telugu politic played an interesting role in various re-writings on the *Rāmāyana* theme. The *Rāmāyana* can be viewed not as a fixed text but as "a multi-voiced entity encompassing different tales on Rama that varied according to historical period, regional literary tradition, religious affiliation, genre and political context" (Richman, 1991:16). Early in 16th century AD, Atukuri Molla, a woman of a lowly potter caste, composed a new version of the epic, known as *Mollā Rāmāyana*. She and her father were Virasaivas, a sect opposed to animal sacrifice and caste discrimination. Her *Rāmāyana* dwells on Sītā's childhood and how Sita choses her husband from among several princely suitors (Tharu, S. and Lalita, K., 1991:94–98). Being composed by a woman, it has a dominant feminine moulding. In the nineteenth century, the Telugu *Bhāskara Rāmāyana* was more of an adaptation of Valmiki's *Rāmāyana*. However, *Śambukavadha*, a drama written by T.R. Choudhari (published in 1920), stirred a political controversy by depicting the killing of the Dravidian Sambuka by Rama as a murder committed by the *ksatriya* Rama at the behest of his *brahmin* advisors. (V.N. Rao, 2000:159)

The earliest Malayalam text is *Rāmacaritam* by Charaman, attributed to 12th century AD. This work mainly describes the events of the *Yuddhakāṇḍa* of Valmiki's *Rāmāyana*. In the 15th century, Ramya Pannikkar wrote *Kannash Rāmāyana* in Malayalam, also based on Valmiki's *Rāmāyana*. Ezhuttachhan recomposed *Adhyātma Rāmāyana* in Malayalam in the 16th century, based on the original in Sanskrit.

The earliest *Rāmakathā* in Kannada is the *Chāvundarāya Purāṇa* or the *Triṣaṣṭisalāra Purāṇam*, composed in c. 10th century AD. This one widely differs from Valmiki's *Rāmāyana* and is largely based on the Jain *Rāmāyana* version of *Uttara Purāṇa*, composed by Gunabhadra. In Gunabhadra's tradition, Sita is described as the daughter of Mandodari. Ravana came to abduct Sita in the guise of Rama. It is Laksmana and not Rama who kills Ravana. Rama attained *moksha* and Sita embraced asceticism (Subbarayachar, U.K., 1967:50). The Jain *Rāmāyana* tradition influenced the Kannada *Rāmāyana* immensely. We find a composition called *Pampa Rāmāyana* (also known as *Rāmacandracarita*) written by Nagacandra in 11th century AD. Following the Jain tradition, Nagacandra also attributes the killing of Ravana to Laksmana not to Rama because that was the last birth of Rama and so he should not be guilty of killing. In the Jain tradition, it was not Valmiki who gave shelter to pregnant Sita but a Jain prince, who aided Sita during the birth of her children. In the end, Sita does not enter the earth but she renounces the world in the Jain fashion. (Sītāramaiah, V. 1980:184).

The most important Maharashtrian *Rāmāyana* is the *Bhāvārtha Rāmāyana* composed by Ekanatha in 16th century AD. This is based on Valmiki's *Rāmāyana, Adhyātma Rāmāyana and Ānanda Rāmāyana*. Among the other *Rāmāyana*s in Marathi, which are considerable in number, we may enlist only a few, namely, the *Rāmāyana* of Madhavaswamin and of Krisnadasa Mudagala (seventeenth century); *Rāmāyana* of Sridhara and of Morapanth (eighteenth century) and of Amrita Rao Oak (ninteenth century).

The earliest *Rāmāyana* in Gujarati are the songs on *Rāmleelā* by Asad in fourteenth century AD. The Rama legend occupied a prominent place during the sixteenth and seventeenth centuries. Some important Gujarati *Rāmāyanas* are by Vishnudasa II, Nakara and Mundana, who composed *Hanumanto-pākhyāna*.

The Pala rulers of Bengal, although professing Buddhism, were liberal patrons and tolerant kings and encouraged poetic traditions of all faith. During their time, Abinandan (nineth century) wrote *Rāmacarita*, and Sandhyakaranandin (eleventh century) composed another *Rāmacarita*, which describes, by means of *śles*, the double story of Rama, the King of Ayodhya, and Ramapala, the King of Bengal. In the twelveth century, Lakshmanasena patronised the great poet Jayadeva, who in his book *Gīta Gobinda* describes Rama in his *Daśāvatāra Sūtra.* An extensive treatment of *Rāmāyana* in Bengali was done by Krttivasa in the fourteenth century. The core story depended on the *Gaudīya* recension of Valmiki's *Rāmāyana*. Krttivasa introduced many new stories, bearing on local customs and sentiments. He was influenced by *Adhyātma Rāmāyana, Yogavaśiṣtha Rāmāyana, Rāmopākhyāna* of the *Mahābhārata* and the *Purāṇa* stories. For example, in the beginning of the story, the fact that Valmiki, who was the dacoit Ratnakara, could not even pronounce the word 'Rama', was taken from *Adhyātma Rāmāyana*. The episode of Harishchandra as depicted by Krttivasa is based on *Devī Bhāgavata* and *Mārkaṇḍeya Purāṇa*. The construction of a *Śiva-liṇga* by Rama, at the time of making the bridge across the sea, does not occur in Valmiki's

Rāmāyana; Krttivasa borrowed it from *Kūrma Purāṇa* (Bandopadhyaya, A.K., 1959:55). In the sixteenth century, a woman poet Chandrawati composed the *Rāmāyana* in Bengali, which is in the nature of folk songs influenced by the *jātrā* (the traditional dramatic performance on an open stage) of Bengal. A curious story was juxtaposed in the *Rāmāyana* tradition by Chandrawati that Sita was exiled because she painted a picture of Ravana on the request of Kaikeyi's daughter.

The *Gaudīya* recension of Valmiki's *Rāmāyana* was the base story for developing the *Rāmakathā* tradition in eastern India, that is, in Assam and Orissa. In the fourteenth century, Madhava Kandli composed the Assamese *Rāmāyana*. He also added a few episodes, in the tradition of Valmiki's *Rāmāyana*, to cater to popular taste, for example, the adventure of Kunji (a substitute of Manthara) seeking Bharata's love, Tara's curse to Rama after Bali's death, etc. Another notable Assamese *Rāmāyana* named *Gīti Rāmāyana* was written by Durgavarain in sixteenth century AD. In this *Rāmāyana,* Sita is described as Mandodari's daughter and Sita offered *piṇḍa* to Dasaratha, etc.

In Orissa, *Rāmāyana* stories were well-known, as seen in the sculptures and the temples of the region. The earliest *Rāmakathā* in Odisi language is that of Sarala Das (fifteenth century), who composed *Vilanka Rāmāyana*. Bulcke (1962:238–39) thinks that the author of this book was Siddhesvara Das and assigns him to the seventeenth century.

Tribal versions of *Rāmāyana* were composed by low-caste poets in the form of folk tales. M.N. Vyas (1993:10) argues that "the social organisation of the civilisations operate in two levels first that of the folk or unlettered peasants, including tribals and second that of the elite or the reflective few. The cultural processes in the former comprise the 'little' tradition and those in the latter constitute the 'great' tradition. Questions inherent in the *Rāmāyana* are many and the thoughtful elites of every age and region, reflected upon them according to their ideas and ideals. The same questions were being raised by the tribal section of society in their folk songs and folk stories; they provided answers with absolute different understanding, so much so that instead of portraying Rama's rival *rākṣasas* as monstrous they claimed their own descents from them and paid their tributes to them as their ancestors." We will deal with these divergent views in the *Rāmakathā* in due course; here, we refer to only a few tribal perceptions and traditions, for example, the Gonds of Madhya Pradesh claim that they are the descendants of Ravana. They worship Meghnath (Meghnada) and perform the Meghnada singing ceremony, to protect themselves from ills and evil spirits. The *Rāmakathā* becomes almost tribalised in the Munda folklore. Sita becomes a tribal girl, Janaka no more than a peasant, and Sita is whisked away by Ravana when she is grazing goats. Rama is not the embodiment of righteousness or an ideal person or an *avatāra*. Rama's treatment of Sita draws adverse comments in Munda folklore. The Gonds of eastern Madhya Pradesh claim themselves as *Rāvanavamśī*. Meghnada and Ravana are the sacred deities of the Kokru tribals (Singh, K.S., 1993a:49–66). It is interesting to note that folk songs were sometimes composed by women as well. Sometimes, these women composers picked up the most touching stories, explaining some forgotten episodes of Valmiki's *Rāmāyana*. Elite classical writers and commentators of the *Rāmakathā* had rarely taken up the issue of Urmila, the bride princess of Laksmana. Telugu women, on the other hand, have treasured the princess in their memories through the popular ballad *Urmillādevī nidrā*, and they sing this on different occasions throughout Andhra Pradesh (Ramraju, D., 1993:77–99). These folk songs and stories are to be further assessed when dealing with the *Rāmāyana* tradition.

The *Rāmakathā* is not only widely popular in India but also in countries outside India, especially in the South Asian subcontinent. The *Rāmāyana* story took various forms in Tibet, Khotan, Indonesia, Siam (Thailand), Burma, Laos and Cambodia. *Rāmakien* appears to be the foremost *Rāmāyana* in the classical tradition of Thailand in eighteenth century AD (Srinivasan, K.S., 1993:29). Sita is described as the daughter of Ravana (possibly borrowed from *Adbhuta Rāmāyana*). Dasaratha (Tosorath in the Thai version) was engaged in a fight with a demon when one of his wives Kaikeyi (Kaiyakesi) helps him in fighting; the king grants her a wish whenever she desires. Later, the king performs a ceremony to beget sons. King Dasaratha gave the fragrant rice, the *prasāda*, of the sacrifice to his queens. Montho (Mandodari) who lived with Ravana, King of Langka (Lanka) smelled the rice and had that sacrificial rice too. As a result, she gave birth to a girl, who was predicted to be destroyer of Ravana and his race. The baby girl was, therefore, abandoned and set adrift in the ocean. She was ultimately found by Chanok (Janaka), who adopted her and named her Sita. The Thai version of *Rāmāyana*, therefore, considers Sita to be the half-sister of Rama. Also, Rama is identified with Visnu, or Narayana, and his brother Laka (Laksmana) is the conch shell and *nāga* that served as Narayana's seat. Brot (Bharat) is the incarnation of Narayana's weapon *cakra* (discus) and Satrud (Satrughna) is Narayana's *gadā* (mace). Seeda (Sita) is the incarnation of Laksmi. Sita, under the spell of a demoness, draws Tosakan's (Ravana) picture and hides it under the bed, which enrages Rama. He orders Laka to take her into the forest and kill her. Because Sita is innocent, Laka's weapon turns into a flower garland. Later, when Rama learns that Sita has not been killed, he begs her forgiveness. Sita, however, rejects him (Sisurang Poolthupya, 1992:26–30). In the Malaya *Wayang Kulit Siam*, a similar portrayal of Sita is available. Here, the same story of Sita drawing a portrait of Ravana is sung in folk tradition. Rama not only banishes her but even beats her eighty times until she is almost dead (Ghulam Sarwar Yousuf, 1992:31–40).

The oldest version of the Rama story in Tibet was found in six manuscripts in Tun-huang (North-west of China). J.W. de Jong (1993:39) informs that even in the Tibetan tradition, Sita is described as the daughter of Dasagriva (Ravana). It was predicted that she would cause the destruction of Ravana and his family; therefore, she was placed in a copper box and committed to the water. She was later found by Indian farmers and ultimately was given in marriage to Ramana (Rama), son of Dasaratha, and was named Sita Devi.

The *Rāmāyana* tradition in Nepal occupies a bulk of the literature, folk songs and dance drama. The story of *Rāmāyana*, described by Bhanu Bhakta, is inspired by *Adhyātma Rāmāyana*. Tulsidasa's

Rāmacarita Mānas retains enormous popularity. It is recited daily by the religious-minded Nepalese, in its original Hindi form. Besides, this has also been translated into the Nepalese language. *Bālum* is their traditional form of dance drama, similar to the *Rāmleelā* of North India. Another form of folk dance, accompanied by discourses, is called *nachāri*, popular in western Nepal, depicting the stories of *Rāmakathā* (K.C. Mishra, 1992:44–49).

The Balinese version of the *Rāmāyana* story is known as *Kākawin Rāmāyana*, or the old Javanese *Rāmāyana*. This composition, however, is not based on Valmiki's *Rāmāyana*; instead, it gathered its episodes from *Rāvanavadha* of Bhatti, who composed his poems in 7th century AD. *Wayang Kulit*, a shadow puppet theatre, is one of the oldest forms of dramatic expression in Bali. Rama stories are its theme. (I.M. Bandem, 1992:59–71).

In Cambodia, the story of *Rāmāyana* is known as *Rāmakerti*. *Rāmāyana* stories were introduced in Cambodia as early as fifth century AD. *Rāmakerti* is also based on the core story of Valmiki's *Rāmāyana*. In mediaeval Cambodia (that is, from fifteenth century onwards), however, Buddhism influenced Cambodian society so much that Rama and other characters of the *Rāmāyana* were remodelled after Buddhist tenets. Rama is made to resemble Prince Siddhartha and he is called Bodhisattva and Buddhankur (Pou, S., 1977:51–96).

The literary version of the Rama story in Malay is known as *Hikāyat Seri Rāma*. It would seem to have been adopted in that form in the Perso-Arabic script, after the Islamisation of the Malay archipelago and peninsula, somewhere between the thirteenth and seventeenth centuries A.D. A notable feature of *Hikāyat Seri Rāma* is that all the chief characters such as Rama, Sita, Dasaratha, Ravana and Mandodari are closely related to each other. Rama is said to have been the son of King Dasaratha and a princess named Mandudari. Rama is said to have been born as the result of his mother partaking of the king's sacrificial meal. Ravana, who hears of the beauty of Mandudari, demands to have her. However, the princess resorts to a stratagem of creating a replica of herself, named Mandudaki, who becomes Ravana's wife. Ravana is also said to have partaken of a portion of King Dasaratha's sacrificial meal; the portion was brought to him by a demon crow. Ravana's consort Mandudaki gave birth to a daughter, who was predicted to be the destroyer of her father's family and thus was abandoned and set adrift on the sea. Eventually, she was found and adopted by Maharisi Kali. She was named Sita, and she married Rama.

A survey of the source material on the *Rāmāyana* indicates the diverse nature of literary and non-literary traditions, spreading from time immemorial to present days, with its pan-Indian context having a global appeal. An attempt has been made here to evaluate the condition of women, as revealed in the epic, through its long period of evolution.

1

The Myth of Sita's Birth

The truth of myth is not the truth of rationality but the truth of faith. Myths reveal different things to different people. In the nineteenth century, the meaning of myth was 'fable' or 'fiction'. Later, scholars believed that myth was 'a story of the hoary past', which had lost its historically documented evidences. However, it remained in the memory of the ensuing generations as a 'precious possession' and, therefore, acquired a sacred, exemplary status.

For the study of myth, a critical historian needs to look at society with a historical perspective, taking into account all the instinctive or intuitive tales and texts of both scholars and believers, in order to make the research objective. The historian must put myths in the context of real time and space, based on records and other historical evidence that have been authenticated by scholars. The process of evolution of a particular myth, with all its modifications and implications, is to be linked by corroborating and counter-checking it with all existing historical sources that are being accepted as part of our cultural legacy and indicate the historiography of the ensuing stages of progression of that society.

Every religious text is studied in the comprehensive format of its society. Texts are interpreted and reinterpreted according to changed notions and values. The role of thought in shaping the culture of a society must be understood clearly. Religious ideas play a prominent role over all social evolution processes. For a theologian and a believer in ritualism, myths communicate the nature of the divine. The leading men and women of myths are considered to be supernatural beings. Theologians and active believers approve of adhering to the examples of mythological heroes because these characters are the revelations of the sacred cosmic power. A mythical hero is believed to be an emissary through whom sacredness is disseminated as an object of worship.

In the earliest literary works, myths were nothing but the allegorical constructions of some natural phenomena. These had no abiding value. Poetry, folklore and art have supplemented mythology as myths found eternal place in the spiritual and sentimental lives of every community. The intelligentsia were fascinated when they observed the beauty of nature, and they expressed this through their poetic imagination. Thus earth, water, fire, wind and sky—different phenomena of nature—were given mythological human forms, with numerous narratives of their supernatural powers. The transcendental self-experience in life provides theoretical glorification and philosophical justification to the natural reflections of early societies, and then a mythical character was moulded with the advanced arrangement of ideology. The forces of good and evil bring antagonism between spirituality and materialism, which needs to be resolved and can be done by creating myths. T.S. Maxwell[1] suggests, "Mythology provides the medium through which mental or spiritual conflict can be defined and sometimes resolved in symbolic terms which transcends the mundane reality of the situation." With the critical approach of historians, the significance of myths has become outstanding. It is applied both in the sense of fantasy, figment of imagination, sacred tradition, exemplary model or even as true story when they demonstrate the existence of obscured memories of the early heroes, male or female, whose laudable feats have been eulogized to the extent of making them mythical characters. Mythological characters are the products of socio-economic and religious transformation of society. Political changes play an important role in modifying their forms. The polarity of a situation, and its attempted perseverance, is an essential part of society that helps in the formation of myths.

Sita's birth is a myth that has undergone many phases of remodelling alongside the changing political, social and economic ethos over the years. Aryans, as represented in the earliest *maṇḍalas* of the *Ṛgveda,* were basically herdsmen and fighters, engaged in expanding and enlarging their occupational realm of pasture land, to embark on a settled agricultural life. In a tribal society, where men were absorbed in hunting, herding and fighting, women controlled the food-producing activities. They formed that axis around which the family and, on a larger scale, society revolved, and women enjoyed liberty and respectful status. Agriculture became the primary mode of subsistence in the later phase of the Rgvedic period, as symbolised in the tenth *maṇḍala*; in the later Vedic literature, it was represented in the *Atharvaveda, Yajurveda,* etc. Sita, as an agricultural deity, was first referred to in the *Ṛgveda.*[2] Later, prayers (*mantras*) of the *Atharvaveda* were composed with the purpose of fulfilling different prerequisites of human society. *Mantras* composed to get rid of ailments were categorised as *bhaiṣyajayāni mantras*. Prayers for long life and good health were known as *ayuṣyāni mantras* and *mantras* for agricultural success and for acquiring animal wealth were called *pauṣtikani mantras*. Prayers for Sita, the *sitāyunjañti mantras*, were part of *pauṣtikani mantras*.

In *Gṛhyasutra*[3] literature, many allusions are found in the accounts of *langala yojanam* (agricultural processing). The tiller draws lines (*sītā*) in the agricultural fields, pours purified butter (*ghee*) in them, chants the *sīra (sītā) yuñjanti mantras* and then feeds the respected *brahmin* guests. '*Sītā*', meaning furrow, was the agricultural deity in the Vedic hymns; she is sometimes characterized as the wife of Indra, the rain god, who filled her up with water, which was a necessity for all agricultural activities. *Sītā,* as part of the agricultural process, became associated with Earth, the female deity, much acclaimed in the Vedic *ṛcās.* In the *Atharvaveda*, Earth is acknowledged as the life-giving mother, who creates and nourishes. Yet, the inherent danger of death and disease prevails in this world. In the *Atharvaveda*,[4] prayers were composed and sacrifices recommended for pacifying and attenuating Earth. *Prithivī* (Earth) is coupled with *Dyaus,* the sky god. He fertilises *Prithivī* with rain, and life sprouts. *Dyaus* and *Prithivī* were considered as universal parents. Eliad[5] has interestingly pointed out, "The fertility of the Earth is bound up with female fecundity hence women became responsible for the abundance of harvest, for they knew the mystery of creation." Later, with the introduction of the plough, agricultural work was associated with the sexual act. Earth, which produces food for the living creatures of this world, was a feminine goddess comparable with the human mother; she is provider of food and shelter to human beings. Vedic hymns praise Earth as the mother goddess, man is born on Earth and after death is assimilated in the earth ("Crawl towards the Earth, thy mother," *Ṛgveda*[6]); while living on this Earth, the agricultural deity preserves the human being.

Not only were prayers offered to *sītā* as an independent agricultural deity during the cultivation process, but *sītā* is also referred to as a part of *pitṛmedha yajña* as well. In *Taittiriya Āraṇyaka* of *Kṛṣna Yajurveda*,[7] it is said that after a funeral, the dead man's last remains were kept in a pot (*asthi kumbha*), buried in the ground and then *sītās* (lines) were drawn around it with the help of a plough. Thus, it is evident that in the Vedic literary tradition, *sītā* did not acquire a human form. She was respected and praised as an exclusive agricultural female deity.

The human form of Sita is known to us through *Taittiriya Brāhmaṇa* of *Kṛṣna Yajurveda*.[8] She is portrayed as the daughter of Prajapati and sister of Sraddha. Sita was enamoured of God Soma (moon) and wanted to marry him. But Soma was in love with Sita's sister, Sraddha. Therefore, Sita had to acquire some special ointment (charm) from her father in order to allure Soma.

The character of this fable is completely alien to the Sita of the later *Rāmāyanas*. The myth of Sita underwent many phases of transformation along with successive changes in the socio-economic scenario. Sita became a special human character and composers of different periods have presented this elusive personage in their own ingenious ways.

The epic *Rāmāyana*, which was fundamentally preserved for generations in the oral tradition, gradually crystallised into a written format. An assortment of oral epics and fables with many local undercurrents were in use in post Vedic literary circles; these were probably consciously worked into the text of Valmiki's *Rāmāyana*. *Sītā*, the agricultural deity of the Vedic sages was conceptualised as the most exemplary character in Valmiki's *Rāmāyana*, and myths were born connecting her emergence from Mother Earth. The *Bhūmijā* (earth-born) Sita myth is originated from the allegorical interpretation of a natural phenomenon. Vedic sires observed the power of Earth to produce life in this world. With the growth and development in agricultural processes and the introduction of the plough to furrow fields, which rainwater filled, as did the water from improved irrigation systems, the production of crops increased many fold. Thus, the newly furrowed land, *sītā*, was beneficial to people and was worshipped as an independent goddess although she remained part of the Mother Goddess Earth. This provided the base for the allegorical conceptualisation of Sita, the heroine of Valmiki's *Rāmāyana*, taking birth in Earth and being found by King Janaka when furrowing land.

The *Rāmāyana* is not a historically substantiated record. Its characters and events cannot be given a precise time-frame within the ancient Indian historical calendar. Neither did the composers of the epic treat the story based on historical incidents as a chronological chain of events. For them, the Rama legend transcends its historicity and was figurative. The *Rāmāyana* may be analysed as an allegory as well. The characters of the *Rāmāyana* may be seen as symbolic expressions of some spiritual, ritual or emotional states, and is often looked at as such. The metaphysical interpretation of the story can well be argued on the basis of the *Chhāndogya Upaniṣada*.[9] The human mind has the tendency (*prakṛti*) to have both a positive as well as a negative approach. There have always been some conflicts at work in the human thought process. Evil, or the negative nature and concept, displaces the good, or positive ideas and propensity, and vice-versa. A great battle takes place in the human mind, in which good ultimately eliminates evil. These diverse philosophical concepts and conflicts were later mythologised as King Rama and his wife Sita, representing the good estimation of human mind and the evil *prakṛti* of human kind being represented by *rākṣasas* and *asuras* that abduct Sita. Brocklington[10] observed that "such transformational interpretations are more readily applicable to the developed stages of the epic than to its origin." He suggests that "myth is a final stage in the development of a hero, whose historicity and particularity are transformed in the popular memory into a mythical and universal form."

The historicity of events and characters of the *Rāmāyana* have always been under the scanner. Sheldon Pollock[11], in his *Introduction* to Valmiki's *Ayodhyākāṇḍa*, views the Sanskrit epic in the "perspective of social and political conditions of northern India in the latter half of the first century BC, the period of coalescence of a hereditary system of hierarchical social organisation and powerful monarchies, governed in theory by the law of primogeniture." It is possible that there is a kernel of historical or semi-historical circumstantial event around which the epic was composed. The social environment of the *Rāmāyana* was soft, subdued and more in accordance with later Vedic notions and *brahminical* ideals. The study of Valmiki's *Rāmāyana* reveals that during the period, as reflected in the epic, Vedic gods were popular, and monarchy had, of course, taken root but was still in its infancy. *Viś* of the *Ṛgvedic* times settled down in *janapadas*. Other than a few cities such as Ayodhya, Mithila, Kiskindha and Lanka, there were very few *mahājanapadas*. Society was more akin to the pre-Buddhist period. The economy was relatively underdeveloped. There is no clear evidence of the use of coins except in one context, that is, when Bharata received presents from his grandfather, which included elephants, horses, blankets, hides and 2,000 *niṣkas*[12].

The Valmiki's *Rāmāyana* available to us now differs on many counts from the original composition of Valmiki that was only passed down through the centuries in the oral tradition. There are many additions, deletions and juxtapositions of old and new ideas in the later versions. The original *Rāmāyana* of Valmiki was composed in a more simple and bardic style. Wherever there is evidence of a new outlook or *ślokas* with long metres and complex *alankāras*, one can accept these as later interpolations. The *Bālakāṇḍa* and *Uttarakāṇḍa* were not parts of the original *Rāmāyana*. The present version of the

Rāmāyana may be grouped under three basic recensions—southern, eastern and north-western[13]. This may have happened due to the long duration over which the epic was 'kept alive'. Besides, the epic remained in the folk-tale format for a very long time; it was passed on through the recitation of bards (*sūtas*). Naturally, with the passage of time, there would be disparity between the expression of phraseology and the text. The epic has been interpreted and reinterpreted by scholars from varied backgrounds, in different ways, over the last several centuries. New queries arose and the old answers were considered irrelevant or non-issues. Inter-cultural conflicts of ideas and values were accommodated to newer renderings of the *Rāmāyana.* Innovations are noticeable in the myth of Sita's birth, due to the systematic transformation of the socio-cultural life as a whole during the last millennium, resulting in changes in human perceptions and ideological values. Valmiki's *Rāmāyana* provided the core story. But our contemporary text cannot be accepted as the 'original' text of the *Rāmāyana*. Analyses of the different sections show traces of many novel elements that were woven into the original composition over the ages. There are so many versions of the *Rāmāyana*, depending on the perceptions and views of people from different cultural/social milieus that were woven into the text. The *Rāmāyana* has influenced the transforming of the pan-Indian tradition and culture with its ideas and structures. Rama and Sita represented the traditional concepts or characters as preservers of universal order and welfare of mankind and were later elevated as cult deities. The polarization element in the myth of Sita's birth is quite evident. Later, re-adaptations took place to satisfy the local ethos of different segments of Indian society. Moral and ethical values of the period and their cultural ideologies influenced the variants and re-modifications.

The *bhūmījā* myth of Sita prevailed in many *Rāmakathās*. In the *Ayodhyākāṇḍa* of Valmiki's *Rāmāyana,* Sita narrates the story of her birth to Anusuya, wife of sage Atri. Sita visits their hermitage during her travails in the forest as she accompanies her husband, Rama, who had been banished from his kingdom. She said, "One day, as Janaka was ploughing the field for the purpose of performing a sacrifice, he found a new-born baby girl in the field and heard a celestial voice that pronounced, 'This is the girl you wished for.' He picked up the baby and named her Sita." The same story can be found in *Viṣṇu Purāṇa*[14], with the addition that Janaka was ploughing the field for the purpose of performing a *putrakamesthi-yajña.* He saw a nymph, Menaka, passing through the sky and desired to have a child from that beautiful nymph. Soon, he found a new-born girl in the field and heard a celestial voice that said, "This is the girl you wished for from Menaka." He picked up the baby and named her Sita.

The story prevailed in many later versions of the *Rāmakathā*, for example, in *Kalika Purāṇa*; in Madhava Kandli's *Rāmāyana* in Assamese; in Krttivasa's[15] *Rāmāyana* in Bengali, and in Visvanath Khuntiya's *Vicitra Rāmāyana*[16] in Oriya. The myth of Sita being born out of the earth was originally a personification of an agricultural process. The *sītā* (furrowed land) of the *Vedas* was associated with Earth, was given a human form and elevated to the status of the wife of King Rama, the lord of the Earth. Valmiki's *Rāmāyana* elaborates the picture of that society, in which the monarchical system was on the rise, and kings were acquiring new landed properties for the expansion of the agricultural economy and for enjoying a more settled life. Naturally, the ideal King Rama of the epic was projected as the husband/master/owner of *sītā,* the furrowed agricultural field, who is associated by birth with Earth.

In the caste-ridden society of the earlier Christian era, social status and high caste birth enjoyed power and privilege in the social hierarchy. However, Sita's *bhūmījā* myth had its shortcomings. The traditionally inherited ideas of a *bhūmījā* Sita failed to satisfy the established conservative, caste-based society, which needed some new and acceptable interpretation of her birth. The assumption that Sita was not born of Janaka's loins but that he only found her on some agricultural land did not give the required respectability to Sita. How can Sita be elevated to a higher stratum if she were not given a royal lineage? She would be abhorred by the guardians of morality and her conduct would be a projection of her low origin. Even in Valmiki's *Rāmāyana*[17], the shadow of this prejudice is clear when

Sita says to Rama, "I receive my name but not my birth from Janaka. I came from the Earth. You devalue my conduct, you who are a judge of good conduct." Kamba, in his composition *Īrāmvatāram*[18], stresses this point very boldly. Rama suspected Sita's purity and even blamed her for sustaining her life in captivity, "After all, she was not born in a family distinguished by goodness but like a worm *(kitam pol)* from the soil." The *bhūmījā* Sita story had an unorthodox flavour, and many *Rāmakathā* composers, who worshipped Sita as an impeccable character, whose historicity they believed existed in 'obscure memories' of the past, could not embrace this allegorical description of Sita's origin. They simply called her *Janakātmajā*, or the daughter of Janaka. *Rāmopākhyāna* of the *Mahābhārata*[19] explicitly states, "*Videharājo janakah sītā tasyātmajā vibho.*" In *Kūrma Purāṇa*[20] and in *Kathāsaritsāgara*[21], she is simply referred to as *Janakātmajā*, ignoring any connection with Earth. The Jain *Rāmāyana Paumacariyam*[22] also refers to Sita as the daughter of Janaka, who was born along with her twin brother, Bhamandala.

The *Rāmāyana* is a story of inter- and intra-group rivalries of Aryan tribes as well as their conflicts with non-Aryans, in the process of expansion and control of the vast Gangetic delta and the southern states of Indian peninsula. The Aryan expansion in southern India had two significant effects. *Brahminical* (Aryan) religious conventions penetrated and, with the influence of Sanskrit on the local languages, these made heavy inroads in the south Indian lifestyle. As a result of this pressure of acculturation and Sanskritisation on the existing social infrastructure as a whole, some efforts were made to bring harmony between southern ideologies and those of the Aryans, who moved south from north. This assimilation process gradually led to the acceptance of the north Indian elite tradition by a large section of society. The influence of acculturation on the tribal or excluded groups made them change their customs and rituals, ideologies and ways of life in the direction of caste-based, higher social norms, and pushed them to claim a higher category within the caste-based hierarchy. This mechanism of submission forced the locals to receive the newcomers as part of society. And acceptance of an external tradition by a community was achieved mainly through the medium of a common language. Learning a language is an integral part of acculturation.[23]

In the course of its long history of conflicting myth of Sita's birth, we find new conceptions incorporated in it. Human relationships and ethics of behavioural patterns had changed considerably due to the Aryan occupation of large areas of non-Aryan regions. The geographical horizon of society had widened, and new racial, social and political zones got into the process of accepting and integrating the Aryan way of life. The mixture of Aryan and non-Aryan cultures provided a wider arena for fabricating new mythological stories linking the classical traditions of the Aryans with the local customs, idols and heroes of other sects.

Sita's character and episodes related to her life were redesigned or recreated by different composers of the *Rāmakathās*, in accordance with time and space of their origin. There were several attempts by composers to describe Sita as the daughter of Ravana, the King of Lanka, claimed to be an intelligent and sensible personality. Ravana was considered to be a hero in the southern states. He was a man of immense physical strength, a devout worshipper of Brahma and Siva, a strong warrior, who carved out a large kingdom for himself. The oldest version of this *Rāvanātmajā* (daughter of Ravana) myth is found in *Vasudevahaṇḍi*[24]. According to this story, Maya, the father of Mandodari, proposed the marriage of his daughter with Ravana. At first glance of this beautiful damsel, Ravana is said to have fallen in love with her. However, the first child of Mandodari was predicted to be the cause of her father's fall. The arrogant Ravana was not disturbed by this prediction, and after the birth of his daughter, he dispatched the new-born to a distant land. Janaka, the king of Mithila, found this baby when tilling the land, adopted her and named her Sita because she was found in a furrowed field.

A similar story is recounted in *Adbhuta Rāmāyana*[25], with a slight alteration. Sita is said to be the daughter of Mandodari, but not of Ravana. The story adds that Ravana used to collect taxes from forest hermits, and if anyone hesitated to pay, he would collect his blood in a pot. There happened to be a sage named Grtsamada, who was collecting the juice of *kuśa* grass in a pot and sprinkling *yajña* water in it for the purpose of generating Laksmi, who would be his own wife. Ravana confiscated the pots and carried these to Lanka; after mixing the contents of the pots, he handed these over to his queen Mandodari for safe custody, telling her that it contained a poison. Soon after, Ravana went to fight another battle where he got involved with other women. Out of jealousy and feeling dejected, Mandodari decided to commit suicide. She drank a few drops of the concoction from the pot, thinking it was poison. Instead, she got impregnated and gave birth to a baby girl. *Adbhuta Rāmāyana* further adds that this girl was Laksmi herself. She had to take birth in a *rākṣasi's* womb because of the curse of Narada. Scared of Ravana's wrath, Mandodari placed the baby in a basket and allowed it to float away in a river. Later, that basket was found by some ordinary farmers of a distant land. They took the basket to Janaka and presented the baby to the king, who named her Sita.

In *Mahābhāgavata Purāṇa*[26], a similar story connecting Sita as the daughter of Mandodari is related (*Sītā Mandodarī garbhe sambhūtā cārurūpinim/Kṣetrajā tanayapyasya Rāvanasya Raghuttama*). Linking Sita to Mandodari was an attractive alternative proposition. As late as the eighteenth century, the Kashmiri poet, Divakara Prakash Bhatta[27], retained this popular rhyme. According to him, Mandodari was originally a nymph, who took the human form merely for Ravana's destruction. Ravana took her as his wife and, in his absence, she bore him his daughter, Sita. She learnt from the baby girl's horoscope that she would likely be the cause of the death of her father; Mandodari then threw the baby girl into a river. The baby washed ashore and was found by Janaka. This story was accepted and became popular. This is obvious evidence of the changing value system in the later phase of the *Rāmakathā* tradition, in which due to acculturation and the impact of *brahminism* on non-Aryan elements in society, some composers, who belonged to the peripheral zone of *madhyadeśa* (middle Ganga basin region) tried to augment their prominence by fabricating the myth that Ravana and Mandodari were Sita's real parents. Sita was now being worshipped as a goddess in the *brahminical* pantheon.

The pan-Indian structure of the *Rāmakathā* was readapted and recreated orally through folk tales and folk-song composers in their local milieu, in terms of their own ethos. Folk tales have opened up new perspectives of interpretation. These have almost 'tribalised' the elite version of the *Rāmakathā*. Sita is a tribal girl, found by Janaka in a drought-hit land, when he was tilling the earth. The interaction of subcultures generated a conflict-cooperation situation. In a tribal version of the Rama story, Rama is not the personification of righteousness. The *Rāmāyan*a theme was recomposed, displaying the new inclination of questioning conventional social practices and views. There was genuine sympathy for Sita. Rama's handling of Sita drew adverse reflections. The pleasures and sufferings of ordinary human beings, their mysteries and afflictions provided a new dimension for reinterpreting the elite *Rāmāyana*. Women sang songs based on the *Rāmāyana* stories; these provide more information on their nostalgic and emotional feelings and mystical thoughts than any other classical works of male authors. V.N. Rao[28] suggests, "Oral traditions in Telugu probably were women's work, as can be judged from the feelings, perceptions, cultural information and general attitude revealed in the songs." Even as late as the sixteenth century, when Bengali poetess Chandrawati[29] composed her folk songs, known as *Sītā Bāromāsī*, she pursued the same storyline. Sita is born of the blood of distressed ascetics, and the death wish of Mandodari. But her name, Sita, according to this story, was given by the fisherman who found the discarded baby in a floating basket. He handed the baby first to his wife, Sata, who dreamt, however, that Laksmi is instructing her to hand over the baby to King Janaka. The fisherman fulfilled this dream with a request to maintain the name Sita, in memory of Sata. The story is more or less a re-narration of *Adbhuta Rāmāyana*. In Awadhi folk songs, Sita is described as the daughter of Ravana, who was abandoned due to sage Narada's prophesy that she would bring calamity on her father. Later, King Janaka found her. In some folk tales, Ravana is considered a man of upright character. A Munda tribal community, known as Timling, and the Gond tribe identify themselves as the descendants of Ravana. The Korku tribe worships Meghnada and Ravana as their deities, who save them from diseases and evils. Naturally, this new ethos of the tribals prepares the ground for accepting Sita as a daughter of Ravana, who was magnanimous and sacred in their estimation. K.S. Singh[30] thinks, "These tribal tales were probably older than the rise of *Vaisnavite bhakti* movement when Rama was glorified as an *avatar*."

Adhering to this *Rāvanātmajā* myth, some compromise formula was noticeable after the rise of the *Vaisnavite* influence. In the Telugu oral tradition, Rama and Sita have been placed on a divine pedestal. Sita is regarded as an incarnation of Laksmi, consort of Visnu, who was born to help Rama, the incarnation of Visnu. She descended on Earth on a lotus flower (the celestial seat of Laksmi) in Lanka. Ravana found her and gave her to Mandodari. They named her Sita. When the girl became 12 years old, Ravana was enchanted by her. But the *brahmins* and the astrologers instructed him to dispense with her soon because she was destined to destroy the family. Therefore, she was cast into water and later was rescued by Janaka, who adopted her and married her to Rama.

This *Rāvanātmajā* myth of Sita's birth is not only part of the native ethnic description of the *Rāmakathās* of Indian origin but also of many of those conceived in the neighbouring countries. These were perhaps influenced by *Adbhuta Rāmāyana*. In the Thai version of *Ramakien*[31], the story of Sita's birth had some modifications. As the story goes, Tosoratha (Dasaratha) was once performing a *yajña* to have children. Lumps of rice were prepared for offering in the sacrificial rites. The fragrance of the rice attracted the attention of Montho (Mandodari), wife of Ravana. She wanted to eat the rice. On her request, her sister-in-law Kakanasun (Taraka) transformed herself into a crow and brought half a lump of that rice for Montho. Later, the three queens of Tosoratha gave birth to four sons and Montho gave birth to a daughter. But Piphex (Vibhisana) and other astrologers predicted that this girl would bring destruction to the family. Therefore, the baby girl was put in a bowl and set adrift on the ocean, until found by Janaka, the King of Mithila. She was named Sita. This version makes Sita a half-sister of Rama and his brothers. The Malay version of *Rāmāyana*[32] has a curious addition that Mandodari was Dasaratha's wife and was the mother of Rama and

Laksmana. Dasaratha had promised Ravana a boon; and Ravana later demanded Mandodari in fulfilment of it. Unknown to Dasaratha, Mandodari, by magical means, created an exact replica of herself, which Ravana took away. It was this replica that was the mother of Sita. In this story as well, she would be Rama's half-sister. A similar story was echoed in Tibetan texts[33], in which Sita, the daughter of Dasagriva (Ravana), was predicted to be harmful for her father, who discarded her by placing her in a box and committing it to the waters. She was later found by ordinary peasants of a distant land, who offered her as a bride to Ramana (Rama), son of Dasaratha. She was named queen Sita by her husband. Several foreign lore relate Sita's *Rāvanātmajā* myth in variant formats that originated in Java, Khotan, Paithan, Cambodia, Siam (Thailand) and other locations. Naturally, this myth had a far-flung popularity.

There existed a moral dilemma in Sita's *bhūmījā* and *Rāvanātmajā* myths. A cult myth conceptualises the triumph of good over evil. Such myths associate the deity as the guardian of universal order and portray him or her as occupied in the welfare of mankind. It can be best accomplished by retaining the theory that she was none else but Sri or Laksmi herself. With the rise of the *Vaiṣṇava* cult, the myth conceptualising Sita as an incarnation of Laksmi gradually overpowered the other mythological tales about her birth. This resulted in the iconisation of Sita. The origin of this Laksmi-Sita-Padmaja myth can be traced back to the *Śrī Sūkta* of the Vedic hymns. Sri and Laksmi were identified, and the features of *Śrī Lakṣmī* expanded with the notion of fertility of Earth. *Śrī Lakṣmī* was associated with the magnanimity of Earth and, therefore, attributed as a necessary asset of the king, the ruler of Earth. *Sītā*, the furrowed land, was soon absorbed as part of Mother Earth, whose bounty was a prized possession of a strong king. With the rise of monarchical power, socio-economic perspectives acquired a new pattern. Now the king controlled agricultural land, enjoyed power and directed the social order. He was the upholder of *dharma-artha-kāma*, the paramount goal in the *brahminical* conception. As a result of this changed ethos, Rama the earthly king of heroic qualities, was invested with full-fledged divinity. Rama was considered an incarnation of

Visnu and consequently his wife, Sita, was elevated to the status of a *devī*. Rama's remodelling as an *avatāra* of Visnu is conspicuously elaborated in the *Purāṇas* and by classical Sanskrit writers from the fourth century onwards. *Agni Purāṇa*[34] begins with the account of the *avatāras* of Visnu and devotes the most space to Rama. In *Uttara Khaṇḍa* of *Padma Purāṇa*[35], Rama was included in the list of *avatāras*. *Adhyātma Rāmāyana*, a part of *Brahmāṇḍa Purāṇa,* provided a significant dimension on the theology of Rama. It presents the story of Rama with a philosophical standpoint, combining the idea of *Advaita Vedānta,* in which Rama is the personification of *Brahma* (the ultimate reality), with belief in Rama's grace. The popularity of Rama story also influenced classical Sanskrit writers. Kalidasa (fourth century AD) in his *Raghuvamśa* and Bhatti (eighth century AD) in his *Uttararāmacarita* (or *Bhattikāvya*) project Rama as an *avatāra* of Visnu. With the elevation of Rama as an *avatāra*, Sita lost the status of an independent deity of Vedic times; instead she was projected as Laksmi, consort of Visnu.

Another factor responsible for the rising popularity of the Laksmi-Padmaja-Sita myth was related to the *bhakti* movement. This myth developed due to the gradual changes noticed in socio-religious perspectives during the medieval period. The *bhakti* movement gained momentum during the Muslim rule. *Sādhus, bauls* and others used to wander around, instead of staying in their institutionalised religious clusters such as *mathas* and *akhārās*. *Sādhu*s, who were not in favour of the then political order of the non-*brahminic* socio-religious milieu, would sing *Rāmakathā* songs for the ordinary people in local languages, to stimulate religious passion in them. *Padmajā* (lotus-born) Sita myths now caught the imagination of *Vaiṣṇavite* poets, and the lotus became associated with Laksmi. The story is well-developed in *Daśāvatāracarita* of Ksemendra. According to this story, Ravana visited a place where he saw a tank full of lotuses. He made a *linga* (phallus) near the tank and worshipped Siva in *linga* form. Subsequently, he found a pretty girl floating on a golden lotus. He picked her up and adopted her as his daughter. The lotus-born *(Padmajā)* girl was none other than Laksmi herself. His wife, Mandodari, heard about a prediction that this girl would be the cause of Ravana's ruin after he falls in love with her. Mandodari discarded the girl to avoid the possible tragedy. The girl in a casket was abandoned in a distant land; later, she was found by Janaka, King of Mithila. An echo of this story can also be traced in *Torwe Rāmāyana*[36]. The poet tried to connect the two birth myths together—*Rāvanātmajā* Sita and *Padmajā* Sita by fabricating this novel idea because Sita, by then, was accepted by common people and in popular mythology as the incarnation of Laksmi. Here, Ravana was not given a paternity status; he only found Sita in a lotus pond and handed her over to his wife. Sita is not counted as *Rāvanātmajā* but *Padmajā.*

Sita as an incarnation of Laksmi, gained ground in popular perception. In *Adhyātma Rāmāyana*[37], Vasistha says, "Rama is really Narayana himself. Requested by Brahma, Narayana incarnated Himself as the son of Dasaratha for destroying Ravana, and the *yogamāyā śakti* of Visnu embodied Herself as Sita, the daughter of Janaka." Again, in the same text, the inhabitants of sage Sarabhanga's hermitage, said, "We know thee to be Mahavisnu, Sita to be thy consort Laksmi." So much so, that Sita became a *devī*, a supreme personification of chastity, a model of eternal loyalty to her husband that her purity was earnestly maintained. Tulsidas, in his *Rāmacarita Mānas*[38], does not dwell on the stories relating to her birth. He prefers not to comment on whether Sita was *bhūmījā*, *Rāvanātmajā* or *padmajā* because for him she was Laksmi incarnate and an object of immense respect. Tulsidas was aware of the *bhūmījā* myth but was reluctant to give it undue importance. In *Mānas*[39], she was called both *avanīkumārī* and *dharanīsutā*. If Rama was *parama brahma*, Sita was his *paramā śakti*. He had to maintain Sita's purity in every detail. Her divine nature is manifested in Tulsidas' description of *chhāyā Sītā*. How can Ravana abduct Sita, the *adyāśakti* of Visnu, who was nobody else but Laksmi herself, whose *pativratā dharma* was not to be challenged. Therefore, in the story *chhāyā Sītā,* adopted by Tulsidas, Ravana only abducts the 'illusory Sita' not the 'real' one. Tulsidas was basically following the trend as set by *Kamba Rāmāyana* and *Adhyātma Rāmāyana*. In the *Aranyakāṇḍa* of *Kamba Rāmāyana*[40], Ravana pays respect to Sita calling her Laksmi and bows to her in reverence, falling at the feet of the goddess. He digs up an area of one *yojana* in length, breadth and depth of the earth. Ravana lifts the entire block of earth with Sita, and places the same over his chariot. Ravana never touches the body of Sita. He is afraid of her. He carries her to Lanka and lodges her in Asoka *vāṭikā*. The same story is retold in *Adhyātma Rāmāyana*[41]. In fact, authors consider that Rama knew Ravana would come and abduct Sita so that the future struggle with him can be ensued. Therefore, he advises Sita to create a replica and hide herself in fire in an invisible form. With these devotional feelings of *Vaisnavite bhakti*, Sita was elevated to the pedestal of Laksmi, and the old myths connecting her 'suspicious' birth were ignored.

The myth of Sita's birth, making her *padmajā*, or an incarnation of Laksmi, was the obvious example of the efforts to deify her by the saint poets of the *bhakti* movement, whose function was mainly to propagate *Vaiṣṇavism.* For them, Rama and Sita were real characters of the hoary past, whose exemplary characters needed to be preserved as per the sacred tradition. Myths were formed not as a truth of reason but as a truth of faith. Rama was transformed as an *avatāra o*f Visnu, taking birth to salvage the evil-ridden earth and Sita, symbolising the descent of Laksmi, was the *śakti* or power of Visnu. The Laksmi-Sita-Padmaja myth, as mentioned, was strengthened more by the regional poets recomposing the *Rāmakathā* during the period of Muslim domination.

The *Rāmakathā* tradition can only be studied methodically by analysing its component parts and *khaṇḍas*, which were absorbed into its texts at various stages of its composition. Modifications of the *Rāmāyana* can only be seen in their own specific context. Variants point out the richness of the narrative of the *Rāmakathā,* which had the capacity to contextualize the heterogeneous components of Indian society. The myth of Sita's birth evolved with the adaptations in social, cultural and political spectra of early Indian societies in different regions. With the existence and consolidation of an agrarian base, the productive utilisation of the land occupied a respectable status in the Aryan mind. Sita symbolised nature and as goddess of agriculture symbolised fertility. Valmiki's *Rāmāyana* picked up this idea and gave a human form to Sita, mythologising her birth from

Earth. In a later epoch, 'monarchy' was strengthened by expansion and occupation of more and more land. The king was visualised as the 'owner'/'husband'/*swāmī* of the agricultural furrowed fields. This concept of politico-economic escalation in monarchical power provided the theoretical background against which Rama and Sita were projected as a model king and his supportive, dedicated wife in Valmiki's *Rāmāyana.* The *Bhūmījā* Sita myth was the outcome of an allegorical interpretation of natural phenomenon, originating in Vedic literature and personified by Valmiki's *Rāmāyana.*

Sita's *bhūmījā* myth lost its literary appreciation with the rise of orthodox trends in the social order. This changed pattern of orthodox society was defined by select groups of elite authors to explain social roles and their related functions, which were regarded as essential characteristics. Further, if someone was regarded by others as an 'exemplary character', it became binding on the part of the authors to describe him/her in accordance with the prevailing social conditions. The *bhūmījā* Sita myth was suspicious and raised questions on her genealogy. Therefore, it is quite logical that the *Janakātmajā* myth gained popularity because it was acceptable to the sentiments of the elitist layer of Indian society. There was an attempt to grapple with the contemporary concern of caste and gender, which had to be answered with honour for the prestigious character of the epic. Sita was, therefore, simply said to be the daughter of Janaka, which provided her a respectable parentage in the eyes of vanguards of morality.

The third myth about Sita's birth makes her *Rāvanātmajā*, or the daughter of Ravana. This myth was mostly elaborated by the authors of peripheral zones or by composers of tribal songs. At a wider level, the epic tradition functioned as a link between the classical tradition and local cultures, which were incorporated into the Rama story with the addition of new episodes. The *Rāvanātmajā* myth was a direct outcome of the subsequent efforts at assimilation made by the local poets, who were influenced by strong south Indian traditions and socio-cultural factors that existed over a long period. The spirit of the north Indian elitist society showed a special creative power of assimilation and revalorisation during the long process of

Aryanisation over a vast area. Myths provide cosmogonic, naturalistic and historic valences. For south Indian composers, Ravana, King of Lanka, was a reverent person. Some tribes of central India even trace their lineage from him or from other members of his family. The formation of lineages can be viewed from the perspective of social mobility of different ethnic groups of the period when the newly assimilated tribes generated an upward movement. Tribal songs express favourable emotional feelings and sympathise with Sita for her power of endurance, purity and loyalty to her husband. In fact, Rama's weaknesses as shown in the north Indian *Rāmakathās*, were a riddle to them. The most ideal character of the Rama story was not Rama but Sita, who can be mythicised as the daughter of Ravana, who represented a non-Aryan race and had, in fact, challenged the expansionist king of north India. The story provides a possible explanation of the mystery of Sita's birth. She was discarded by her natural mother Mandodari, due to the terrible forecast, and was later found in the field of a distant land by Janaka. The abandoning of an unwanted child by a mother, scared of social stigma or injunctions, was not uncommon. We find a similar story of Karna and his mother Kunti in the *Mahābhārata,* wherein Kunti sets her son adrift in a river because she was terrified of social sanctions. The *Rāvanātmajā* myth, thus, also gained popularity in southeast Asian countries such as Thailand and Malaysia.

References

1. Maxwell, T.S., 1997:221.
2. *Ṛgveda,* X.4.57.
3. *Kathak Grihya Sūtra*, 71.1.6; see Bulcke, Camille, 1962:14–18.
4. *Atharvaveda*, III 17.4; III.17.9; X.1.44–45.
5. Eliad, M., 1959. vol. I:40–41.
6. *Ṛgveda,* X.18.4.
7. *Taittirīya Āraṇyaka of Kṛṣna Yajurveda,* VI. 6; see Bulcke, C., 1962:13.
8. *Taittirīya Brāhmaṇa of Kṛṣna Yajurveda,* III.3.10; see Bulcke, C., 1962:6.

9. *Chāndogya Upaniṣad,* I.2.1–11.

10. Brocklington, J.L., 1984:12.

11. Pollock, S., 1991, Vol. II, *Ayodhyā Kāṇḍa,* II.64.17–18.

12. Bulcke, Fr. Camille, 1962:20–25.

13. Valmiki *Rāmāyana,* Eastern recension, III.4. (see Chand, H., 1928:790); North Western recension, III.2. (see Dayananda Mahavidyalaya edition, Lahore, 1923), (see Bulcke, C., 1955–56:66–94).

14. *Viṣṇu Purāṇa,* IV.5 (see Wilson, H.H., 2007).

15. Krttivasa *Rāmāyana, Ādi Kāṇḍa,* 94.

    bhumi hoite ei kon svahaste langale rājā yajnabhumi case, Urvasi caliy*ā* j*ā*ye uparākāse

    Tāhāke dekhiyā kāme Janaka mohita, hotāt risir viryya hoilā skhalita

    Daivayoge prithivi achilā ritumati, risiviryya poriyā hoilā garbhavati

    Dimborupe bhumi modhye chilo bohukāle, bhāsiyā uthilā dimbo lāngala sirale

    Cāsā yār janma, tava kanyā bote ai koriha pālana.

16. *Vichitra Rāmāyana* (Odissi), *Ādi Kāṇḍa,* 21.6–8. According to this, once Janaka saw nymph Menaka passing through sky when he was performing *tapa* in a forest. He wanted to have a girl like Menaka, but she said that she cannot take birth as a daughter of Janaka. But he can find a babe if he goes to a designated place near the southern sea where Vedavati's dead body is lying. Vedvati had been raped by Ravana and had taken the vow of destroying him. Janaka went in that spot. He ploughed the land to perform a *yajña,* and a girl child was found in that land. Janaka adopted her and named her Sita.

17. Valmiki *Rāmāyana,* VI.119.15.

18. Kamba *Irāmvatāram,* VI.37.395–397.

19. *Mahābhārata, Rāmopakhyāna,* III.258.9 (see Sukhtankar, B.M., 1941:422–88).

20. *Kūrma Purāṇa,* earlier part, 21.18.

21. *Kathāsaritasāgara,* X. 1. 60.

22. *Paumacariyam,* II.22.5–6.

23. Srinivasa, M.N., 1966:6.

24. *Vāsudevahaṇḍi* of Sanghadasa, II.240–246.

25. *Adbhuta Rāmāyana, Sarga,* VI.21; VIII.14–36.; (see Grierson, G.A., 1926. *BSOAS* iv:11).

26. *Mahābhāgavata Purāṇa, 64.*

27. Grierson, G.A., 1930. *The Kashmiri Rāmāyana, vs* 1033.

28. Rao, V.N., 1991:118–121.

29. Sen, D.C., 1920; and Sen Nabaneeta Dev, 2000: 183–191.

30. Singh, K.S., 1993b:52.

31. Srinivasan, K.S., 1993: 29.

32. Zieseniss, A., 1928:12, 71.

33. Thomas, F.W., 1929: 193–212 ; and Jong, J.W., 1993:II.39.

34. *Agni Purāṇa*, Ch 5–11.

35. *Padma Purāṇa, Uttarakāṇḍa,* 269–271.

36. *Torwe Rāmāyana,* I.16 (see Rice., E.P., 1921).

37. *Adhyātma Rāmāyana,* III.2.15–16.

38. Tulsidas *Sri Rāmacarita Mānas,* II.23.1–2; II 64. (Tulsi may have borrowed this story from the *Purāṇic* tradition such as *Brahmavaivarta Purāṇa,* 14:34–38.

39. *Ibid,* I.186; I .246.

40. Kamba *Irāmvatāra, Araṇyakāṇḍa,* IX.876–879; IX.950.

41. *Adhyātma Rāmāyana,* III.7.38–65; III.7.1–3.

2

Gender Dynamics in the Institution of Marriage

Valmiki's *Rāmāyana* provided the axis along which composers and poets of various regions and periods weaved the story of Rama and Sita, according to their respective perception and imaginative expression. A systematic, regional and period-based study, exploring and questioning the *Rāmakathā* is presented here. Perforce, one has to be selective in one's approach when focusing on the topic, considering the fact that there exists such a large number of retellings of the main story, which, in turn, have provided us with an even larger number of interpretations. Despite the maze of variants, only the versions of the *Rāmakathā* that are being widely accepted and have left a lasting mark on the human mind have been examined here.

All the texts, by and large, were male-dominated and *brahmin*-oriented. The close coupling of gender and literature is crucially important in the critical interpretation and understanding of the positive and negative aspects of the position of women, according to a historical synthesis. That women did not open the very texts that laid down the criteria for their behaviour reflects their attitude and status in the socio-economic forums then. Women usually played insignificant roles in the male-dominated literature of that time. Their contributions were completely under-valued. Their voices have scarcely been recorded in the written texts. *Brahminical* scribal groups, in general, neglected the versions relevant to women's challenges, if any, and painted them as passive spectators of their providence. Women were evaluated by men, who had their own scales of assessments, according to the *Rāmakathā* tradition. Women were considered peripheral; their roles were insignificant and were not considered worth recording.

Men and women are quite distinct—physically, mentally and emotionally. Social laws are expressions of biological facts. Social norms have their cause and origin in Nature. In 1913, a British doctor named Walter Heape[1] explained the 'two-sex' view of the differences. He says, "The reproductory system is not only structurally but functionally fundamentally different in the male and female. And since all other organs and systems of organs are affected by this system, it is certain that male and female are essentially different throughout…They are complementary, in no sense the same, in no sense equal to one another; the accurate adjustment of society depends on proper observation of this fact." If sexual diversity generates two different classes in society, either uncompromising patriarchy or innate natural matriarchy would reduce the resulting impasse. The 'two-sex' model can only generate a relationship of mutual trust and understanding if either the patriarchal form or the matriarchal form has ascendancy over the other. This leads to the crucial issue of the right to control the descendants. Patriarchal society constructed its demands about the subordination of women on appeals to the sciences of female anatomy and biology. Men, who emphasised their physical strength, considered that rationality, objectivity and capability to perform their functions were the qualities of men whereas the physically weaker section of society, that is, the women, embody disorder and are obsessed by their emotions. Women's nature (*strīsvabhāva*) is regarded as inherently mysterious and also unconquerable. At the same time, some 'negative' qualities of women were treated at par with that of men. They can be equally passionate, equally ruthless and insatiable in terms of sexual behaviour. This attitude in terms of sexual relationships is to be accepted as a reflection of natural instincts and emotions.

Interestingly, male intelligentsia had unconsciously accepted that female energy was stronger than that of men, and consequently many natural faculties of human beings or different phenomena of the universe were given a feminine identity. For example, men have controlled the power of speech through cultivating and advancing the language and its expressions but the 'power of speech', itself called *Vāgdevī*, is a feminine entity. Goldman[2] points out the sacred Vedic word, *vāc* (speech), comes to be represented not only as the feminised energy that animates the otherwise disempowered male divinities but as a 'well-dressed wife', who reveals herself only to those *brahmins* she choses[3]. The unification of the human and the cosmic 'power' is the essence of *Vedānta* philosophy. But the 'power', which may be assigned any name by some definite bearer from whom it emanates, is given a feminine identity. *Śakti*, a female deity, is considered to be the source of all universal manifestation. The Hindu philosophy considers Nature (*prakṛti*) as the active female counterpart. It is undifferentiated substance whereas the cosmic person (*puruṣa*) is the inactive male aspect. The unification of *puruṣa* and *prakṛti* underlies the belief regarding biological conception. Women represent the equation of *śakti* + *prakṛti* (that is, power + nature). Uncultured, undifferentiated power (*śakti)* is dangerous. Therefore, men from ancient times, recognised feminine strength and tried to subjugate feminine power on the pretext of maintaining patriarchal social norms and order. There is no society, with one or the other form of religious belief, which underpins its forceful code of behaviour. Religion was a sure part of the masculine power formation within which social contact was gendered and class stratified.

The concept of the 'mother', the creator and originator of this cosmic world, was considered supreme. The masculine craving for domination, a hypothetical replacement of patriarchal superiority over matriarchal reality, forced men into theorising women as parallel to the soil (*kṣetra*) from where life sprouts. Leela Dube[4] has explained the relation between the seed (*vīja*) and earth (*kṣetra*) symbolism using the facts of biological reproduction. She says, "The seed symbolises the father's contribution and the field represents the part of the mother. The seed is contained in the semen which is said to bear a relationship with blood. The quantum of semen, according to traditional belief, bears a proportion to the total volume of blood in the male body. The child, thus, shares its blood with his father. A male child has the potential of being the transmitter of the same blood to the next generation. In other words this would allow of continuation of the blood line. Blood of a female child cannot be transmitted, for she produces children (for her husband), by providing the field in which he sows his seed." She further suggests, "Men are plagued with a dilemma. On the one hand male participates through sexual intercourse in the creation of life and on the other hand he plays no role in the bearing and birth of this life. They are excluded from the primordial role of life regeneration. Men may long for women sexually and need them for the generation of offspring, but they abhor the consequences whereby their contribution to the latter is ended." Meillassoux[5] theorizes emphatically, "Women's reproductive functions became the source of their subjugation by men. Since women were the sole agents of genetic reproduction, men in order to establish control over the progeny, who socially and economically inherit the asset and maintain the continuity of the caste/class/family inheritance, protected, guarded and subordinated the feminine power, so that they can have control over the socio-economic infrastructure."

Gradually, women were relegated to an inferior position because it was argued that the male sperm, or *vīja*, is the real regulator of the new birth, not the female womb, or *kṣetra*, which is just the bearer of that *vīja*. Equipped with this hypothesis, the control of the *kṣetra*, or women, became an essential stride forward; and man, having explained the relationship between the *vīja* and the *kṣetra*, can only own the product of his germination if the *kṣetra,* or woman, is under his sole control. Both sex and reproduction are basically masculine activities. The female principle is conceived of as passive, a receptacle for and conveyance of male sexual and procreative energy. Man's contribution to human conception is greater than that of a woman's. Therefore, a father's jurisdiction over his children is considered unconditional and uncontroversial. Given the status of superiority of husband to wife, it is considered normal that brides reside virilocally and amalgamate themselves and their children with their husband's line. In the patrilineal system, a woman's children belong to her husband's kin only and, if she departs from her family, she must leave her children with her husband or his kin, otherwise her children will survive as non-kin in her own group. This system existed in the story of Lava and Kusa. When Rama recognized them as his prodigy, Sita handed over her children to their father because they rightfully belonged to him.

Pankaj Singh and Jaidev[6] argue, "The rule is to see women as *kṣetra* (field) or *dharā* (place) a site for man's work conquest and control. What a woman felt or how she saw is universally erased, her feelings and perceptions all tend to be mediated and presented through a controlling male narrative." This ideology was self-contradictory, whereby the 'invisible' controls the 'visible'. The father's 'invisible' contribution becomes pronounced over obviously identifiable and confirmed contributions of the mother. Although the mother is essential, she cannot give social identity to her progeny. The child obtains legality from his father.

We are told that marriage is important for two reasons. One, no ritual is complete unless the wife be present for it. Etymologically, *patni* is the one who performs rites. Second, the primary objective of the marriage is reproduction. To continue the family lineage, man was to beget a son with his legally wedded wife of the same agnate group. If a man does not have a son, he cannot perform his mundane and religious duties in this life. To ensure this necessity, a childless man is expected to perform all types of rituals. The powerful kings did *aśvamedha* and *putreṣṭhi yajñas* to have a son. The *aśvamedha yajña* was performed by an already powerful king to extend, consolidate and display his political and military superiority. In such royal rituals, the king was the sacrificer and his wife (*patnī*) was a co-participant. The chief queen had a more important role to play. She was called *mahiṣī*, or 'great female buffalo'. At the climax of a lengthy and elaborate ritual, the *mahiṣī* copulates with the just slaughtered horse. Although she is covered by a linen cloth, the text leaves no doubt as to what she is supposed to do physically, and this ritual is not merely symbolic. This custom was recorded in older texts as well, for example, in *Śatapatha Brahmāna*[7]. The *Mahābhārata*[8] says similarly that after the horse sacrifice, Draupadi had to lie down beside it for three minutes, according to the rule of the ritual. When Dasaratha performed the *aśvamedha* and *putreṣṭhī yajñas*, however, not only did Kausalya have to spend one whole night with the horse but the other wives also mated with it[9]. This horse sacrifice was undertaken because of the childlessness of the queens, and soon after this *yajña*, all three queens were fortunate to fulfill their dreams. Sexuality and fertility were combined through such rituals, and all three queens of Dasaratha became pregnant with sons. For the sake of a son, man could invent any ritual and give it a religious garb, and women accepted it as an obligation and duty to cooperate in such acts. If a woman could not bear a child through her husband, she was advised to go through the indignity of *niyoga,* wherein she copulates with a chosen person, either brother-in-law or a highly revered priest, so that the family lineage could be continued. Such examples of *niyoga* are available in the *Mahābhārata* although not in the *Rāmāyana*. In general, in patriarchal societies, man is not satisfied with only authority over the womb of his wife but he also has to be assured that the child that womb begets has to be his. Women and her procreative capacity were treated as the private property of her husband.

To assert male control over dominant feminine energy and power, the concept of marriage as an institution was initiated. From the times of the earliest literary works, formulated and controlled by male scribes, women had been projected as the source of evil, whose infatuation can spoil the patriarchal control over society. Social morality meant regimenting women's sexual communications, to fit the tradition of harmony of social order. Jurisprudence in every civic society accepted an inherent nature of women that clearly reflects society's mistrust of female sexuality. They constructed all possible rules to control female sex, to safeguard the purity of the linage.

The stereotyped exemplary nature of woman's chastity, particularly in ancient India, is considered sacrosanct within the confines of marriage. Uma Chakravarty[10] argues, "Through prescriptions of *strīdharma*, or duty of the ideal wife, who was expected to be totally devoted and subservient to her husband (*pativratā*), *brahmins* on the one hand and members of the ruling clans on the other have tried to maintain masculine identities—as these were related to the transmission of social attributes from the generation of men to another." Although in several literary sources, woman is represented as the embodiment of all elements of beauty, she is not given any space to express her sexuality. Her body and feelings had to be cultivated, according to the discipline of the 'male-oriented *brahmin*-controlled' norms. Even in marriage, which was regarded as the ultimate destiny of woman, their duty overrode conjugal desire. Their expression of excessive passion was considered 'shame' for her and for her family, who had mapped out her upbringing. She is revered and worshipped under regulated sexuality, as a wife or as a mother. However, as an unrestricted individual entity, she was considered a dangerous evil. In the *Rāmakathā* tradition, stereotypical statements support this view. In Valmiki's *Rāmāyana*[11], Agastya says to Rama, "It is the nature of woman from the beginning of creation that they become attached to persons in affluence but leave them in adversity. In their attachments they are unstable like lightning, in snapping affection they are sharp as weapon and in the evil they are quick as the wind or the winged bird." "Instability is a matter of course in women[12]." Gradually, women absorbed these ideas as their own and experienced them as the basic characteristics of women in general. Kausalya says to Sita, "Fickleness of women is their own characteristic[13]."

From the very beginning, a girl child was considered a burden on the family and the foremost duty of a father was to get her married 'suitably'. A daughter was a misfortune because to safeguard her virginity was a difficult commitment. Unlike celibacy in males, which represented their own self-control, the virginity of girls implied control over her orientation by her kinsmen. The loss of virginity is, therefore, a loss of prestige for them. 'Holding on' to daughters may begin early with special fondness and pampering accorded to them in childhood by their fathers, but the satisfactory demonstration of this tendency to 'hold on' is seen in the safeguarding of the unmarried daughter's virginity. The most complicated form of the sexually controlled daughter/sister is to be seen in the institutionalised 'sacred maid' found throughout aristocracy. What is symbolised by her virginity is not her own self-control but the control of her kinsmen over her behaviour. A daughter's or sister's virginity, thus, represents the kinsmen's 'hold' on her, necessary for maintaining the purity of descent, which can only attract desirable bridegrooms from distant parts of the land. Controlling women's sexuality in a patrilineal society was necessary to ensure that the child born to a man indeed belongs to the same blood as the agnate group. The ability of a householder to control his women is one of the indicators of his strength. Stories of the *Rāmāyana*[14] provide ample examples to support this view. Janaka stresses on the purity of his daughter Sita when giving her in marriage to Rama; Ravana was distressed to find out that his sister Chandranakha (Surpanakha) had absconded with Khara Dusana and crossed the boundaries of virginity, and lamented for the loss of his own prestige[15]. Here lies the possibility of sorrow and misfortune for a parent. Valmiki expresses it woefully in thc *Rāmāyana*[16], "To be the father of a daughter is an affliction for him that seeks after honour, and no one knows who will take a maiden to his home. The mother's kindred, the father's and they whom she goes in marriage—three families are brought over into danger by a daughter."

Ancient social laws, as prescribed in the *Dharmaśāstras*, insist that girls should be given in marriage at quite a young age whereas boys were expected to marry only after completing their education. Manu[17] prescribed that a man of 30 years shall marry a maiden of 12. Codifiers advocated the marriage of girls before they attain puberty. Yajnavalkya[18] laid down the rule that if a father does not perform *kanyādāna* in time, he will be accused of womb killing at each menstrual cycle of that girl. *Rāmakathās* followed similar social obligations. In Valmiki's *Rāmāyana*[19], we find Sita's marriage took place when she was six. Vinita Chandra[20] rightly points out that the male-oriented social order prescribed a young age for a girl's marriage with the purpose of keeping women in 'a subordinate position' and to force them 'to spend their lives in the performance of domestic duties'. By adhering to her preordained disposition and destiny, a woman is expected to function strictly under the socially sanctioned, *dhārmic* ways. Her voice, expectations, desires and opinions were pushed to the background in relation to the daily routine of a family. To be a wife of someone was the prime objective in woman's life. Valmiki in his *Rāmāyana*[21] says, "Without string there is no lute, without a wheel no chariot, without a husband no woman is happy." Serving the husband was considered more religious than even observing fasts[22]. Sita says to Rama, "Father and mother have advised me to follow the husband in prosperity and in adversity[23]."

Law-givers prescribe marriages according to the direct order of the respective castes. The marriage of a higher *varna* man was discouraged with a woman of a lower *varṇa* (*anulomavivāha*), but was not altogether prohibited. The reverse of it, that is, *pratiloma* marriages, or the marriage of a higher *varna* woman with a lower *varṇa* man, was denied by all codifiers[24]. Dasaratha's third wife, Sumitra, was of the *vaiśya* caste, according to the northern recension of Valmiki's *Ramayana*[25] and was given a lower social status.

The *Dharmaśāstra*s have recognized eight forms of marriages—*brahma, ārṣa, prajāpātya, daiva, gandharva, asura, rākṣasa* and *paiśāca*[26]. The texts differ in their views of legality and desirability in the marriage types. Most of them condemn the *rākṣasa* and *paiśāca* types of marriages. The most interesting point, however, in all these marriage types is the fundamental issue of exchange. Women are considered to be a symbolic object in such exchange processes. The giver and the receiver of brides are men. A bride is just a gift item, being a channel of relationship rather than a partner to it, and men are the trading partners. Manu refers to *kanyādāna* in the *brahma*, *sutādānam* in the *daiva,* and *kanyāpradānam* in the *ārṣa,* the *prajāpātya* and the *asura* forms of marriages. Taking gifts implies that the willing recipient has a mastery over the received gift article; in other words, a bridegroom's authority over his bride is accepted from the very beginning of their conjugal life. In *daiva* marriage, the daughter is gifted to a priest, who has performed the rites correctly. The story of Santa in the *Rāmāyana*, who was given in marriage to Rsyasrnga, asserts the prevalence of this type of marriage. She was gifted and married to this priest so that he performs the required *yajña* and save the kingdom from a persevering drought. Only in the *prajāpātya* marriage is the ceremony performed with the *mantra* "Together do ye both practice *dharma*." This may indicate that here the marriage was conceived as an equal nature, a partnership between the equal parties. Although, even here, the bride is given over to the bridegroom as a gift item *(dāna)* and thus reduced to the subordinate position from the very beginning of her married life.

The *gandharva* marriage, though referred to in the epics, was not much appreciated. Lawgivers maintained that before marriage, maidens remain under the protection and control of her father and male kin. Naturally, the question arises whether a maiden had any legal standing to give herself away to a man without the acceptance and support of her father? King Kushanabha's hundred daughters clearly comment that they cannot have any choice of bridegroom by themselves. It is the privilege of their father to find a suitable groom for them. The *asura* form of marriage, which involved the taking of a bride price by the maiden's relatives, is defined by lawgivers as one in which the bridegroom receives the maiden after having given wealth to the father or kinsmen of the bride[27]. Such a marriage was acceptable by Manu for *kṣatriyas, vaiśyas* and *śūdras* but was forbidden for a *brahmin* male. There are a few references to gratuity being taken by the father of the bride such as Kaikeyi in the *Rāmāyana*.

In the persistent patriarchal *brahminical s*tructure, women were systematically excluded from all religious rituals because they were considered basically impure due to their menstrual blood, and woman's sexuality was held to be violent and dangerous for men[28]. The father or a male member of the family decides a girl's fate. They look for a socially acceptable suitor, through the male priests. Male priests played a significant controlling role in arranging marriages. Sita's marriage was arranged by her father; however, interestingly, there were three other marriages arranged on the same occasion[29]. Urmila was given to Laksmana, Mandavi to Bharata and Srutakirti to Satrughna. All these marriages were settled by the family priests, Visvamitra and Vasistha. No question was even raised about its propriety. It was an accepted social norm that maidens can be handed over to a suitable person by their male guardians or the male family priests. Opinion of any female relative, even mother, was not considered indispensable.

The patriarchal cultural machination was intended as a controlling and disciplining device. Family unity and harmony were the most important factors in the choice of the arranged marriages. The personal choice of a maiden had to be sacrificed in favour of social considerations. This oppressive patriarchal agency was in direct conflict with love marriages. *Gandharvavivāha*, though sometimes alluded to among the *kṣatriya*s, was not appreciated as a form of marital alliance by the *brahmins*. The custom of taking bride price (*śulka*) from the bridegroom existed within royalty. The King of Kekaya, conferred his daughter Kaikeyi to Dasaratha only after extracting from him an assurance to confer his kingdom to her progeny. Kaikeyi was not an ordinary girl. She was extremely beautiful, much younger than the old king Dasaratha and a highly accomplished woman too. She had knowledge of warfare. According to *Adhyātma Rāmāyana*[30], Kaikeyi participated in a battle against the *asura*s, along with Dasaratha; when, during the battle, the axle of the chariot broke, she kept the chariot on wheels by putting her finger in the hole of broken king-pin. She knew how to treat wounds. Kaikeyi was remembered even by later *Rāmakathā* composers as a woman of extraordinary capabilities. Krttivasa[31] describes her as '*astrosanjīvanīvidyājāneKaikeyi*'. She could suck off the pus-filled nails of the king and cure his wounds. But even such a qualified and skilled lady did not ever think of expressing her own judgement against her father's decision when he planned to marry her to a much older man.

Hindu ethics emphasise submission and deference to elders, faith in parents' judgement and the ultimate surrender to destiny. Woman was not entitled to any independent judgement. Her chastity was too inviolable to be protected and this can only be ensured within the confines of marriage. The Jain *Rāmāyana Paumacariyam*[32] gives a similar version about Sita's marriage. According to this story, Rama helped Janaka in a battle against *mlecchas*. Therefore, Janaka was determined to give Rama his daughter. The parents of a maiden treated her as a mere object that is to be used to enhance the father's political and/or temporal ambitions. In most of the canonical *Rāmakathā*[33] texts, Janaka calls for the condition of a martial test as the bride price. It is a variant of the *asura* form of marriage because the father is assuring himself of military help from his future son-in-law, in case of need. The *asura* form of marriage is not appreciated by codifiers. Law-givers have directed the path; Manu[34] says, "The man to whom her father or with her father's consent, her brother gives her away, she should obey him when he is alive and not be unfaithful to him when he is dead." Women's freedom of expression, especially on matters of their marriage, was a taboo. The story of King Kushanabha also elucidates this point. The king had a hundred daughters. When they were playing in the garden once, the wind god saw them and fell in love with them. He proposed, but the girls clearly discarded his proposal, saying, "We will marry alone that person who will be selected by our father, as we cannot indulge in the liberty of selecting our own life partner[35]." This example of Kushanabha's daughters was also cited in the Telugu *Ranganatha Rāmāyana*[36], in which they reaffirmed the ideology of a father's absolute power in selecting grooms for his daughters. All the marriages alluded to in Valmiki's *Rāmāyana* were arranged by the male guardians of maidens. The *svayamvara sabhā* organised by parents did not leave any space for the girls to exercise free choice because they were preconditioned to their fathers' decision. For well-bred girls of aristocratic families or families of higher social strata, the expression of their preferences of grooms was considered belittling. Following the trend of Valmiki's *Rāmāyana*, the Sita of *Adhyātma Rāmāyana*[37] saw Rama for the first time in the *svayamvara sabhā.* No premarital meeting is alluded to. In the *Ranganātha Rāmāyana* as well, there is no description of a premarital meeting of Rama and Sita. Even the late composers of the *Rāmakathās* preferred to present Sita's timid, unassertive and docile characteristics. Similarly, in the Odisi *Rāmāyana*[38], Sita got her first glimpse of Rama only in her *svayamvara sabhā*. She felt instant attraction to Rama; however, she was anxious because she thought the slender man may not be able to fulfill her father's condition. But she did not have the courage to convey her worry to her parents. She could only communicate her anguish to her friends, "*Kijāni vidhātā ki koribo sakhi.*" Girls fall back on their destiny in all such situations. Tulsidas[39] relates the episode with a delicate portrayal of Sita. Although she met Rama for the first time in a pleasure garden in Mithila before the *dhanurbhanga* ceremony, and was forthwith attracted to him, she prevailed within the sanctioned limits of decorum. She hesitated to reveal her feelings even to her close friends.

In later *Rāmakathās*, a variant is presented related to this episode. Influenced by the classical drama literature of the Gupta and the post-Gupta times, many composers gave a passionate description of the pre-marital budding love between Rama and Sita. This variation of the story can be traced in *Kamba Rāmāyana*[40], *Ānanda Rāmāyana*[41], the *Rāmāyana* of Krttivasa[42], the *Rāmāyana* of Madhava Kandli[43] and *Bhuṣuṇḍī Rāmāyana*[44]. However, some *Rāmakathā* composers introduced a few innovative ideas about women's role in the selection of their husbands. *Adbhuta Rāmāyana*[45] was bold enough to suggest that women were at liberty to choose their prospective husbands through the fair and free *svayamvara* mode. The story deals with King Ambarisa's daughter, Srimati. One day, the saints Narada and Pavata visited King Ambarisa and saw his daughter. Both asked for her hand in marriage. The king was puzzled and ultimately left the decision to his own daughter by arranging a *svayamvara sabhā*. Srimati did not choose any of them and garlanded Visnu instead. It was her own independent choice and her selection was accepted by her father. Thus, some progressive *Rāmakathā* writers asserted a comparatively courageous outlook about maidens selecting their life partners. In the Assamese *Rāmāyana* of Madhava Kandli[46], Sita shows an independent frame of mind and courageous behaviour. She was determined to achieve her goal. She tells her father frankly, "Leave aside your vow and marry me to Rama." This changed perspective in the behaviour of Sita reflects the social ambience of the composer, who was away from *brahminical* orthodox impediments.

The word to be noted in a marriage rite is 'give away' (*dāsyati*). A daughter is like any inanimate object. She is to be 'given away' by her father to the groom, along with other dowry articles. Dowry was a type of marriage payment, wherein property or wealth was transferred across kinship groups. However, whereas brides leave their natal homes after marriage to live with the husband's group, they cease to exercise their rights to inheritance. Women did not get landed property from their parents as a part of the dowry, which usually comprised moveable property. Dowry forms a complex type of stratification. Girls are gifted (*dāna*) away along with other animate and inanimate objects by their fathers to the bridegrooms at the time of marriage. They are treated as property by their husbands. Their reproductive use is the basis of their value in this exchange system of marriage. They were a source to increase family progenies and thus to expedite human resources in an agnate social group. Girls practically did not have the right to utilise the dowry items given to her by her parents as she wished. Dowry may comprise human workforce, animal wealth, cash and ornaments. Human and animal workforce and cash money, given to a bride, were used by her husband's family.

Women had the right to handle and enjoy her personal ornaments and dresses, which the *Rāmāyana* refers to as *kanyādhanam.* Other things, in fact, go to the husband's family. A few personal maids were, however, given to bride for her personal attendance like Manthara was given to Kaikeyi. A woman does not usually control her cash presents and they may be appropriated by her husband or his male relations. Did women have the liberty to dispose of their ornaments freely without taking prior consent of their husbands? We find Rama asking Sita to distribute her ornaments, etc., to the wives of priests when leaving for the forest. It was Rama's decision, not Sita's. However, most women more or less had the liberty to operate their own jewellery. Anusuya handed over her own jewellery to Sita of her own free will not because her husband had asked her to do so. Similarly, Kaikeyi freely gave her jewellery to Manthara, when she was pleased with her. Kausalya also gave her jewellery, according to her own free will. She even donated cash to the priests and her helping maids, without any prior permission from her husband. Therefore, that women had the full freedom to enjoy the jewellery they got from their fathers or husbands is an acceptable fact. If, however, the girl chooses the groom by herself, she was not allowed to take with her any ornaments given to her by her parents. Manu says if she carries them away, it will be regarded as theft. Kautilya in his *Arthaśāstra* also confirms this. Manu gives husbands full right over the *strīdhana.* According to him, a husband has full right over the *strīdhana* if he marries according to the *brahma, daiva, prajāpātya* and *ārsha* types of marriage. If, on the other hand, he marries according to the *gandharva,* the *paiśāca* or the *rākṣasa* types, he cannot have right over the *strīdhana.*

No landed property was given as dowry. Girls do not have right over her father's immovable estate. A girl without a brother, of course, had a right to inheritance as *putrikā*. She would, however, be discharging her duties as a trustee of the inheritance, which is her son's. Most daughters inherited their mother's property called *yautaka.* Unmarried daughters had a share in the father's property, and after the father's death, brothers were expected to share their property with her, till she got married. Married women were often given presents by their husbands, over which they had full right. Dowry prevailed in the *Rāmakathā* tradition as part-and-parcel of the marriage ceremony. In every version of the *Rāmakathā*, this custom acquired prominence, overruling all regional variations, if any. This can be compared with gift exchange, *dakṣinā* or *dāna*, which constituted social and material transactions, forbearing the system of distribution. Goods, animal wealth, precious metal and jewellery, along with human workforce were gifted by the bride's father to the groom, his family and the priests. The *Rāmakathā* tradition was simply following age-old customs, which may have prevailed since time immemorial. Sukumari Bhattacharya[47] notes, "Women were being treated as chattel ever since the later Vedic period. Such gifts were given to priests. Evidently the human workforce was enjoyed by them and then sold as slaves or prostitutes." In Valmiki's *Rāmāyana,* some statements hinting at respectability can also be traced, for example, during the marriage rites, Janaka says to Rama, "*Iyam Sitā mama sutā sahadharmacārī tava. Praticcha ca iman bhadram te pāṇigrhanisvapāṇinā. Pativratā, mahābhāgā, chāyevānugatā tava*[48]." The bride though given a respectable and solemn position of being a *sahadharmacārī*, her position was not that of an equal, who would share the burden of family life as her husband's compatible partner. She was, on the other hand, considered a follower of her husband like a shadow (*chāyevānugatā*), with no individual entity. Although husband and wife are believed to be two parts of one whole, they were not placed on an equal footing, especially with the gradual acceptance of the concept of *pativratā* by the society.

Daughters were reared, educated and trained in the family tradition, social norms and obligations by their mothers and other senior women of the family. However, when the question of marriage arose, mothers were relegated to a secondary status and fathers always dominated the events. Women's role in their daughters' marriage remained restricted to some locally practised rituals known as *strīācāra,* which were not an essential part of *brahminical* religious rites. Valmiki's *Rāmāyana* did not mention the mothers of Sita and her cousins, who would have played some nominal part in her actual marriage ceremony. The views of mothers were not of much importance in the selection process of the grooms for their daughters. Even in a later retelling of the *Rāmakathā*, for example, the *Adhyātma Rāmāyana*[49], the descriptive part of the marriage rituals of Rama and Sita depicts that it is only the father who gave away his daughter to the groom. The father presents the dowry to his son-in-law, according to his status and position. Women slaves were part of this dowry[50]. According to the *Adhyātma Rāmāyana*[51], Janaka gifted 300 female slaves along with animals, jewellery and other items as part of the dowry.

The dominant role played by a father in the marriage of his daughter continues to be an integral part of our socio-cultural norm. In the later *Rāmakathās*, especially if it were composed by a *brahmin* male, this conceptual attitude was reflected with more convincing stories. Tulsidas[52], a poet of the mediaeval period, revealed a similar attitude wherein a mother's role was insignificant in his *Rāmacarita Mānas (Mānas*). So much so, when Sita's mother saw first Rama, she immediately fell for him and got worried whether such a tender looking young boy would be able to fulfill the demands of Janaka's vow. But she had no courage to talk to her husband or impel him to withdraw his vow and let Sita marry this solemn looking young man without any such pre-condition. She could only express her wish to her friends (*sakhis*) and ask them to go to Janaka and counsel him to abandon his pledge. *Brahminical* doctrines, which created the male-dominated social order, also percolated through to the southern *Rāmakathā* traditions. In the Jain *Rāmāyana Paumacariyam*[53], there are many allusions of marriage, in which the father gets his daughter married, following rituals similar to those for north Indian royalties narrated in the *Rāmāyanas*. In *Paumacariyam*, Sugriva gave away his daughter Padmaraga in marriage to Hanuman, in a similar fashion.

An authoritative paternal attitude was also the practice followed in most cases when getting sons married. Dasaratha, the father of the groom, was in his court when messengers from Mithila arrived with the message of Rama's success in breaking the *Śivadhanuṣ* and Janaka's invitation for the forthcoming wedding. Dasaratha announced the great success of Rama in the court and to his sons but the poet did not bother to add a line about passing of this message to his queens. Dasaratha came to Mithila to attend the marriage along with his high officials, army and *brahmin* associates such as Vasistha, Vamadeva, Javali, Kasyapa, Markandeya, Katyayana and others[54]. But no queen or women accompanied the marriage party. The groom's party has always been placed on a high pedestal in all such occasions. As was the convention, the bride's parents were expected to wash the feet of the guests as part of welcome gesture[55]. The groom's party was received with conspicuous honour[56]. The mothers of Rama, Laksmana, Bharata and Satrughna were only mentioned when all four bridegrooms returned from Mithila with their respective brides. The queens of Dasaratha received the brides inside the palace, performed some rituals, auspicious ceremonies and directed them to seek blessings from the household deities as per family traditions[57].

This attitude changed with the later composers of different *Rāmakathās*. However, a few *Rāmakathā* texts, emerging from different social milieu, especially due to the influence of heterodox movements of Hinduism, departed significantly from the dominant *brahminical* traditions. The newly emerging popularity of classical Sanskrit writers, who composed exotic literature, befitting the luxurious lifestyle of Gupta and post-Gupta monarchs, brought a change of trends in literary works. In drama, particularly, women were presented as embodied representations of celestial beauty, which held a spiritual core behind the sensuous masks. The orthodox writers, however, rated excessive passion and the physiognomy of beauty in women as shameful and an indicator of loss of virtue. Romantic drama literature, however, gave prominence to a new supporting character in the episodes, called *sakhi,* a sweet-tongued, intelligent companion of the heroine. They changed the forbidding attitude of the earlier writers. Women characters started becoming an integral part of any ceremonial occasion. Their active participation in public life, reflected through women actresses, dancers and entertainers, became a common feature. The traditional role of a woman, either as a conventional housewife or a temptress and prostitute, expanded now far more. The concept of women as passive partners, termed as housewives, and used as companions by men to sustain family lineages and to promote their so-called sectarian religious ends, then onwards significantly changed.

Another important phenomenon was the rise of the *Kṛṣna bhakti* cult. *Kṛṣna leelā* of *Bhāgavata Purāṇa*, describing the childhood games and youthful love of Sri Krsna and Radha, captured the poetic minds of Rama worshippers too. Although Rama, a self-controlled, upholder of righteousness and promoter of *Sanātana dharma*, could not be completely transformed in the Krsna-style amorous character, some romantic episodes, reflecting the contemporary literary trend, were added in the later *Rāmakathās*, which depicted another world, where women were presented in a more liberal social environment.

The *brahminical* tradition of patriarchal dominance faced the most formidable challenge from Tantric theology, which developed the idea of the cosmic feminine principle of a goddess, providing her equal divine power for giving birth to creation. The contradiction between the glorification of goddess *Śakti* and the subordination of women to male supremacy was vivid. Attempts were made through heterodox literature to free women from her constraints, without tampering with her honour in the social compass.

The gradual liberalisation of attitude to women happened with the expansion of the *brahminic* culture in the southern region of the country. The Tamil *Rāmāyana Irāmavatāram*, written by Kamba in the twelfth century of the Christian era, primarily revealed two trends: the *bhakti* trend of the contemporary society and the cultural undercurrent of Tamil society. It demonstrates the interplay of cultures of different communities—the so-called, value-based aristocracy of northerners, or the Aryans, the forest dweller clans of the *vanaras* and the strong-featured, mighty *rākṣasas* of the southern region. Kamba was influenced by the *Vaiṣṇava bhakti* cult, in which Rama was considered an *avatāra* of *Viṣṇu*. However, Rama himself, as depicted by Kamba, seems to be ignorant about this till Sita's fire ordeal when *Brahmā* and *Śiva* reveal this truth to him. Rama's actions in the epics do not present him as a superhuman being but as a normal mortal, who is inflicted with many weak characteristics. The poet described his hero and his socio-cultural surroundings as perfectly mundane episodes, reflecting the social behaviour, expectations, prejudices, customs and norms befitting of life between the tenth- and twelfth-century Tamil society. Women across the Vindhyas were more liberated, independent-minded, and capable of asserting their views to their male partners. The traditional image of the 'good' woman, which in the north Indian *brahminical* tradition meant an utterly subservient and subdued woman, was not portrayed in the south Indian *Rāmakathā*s of the middle ages. Women, on the other hand, could express their views and still remained unsoiled. They expressed their views about their marriages and conveyed a liberal sexual behaviour.

However, one should not underestimate the non-literary compositions of the *Rāmakathā* tradition, which survive in the folk songs and the folk tales of every part of India. The composers were mainly ordinary women singing their *Rāmakathās* while sowing seeds in the fields, rearing children, celebrating festivals in village gatherings, or during some marriage in the family. These folk songs brought some unexpected reinterpretations of the *Rāmakathā*. They were predominantly women-oriented, reflecting the pain and agony of the women characters of the *Rāmāyan*a. They retold the whole story from a woman's point of view. V.N. Rao[58] provided an in-depth view of these *Rāmakathā* songs. According to him, it is interesting to notice the importance of women at all social events; at every important juncture, women either take the initiative themselves to act or advise their husbands or menfolk to take a specific step. The position of men is presented as titular whereas the real power rests with the women. A comparative study of earlier and later *Rāmakathās* will elucidate this view.

In all the traditional *Rāmakathās* such as Valmiki's, Sita did not see Rama before he broke the *Sivadhanus* because modesty was an essential quality for girls born in a high society. In *Adhyātma Rāmāyana*[59], a similar story is repeated, wherein Sita, the bride, was 'given away' to Rama, the groom, before they even had a glimpse of each other. In later *Rāmakathās*, however, Rama and Sita's love-at-first-sight episode became very popular. Kalidasa introduced the eroticś description (*sṛngāra rasa*) in literary compositions, with immense success. The successive poets of the *Rāmakathās* composed similar literary works imbued in romantic expression. Kumaradasa[60], a poet in the eighth century CE, wrote *Jānakīharan*, in which Rama and Sita's love before marriage is delicately presented. In Bhavabhuti's *Mahāvīracarita*[61] (8th century CE), Visvamitra invites Sita and Urmilla to his *āśrama*, where pre-nuptial love was ushered in between both the pairs, Rama–Sita and Laksmana–Urmilla. *Ānanda Rāmāyana*[62] also refers to the 'love at first sight' incident. Sita fell in love with Rama as soon as she saw him in the *svayamvara sabhā*. For Rama *bhakta* Tulsidas[63], Rama was an *avatāra* of Visnu, a '*puruṣottama*' and beyond any trace of criticism, and Sita, his consort, was incarnation of Laksmi; her each action was worthy of worship. He described this episode of the Rama-Sita meeting in a pleasure garden before their marriage with tender feelings, '*Lochana mag rāmahi urāni, dinhe palaka kapāṭa sayāni.*' But there, Sita was still wrapped in timidity and modesty. She was incapable of expressing her emotional feelings even to her intimate friends because for a *brahmin* composer of northern India 'modesty/*lajyā*' was valued as the greatest beauty of woman. (*Jab siya sakhinha prembas jānī, kahi na sakahin kachu mana sakucānī*[64]). This hesitation, however, is not so evident in the Tamil *Rāmāyana Irāmvatāram*[65]. The liberal attitude of the south Indian poet clearly depicted Sita falling in love with

Rama as soon as she saw him and before they got married. In the Bengali *Rāmāyana* of Krttivasa, Rama saw Sita first on the roof-top of Janaka's palace. Sita's maids went to Rama with several pictures, each of which indicated Sita's pain in love. Rama took the brush himself and painted below the picture, showing equally his own depressed condition due to separation. They interchanged their thoughts by means of such picture drawings[66]. Krttivasa[67] depicted the 'love at first sight' scene, in which Sita's friends (*sakhis*) played a major role, delicately. Similar anecdotes were incorporated in the other *Rāmakathās* of the mediaeval period. Maithili *Kalyāṇa Nāṭaka*[68] and *Ānanda Rāmāyana*[69] showed Sita's fondness for Rama before he became her husband. *Bhuṣṇdī Rāmāyana*[70] concocted a romantic story, to enhance the beauty of this incident, and gave it another dimension. Here, Rama sent a bird with his picture to Sita, seeing which Sita suffered the pangs of love. Sita and Rama's 'love at first sight' episode gathered such popularity that even in the neighbouring countries, it took over the imagination of local composers of the *Rāmakathas*. The temple of the emerald Buddha in Bangkok has an outer gallery, which has a grand mural painting, running into 178 sections, so as to cover the entire *Ramkien* as told by Rama I of the Chaki dynasty of Thailand. The episode of Rama and Sita having a glimpse of each other, before their marriage, is depicted in one of the murals.

The Rama *bhakta* cult was more tradition-bound than the Krsna *bhakta* cult. Timid, restrained women folk are an essential element in Tulsidas's *Mānas*[71]. He described the ordinary town women of Mithila peeping from their windows, to enjoy the sight of Rama and Laksmana when they arrived in their city (*jubati bhavan jharokhanhin lagi, nirakhahin Rāma rūpa anurāgi)*. The eroticism of the Krsna *bhakta* cult made a remarkable contribution on the Rama *bhakta* cult. Ordinary town women in the Bengali *Rāmakathā* forgot the orthodox prohibition of tradition and rushed to see Rama and Laksmana when they arrived in their town. This reminds us of the exact behaviour of the *gopis* of Vrindavana in the poems of Krsna *bhaktas*. "*Srī Rāma ailā suni jotek juboti, bhule nija griho kormo gurujana pati, keho dhāye ekpode āltā mākhiyā, aar jon je ekore nupur poriyā*[72]."

The liberal attitude of the later *Rāmakathā* writers can be seen in their description of the *dhanurbhanga* (breaking of bow) ceremony as well. In Valmiki's *Rāmāyana*[73], Janaka's decision about who will marry his daughter was his personal whim. *Dhanurbhanga* was his vow. This tradition was followed by many *Rāmakathā* composers. *Ādhyātma Rāmāyana*, *Padma Purāṇa*[74], *Devī Bhagvata Purāṇa*[75], *Kashmiri Rāmāyana*[76] and *Paumacariyam*[77] are some of the important compositions, which indicate the paternal authoritative attitude of Janaka and how he imposed his command on his wife, daughter and her other suitors without any compromise. There may be different versions of the *Rāmakathā* traditions about how Janaka got hold of this bow, who gave him this bow, why gods instructed him to make such an inflexible pledge, but these are the questions beyond our present purview. Here, we want to highlight that in orthodox *brahmin*-oriented *Rāmakathās*, the mother's role and the girls' opinions were all non-issues. Tulsidas[78], a *brahmin* poet, could never transgress this barrier. Sita's mother is timid, hesitant and had no courage to express her own feelings to her husband about the selection of a groom for her daughter. Tulsidas puts the situation very courteously. Sita's mother, after seeing the delicate prince Rama, approved of him and ardently wished for him to be the winner of *dhanurbhanga* pledge of her husband; she was worried whether such a young boy would be able to fulfill Janaka's demand because stronger and older kings failed even to move the bow. She was scared of her husband's adamant attitude. She did not dare to persuade her husband to change his mind. She only expressed her impressions to her *sakhis*, the only support for a terrified queen; they could possibly rescue the situation by speaking persuasively to the king. In the later *Rāmakathās*, new stories were concocted or added to justify Janaka's pledge. According to *Ānanda* Rāmāyana[79], Sita herself while playing as a child had picked up the *Śivadhanuṣ*; therefore, Janaka took the vow that he would only marry her to a person who could break it. This changed attitude was a visible inclination towards the Tantric theory of women's empowerment in *Bhāvārtha Rāmāyana*[80]. In Valmiki's *Rāmāyana*[81], Dasaratha received the news of Rama's success in breaking the bow, in his court. He made an announcement to his courtiers and his sons, Bharata and Satrugna. There is no reference to the news being passed on to the queen mother, Kausalya, or about when or how the queen received this joyful tiding. In fact, in Valmiki's *Rāmāyana*, a mother's joy was of no consequence. This omission was somewhat modified by later re-interpreters of the *Rāmakathā*. The relatively less orthodox writer, Tulsidas[82] says, "*Rājā sab rāni sab bolai, janaka patrikā bāci sunāi.*" The women of Ayodhya dressed up in their fineries and expressed their joy in receiving the news of Rama's forthcoming wedding. Their exuberation and joy were confined to the limits of their homes (*Cadhī atārinh adekhahin nāri, liye ārati mangala thārī*)[83].

In Valmiki's *Rāmāyana*, women did not take part in marriage processions or parties[84]. Neither did Tulsidas give the queens of Ayodhya the privilege of joining the wedding procession to Mithila. They stayed in their *antaḥpura* till the couples returned to Ayodhya. They only received the brides and performed the rituals according to the *kularītī* (customs of the family) and *nigamanītī* (as prescribed in the Vedas)[85]. A more liberal attitude of the *Rāmakathā* writers can be found in south India, such as in *Kamba Rāmāyana*[86] and *Udāra Rāghava*[87]. The queens of Dasaratha proceeded towards Mithila with the marriage procession. The grooms' party had full freedom to enjoy the company of female attendants, even copulating with the accompanying damsels on their way to Mithila. In the older version of the *Rāmāyana*, the marriage ceremony in Mithila was completely a male-dominated affair. This attitude was challenged in some *Rāmakathās*, which recounted the events, according to contemporary local customs. In Tulsidas's *Mānas*[88], Sita's mother had some role to play, incorporating the local tradition of Uttar Pradesh. Tulsidas described Sita's mother and her female attendants receiving the groom. With the auspicious ritualistic things in her tray, she did the *arati* of the groom and performed a ceremony called *parchan utāran*[89]. She participated in the rituals, in accordance with the Vedic marriage ceremony, sitting on the left side of her husband and handed over the *mangalakalaśa* with her husband, the king, to the groom[90]. The *strīācāra,* which she performed, was much more elaborate than what Sita's mother did in Valmiki's *Rāmāyana*. Similarly, the Bengali

Rāmāyana of Krttivasa[91] provides us greater visual details of the Bengali customary marriage. The *sakhis* of Sita dress up the bride, accompany her to the marriage altar, and ask the groom's party to bring the groom to the ceremonial platform.

North Indian *brahmins* carried a strong bias against the south Indians, citing linguistic and racial differences. Beyond the Vindhyas, the south Indians were considered to be 'jungle dwellers', who spoke and wrote an incomprehensible language, were dark skinned, anti-*brahmins* and destroyers of *yajña*s. They were categorized as *rākṣasas* and *asuras*. Their women were voluptuous and shameless. They indulged in free sex and were habituated to initiating their own marriage proposals. The glaring example of this is the basis on which the character of Surpanakha was developed. In both Valmiki's *Rāmāyana* and the *Adhyātma Rāmāyana*[92], Surpanakha proposes to Rama. She says, "Oh Rama, come along with me. We shall have a very enjoyable life. I who am in the grip of passion cannot remain separated from you (*Kāmārta aham nasaknom ityaktum tvam kamalekṣanām*)." In *Bhattīkāvyam*[93] too, Surpanakha appeared in a beautiful form, hiding her ugly features and made advances to Laksmana. *Paumacariyam*[94] provided an explanation for Surpanakha's illegitimate passion. She made all these advances because she wanted to take her revenge on Laksmana, who had killed her son Sambuka. Tulsidas[95] made similar derogatory remarks about this *rākṣasa* woman, who seeing Rama, was overwhelmed by passion and proposed marriage. Surpanakha was not the sole representative of the daring female *rākṣasa*. The Jain *Rāmāyana Paumacariyam*[96] tells the story of how Lanka Sundari, the guardian of the city of Lanka and strong enough to resist Hanuman's entry, was filled with passion and asked Hanuman to marry her. In the same text, *gandharva* girls marry Ravana, out of their own personal desires. In short, it seems that non-Aryan women, categorized as *rākṣasis, vidyādharis*, or *vānaris*, had stronger personalities and decided about their own marriage; they did not always play mute receptors of their destiny, imposed on them by their male guardians. Sometimes, we see non-Aryan women were active as major power brokers, expressing better political wisdom, which helped mould their own fortunes through marriage alliances, for example, Tara choosing her partner Sugriva after Bali was killed. In most cases, however, the husband defined the prescribed ideology of subordination, and women remained salient passive performers.

The *Rāmakathās* present Ravana as an expansionist, who built a huge empire through waging successful wars. The captured wives or queens of vanquished enemies were brought to Lanka as war booties. Their movements were restricted, to avoid rumours and gossip. They were always guarded against any attacks from rival groups. Sometimes, victorious kings married them but they were largely confined to a room or a quarter meant for sex-workers. Consequently, the warriors became the providers of the women, and the captive women became the decisive instruments of social reproduction. The king's harems—Janaka's, Dasaratha's, Ravana's or Sugriva's—had numerous wives/*dāsis*/concubines and women without any socio-economic or marital rights to protect them from their master's atrocities. Although, force may not have been actually used against them, they could have been exploited or have become victims of religious terrorism, fear of superstition and sense of guilt. The wife was expected to be passive—like Earth, she must receive the seed passively, nurture it inside her womb, and not dare to think of owning the offspring because the owner of the seed (father) owns the ultimate product (child).

In tribal *Rāmakathās*, the women's role in marriages was well-defined. Folk songs, mostly composed by women of different communities other than caste Hindus, gave it a more feminine orientation. In these lyrics/songs, the mothers of the bride and the groom separately played decisive roles. The bride's views were expressed through her confidence in her mother. There are several examples of women arranging the marriages of their daughter, son or husband. Vidya Bhusan Singh[97] in his study of Indian folk literature presented a detailed account of women's role in marriages. He identified some popular folk songs in Hindi, which described Dasaratha's grief of not having any progeny and how Kausalya persuaded Dasaratha to have two more marriages, which would give him some hope of being blessed with a child. One of them was with her own sister Sumitra. When the king failed to beget a child from

Sumitra, Kausalya then urged the king again to marry Kaikeyi. This authoritative decision-making role of Kausalya lends a completely different colour to the story. Nowhere in any version of the *Rāmakathās,* written by a male composer, was so much importance bestowed on to her character. In Valmiki's *Rāmāyana*[98], Rama informed Bharata that when Dasaratha married Kaikeyi, he promised Kaikeyi's father as *vivāhaśulka* that the kingdom would go to Kaikeyi's son alone and not to any other son of his. This demand of Kaikeyi's father was politically motivated. In Krttivasa's *Rāmāyana,* Sumitra is described as the daughter of a Simhala king, who had approached Dasaratha with a marriage proposal. Kausalya's role as the prime negotiator in Dasaratha's second marriage is narrated nowhere, except in the folk song referred to by Singh, which happens to be by a woman composer.

Another folk song, quoted by V.B. Singh[99], narrates Kausalya's anxiety to perform Rama's marriage. In these folk songs, Sita not only meets Rama in a pleasure garden but also opens up her love for Rama to her mother. These women composers completely changed the earlier male-dominated concepts of the Rama-Sita marriage. Here, women were outspoken, persuasive, owned rock-like determination that was reflected in the wedding rituals. V.N. Rao[100] points out, "The women who sing these songs have not sought to overthrow the male-dominated family structure; they would rather work within it. Their interest is rather to make room for them to move."

Myths and legends have idealised women in the *Rāmakathā* tradition. Marriage was considered sacrosanct in the life of a woman. The ideal woman was selfless and did not express any desire of her own. She was a passive instrument, to be controlled and guided by her male relatives. They were granted no power by formal social dispensation, to express their views on the likes, desires or opinions in matters related to marriage. The theology of subordination dominated the essential qualities of *strīdharma*. Their functions were confined to 'motherhood' and 'home-making'. Men perceived disaster if ever woman expressed her views in public. Gradually, the woman's position transformed, in accordance with the changed social scenario by later interpreters of the *Rāmakathās.* In the erotic, Sanskrit literature of the Gupta and the post-Gupta times, the Krsna *bhakti* movement and Tantric rituals were decisive in moulding marriage rituals according to the time and space. The maximum transformation in marriage-related Hindu rituals can be perceived in folk songs, mostly composed by tribal and village women-folk. The *Rāmakathās* required to be treated according to the imagination, feeling and understanding of each individual composer, who composed or recomposed it, in written or oral format.

References

1. Referred by Laquer T. 1990:220.
2. Goldman, R.P., 2000:85–87.
3. *Ṛgveda*, X.7.14.
4. Dube, Leela, 1986a:75; 1986b: 22–39.
5. Meillassoux, C., 1986:15–21.
6. Singh, Pankaj, and Jaidev, 1999:3–5.
7. Eggling in his translation of *Śatapatha Brāhmana* XII.5.2 and Keith in his translation VII.4.19.d–k. omit this part of the text saying, "the verses are not translatable."
8. *Mahābhārata*, XIV.91.2.
9. *Rāmāyana*, I.13.27–28.
10. Chakravarti, Uma, 1999, Introduction:10.
11. Valmiki *Rāmāyana*, III:13:5–6.
12. ——, III: 45: 30-32.
13. ——, II:39 : 23.
14, ——, VII: 9: 10-11.
15. *Paumacariyam, Vidyādhara Kāṇḍa,* xii.3–4.
16. Valmiki *Rāmāyana*, *VII .9.7-10.*
17. Manu, *Dharmaśāstra*, II.67.

18. Yajñavalkya, I.3.64.

19. Valmiki *Rāmāyana*, III.47.4. According to Bombay edition, I.77.14, and North Western edition of Valmiki's *Rāmāyana*, Sita was married to Rama after she reached her puberty. For different views, see Brocklington, 1984:168–69 ; Jayal, Sakambari, 1966:43.

20. Chandra,Vinita, 2010:54.

21. Valmiki *Rāmāyana*, II: 39:29-30.

22. ——, II: 39: 20-25. ; II. 27. 9-23.

23. ——, II: 27: 10.

24. Manu, *Dharmaśāstra*. X.5.

25. The Northern recension of Valmiki's *Rāmāyana* calls her the *karani suta* of Vamadeva (I 14.4). Monnier William's *Sanskrit Dictionary* (p. 254. col.1) says, "the *Karani* refers to the offspring of an outcaste *ksatriya* or of a *vaisya* women by a *ksatriya* or of a *sudra* woman by a *vaisya*." (see Ghurye, 1979:59).

26. Manu, *Dharmaśāstra*, III.27–34; Narada, XII.38–39.

27. ——, III.31; Narada. XII.38–39.

28. Gupta, Samjukta Gombrich, 2000:91.

29. Valmiki *Rāmāyana*, I:72.1–7

30. *Adhyātma Rāmāyana*, II:2:69–70.

31. Krttivasa *Rāmāyana*, *Ādi Kāvya*, 76–78.

32. *Paumacariyam*, *Sandhi*, XXI.3–4.

33. Valmiki *Rāmāyana*, I:65:15–19. (tr. Goldman, 1996:249).

34. Manu, *Dharmaśāstra*, V.151.

35. Valmiki *Rāmāyana*, I:32:11, 15, 21–22.

36. Ranganatha *Rāmāyana*. I.970–990

37. *Ādhyatma Rāmāyana,* I:6:28–32

38. *Vicitra Rāmāyana,* I:42:7.

39. Tulsidas, *Rāmacarita Mānas*, 231:4.

40. Kamba, *Irāmvatāram*, I:10:590–593.

41. *Ānanda Rāmāyana*, I:3:111–120.

42. Krttivasa *Rāmāyana*, *Adi Kavya*, 60–61.

43. Kandli, Madhav. *Assamese Rāmāyana*, I:39.

44. Singh, B.P., 1980:475–504.

45. Grierson, G.A., 1926. *Bulletin SOAS*, IV:11; and 1928, *Bulletin SOAS*, V: 285.

46. Kandli, Madhav. *Assamese Rāmāyana*. I:40:37–43.

47. Bhattacharji , Sukumari, 1999:221.

48. Valmiki *Rāmāyana*, I:73:26–27.

49. *Adhyātma Rāmāyana*, I:6:52–56.

50. Valmiki *Rāmāyana*, I:74:3–5.

51. *Adhyātma Rāmāyana*, I:6:76–78.

52. *Mānas, Bāla Kāṇḍa*, *dohā*:255, *chaupai*:1–4.

53. *Paumacariyam*. I:20:12.

54. Valmiki *Rāmāyana*, I:69:4–6.

55. *Adhyātma Rāmāyana,* I:6:29–32.

56. Valmiki *Rāmāyana*, I:69:9–10.

57. ——, I:77:11–13.

58. Rao, V.N., 1991:114–136.

59. *Adhyātma Rāmāyana*, I:6:28–32.

60. Kumardasa, *Jānakīharan*, *Sarga*, VII:1:3–4. (Published in *BSOS*, Vol. IV:285. Quoted by Bulcke, C., 1962:193–94).

61. Bhavabhuti, *Mahāvīrcarita*, Act. I. (quoted by Bulcke, C., 1962: 205) .

62. *Ānanda Rāmāyana*, I:3:111–120.

63. *Mānas, Bāla Kāṇḍa, dohā* 232, *chaupai* 4.

64. ——, *dohā* 231, *chaupai* 4.

65. *Irāmvatāram*, I:10:590.

66. Sen, D.C., 1920 (reprint 1987):112.

67. Krttivasa *Rāmāyana*. I : 134.

68. *Kalyāṇa Nāṭaka:anu*, 239. (quoted by Bulcke, C. 1962:286).

69. *Ānanda Rāmāyana*, I:3:111–120.

70. Singh. B.P., 1980:475–504.

71. *Mānas, Bāla Kāṇḍa, dohā* 219, *chaupai* 2.

72. Sen. D.C., 1920:(reprint 1987):107.

73. Valmiki *Rāmāyana*, I:66:15.

74. *Padma Purāṇa, adh.*, 112.

75. *Devī Bhāgvata Purāṇa, skanda* 3, *adh.* 28.

76. Kashmiri *Rāmāyana*, *Bāla Kāṇḍa,*, *5*. (See Grierson. G.A., *Bulletin SOAS*:V:285.)

77. *Paumacariyam, Ayodhyā Kāṇḍa*, XXI:12.

78. *Mānas, Bāla Kāṇḍa, dohā* 256*: chaupai* 4*; dohā* 257, *chaupai* 1–3.

79. *Ānanda Rāmāyana*, I:3:58–60.

80. *Bhāvārtha Rāmāyana*, I:17.

81. Valmiki *Rāmāyana*, I:68:11–18.

82. *Mānas, Bāla Kāṇḍa, dohā* 294, *chaupai* 1.

83. ——, *dohā* 296, *chaupai* 1–2; *dohā 300*, *chaupai* 2.

84. Valmiki *Rāmāyana*, I:68.

85. *Mānas, Bāla Kāṇḍa, dohā* 349, *chaupai* 1–2.

86. *Irāmvatāram*, I:13.

87. *Udāra Rāghava*, III:103.

88. *Mānas, Bāla Kāṇḍa, dohā* 323, *chaupai* 1–2; *dohā* 327, *chaupai* 1–2; *dohā* 335, *chaupai* 3.

89. ——, *dohā* 318, *chaupai* 1–2.

90. ——, *dohā* 323, *dohā* 1, 2, 3.

91. Krttivasa *Rāmāyana*, I:147.

92. *Adhyātma Rāmāyana*, III:5:11.

93. *Bhattīkāvya*, IV:15–18.

94. *Paumacariyam, Ayodhyā Kāṇḍa*, 36:6–12.

95. *Mānas, Araṇya Kāṇḍa, dohā* 16, *chaupai* 2–5.

96. *Paumacariyam, Sundara Kāṇḍa*, 48:7–15.

97. Singh, V.B., 1991:44–45.

98. Valmiki *Rāmāyana*, II:107:3–4.

99. Singh, V.B., 1991:43–44.

100. Rao, V.N., 1991:133.

3

Humiliation, Abuse and Discrimination of Women

Cynicism prevails and questions have been raised about whether a totally egalitarian relationship between the sexes existed because it is difficult to prove that there ever was such a community wherein an egalitarian economy with collective and communal ownership of resources prevailed in India even before the rendering of the *Rāmakathā* stories occupied the popular imagination. In the earliest literary memory of the Vedic *mantras*, woman was regarded and respected as the creator of the human race. The myth of Aditi and her sons, the Adityas, was preserved in the *Ṛgveda*. Aditi was acknowledged there as the divine mother of all the Vedic gods. Aditi's womb has been associated with the naval or the centre of Earth, *Prithivi.* Visnu was believed to have sheltered her womb from which this world and its creatures materialised. The ancient Indians believed that there is "a pulse of the mother heart, the pulse of the energy of compassion, love and protective attitude, all that is associated with the idea of mother, behind the universe, so they spoke and sang of God as mother, as *parāśakti*, the Supreme Energy, or *parāprakṛti*, the Supreme Nature from which life originated and was sustained[1]." Similarly, the mundane mother strengthens the life of a child by imparting warmth and nourishment in her womb, and continues to do so by feeding the child with her milk. She is the sustainer of life and the contributor of nourishment to a child. Ideological statements covering the mother's role were recognized by the male elite of all ages. A common belief in society, according to Manu[2], was that Laksmi dwelt in maidens, who are the personification of chastity and, therefore, auspicious in every social occasion. He further commented, "Where women are revered, there the Gods rejoice, but where they are not, no rites bear any fruit." *Manu Smṛti* accepted that women have such qualities as inherent purity (*tesam svabhāvikā sucivādi guṇānām avagamat*) and the *Viṣṇu Purāṇa* asserted that women are inherently blessed with good fortune (*strīnām svabhāvato dhanyatvavagamad api*). This idea prevailed in the various *Rāmakathās,* both in the earlier and later expositions. Valmiki refers to unmarried maidens as an indispensable requisite for the coronation ceremony of Rama. Similarly, *Adhyātma Rāmāyana*[3] says, "Virgins were mandatory to be stationed at the main gate of the palace on auspicious occasions because they were considered lucky." The 16th century poet Tulsidas[4] was a great devotee of Rama and worshipped him as an incarnation of Visnu whereas Sita was alluded to as Laksmi, the inner power (*śakti*) of Visnu himself.

This, however, was a facade behind which the real face of a mundane woman was hidden. The truth was that *dharma* had not been very kind to women. The patriarchal family tradition, which governed the caste-ridden social system, did not permit women to benefit from all these elevated illustrations of her image that reflect the ingenuity of some of the ancient composers. A lofty image of the divine feminine did not bear any corroboration in the real social plane where she was downgraded to a humble status. Conventional texts of early India did not acknowledge the feminine gender as a meaningful segment of society. Men were accorded primacy and legitimacy in the construction and process of social evolution. Women were dealt with insignificance and passivity. Women were ignored, relegated to limited spheres and were largely misrepresented. In male monopolised cultures defined by the male-centred hierarchical ideologies, women's conceptions were merely secondary.

The established and accepted goddesses in the Hindu mythology were those who were conventionally married and who had transferred control of their sexuality [power (*śakti*)/nature (*prakṛti*)] to their husbands. Goddesses were worshipped regularly as mothers, rather than as wives; they were considered protectors and, therefore, a goddess was called 'a mother' rather than 'a wife'. This concept of transforming womanhood to universal motherhood was gradually modified by the altering patriarchal formation of society, in which the father cult prevailed. Hindu ideologies presented an important duality. On the one hand, woman was fertile, benevolent, and a bestower of life and love. She was *parāśakti*, energy personified. She was the energizing principle of nature. All creation and all the power of the world were based on femininity. She was the Mother. If this *śakti* or *prakṛti*, or the power of nature, however, was uncontrolled, it would bring devastation to the world (power + nature = danger). So *puruṣa* is the cosmic person, the spirit, the male counterpart, who controls *prakṛti* within a coded system. The unity of *puruṣa* and *prakṛti* (spirit of the cosmic person and the undifferentiated matter of nature) underlay biological conception. Therefore, the common perception was that woman was the field or the earth into which man put his seed. Woman was the active female counterpart (nature) and cosmic *puruṣa* was the inactive male aspect. Women's contribution to biological reproduction, however, was underestimated. The worship of woman energy (*parāśakti*) was not really an acknowledgement of female empowerment because woman was confined to stipulated preconditions. Only married women, not single women or widows, and, specifically, the mother of a son was worshipped as a goddess. Therefore, the Vedic lore of worshipping female deities did not necessarily imply an exalted social status for women in society.

In the earliest version of the *Rāmakathā*, as composed by Valmiki, the patriarchal social fabric had become the assertive feature. In a male-dominated social formation, man's command and ownership of his female counterpart established the capacity of his lordship. Motherhood and its adorable aspects were minimised and were limited to contextual references. Instead, the negative forces of feminine power came to the forefront. Motherhood was related with legitimate procreation and it had many biological stages such as menstruation, copulation, pregnancy and childbirth. During menstruation and the post-delivery stages, women were considered unclean. As a result, rituals and *mantras* were formulated with the objective of purification of a mother. Thus, *mantras* and rituals occupied paramount status during childbirth and, sometimes, they were considered more important than the biological processes involved with it. In the *Rāmakathās*, Dasaratha performed ritualistic *yajñas* for the purpose of acquiring sons. The performance of the *putreṣṭhī yajña* by King Dasaratha found its place in every retelling of the epic. Millassoux[5] offered a challenging suggestion by arguing that because women were the "sole agents of genetic reproduction", the fruit of reproduction, the children, was directly craved for and, "women were brought under subjugation in order to establish control over the progeny." Men pined for control over women to ensure the purity of the *brahminical* structure. During pregnancy and childbirth, sex segregation was primarily done to maintain the purity of the household, but women bore her anxiety, depression and feeling of isolation alone because she could never expect her husband to extend psychological support to her.

The basic notion that prevailed in all *Rāmakathās* was that women were a different kind of human species. Nature had, of course, created mankind unequally. Opportunities offered to men and women were different. As a result, their overall development became disproportionate. "But to create adverse social conditions, frustrating and impeding the fair opportunities for physical and mental development of women meant that society considered them of unequal merit. Inequalities in the social context are not provided by nature but culturally constructed by human beings, under particular historical conditions[6]." Women were considered a large undifferentiated species, whose entity was inferred rather than detailed, and who were mostly peripheral to central discussions. Their dissimilar status was projected in every sphere of their lives—social, moral, religious, economic or political; this was not gauged on the scales of nature but on the scales of male analyses of social restrictions. The persevering patriarchal structure that was consistently embedded in society helped inculcate an acceptance of endless social stratification. Gender issues revolved around the unequal status given to women, who were considered to be inferior in every walk of life, irrespective of their social, economic or educational background. Reasoning and sensibility of the mind were associated exclusively with the masculine nature whereas women were considered the personification of emotion, disorder and unbridled behaviour. Women's bodies and minds needed to be regimented to fit into and adjust with patriarchal social traditions. This was termed *dharma*. Manu[7] says, "No rite is performed for women with the recitation of ritual formulas that is the well-established rule." Without the strength of ritualistic formulae, women were 'untruth'. The mere fact of femaleness was seen as proof of sin. Manu and the *Mahābhārata* both asserted that being born a woman was the result of particular sins in previous births. *Dharma,* as specified by the codifiers of ancient India, was based on socio-cultural and historical circumstances rather than on the personal question of faith or the notion of spiritual value. Society formulated those conceptions of *dharma* that underpinned its dominant value system. Women were classed at a lower rung of Hindu society, barring them the privileges which the men of the same family enjoyed. As early as the period of *Śatapatha Brāhmāṇa*[8], women were linked to creatures such as dogs, vultures and *śūdras*. Women did not have the right to Vedic education and the *upanayana*[9]. Manu prescribed the same rules for purification of women as those for *śūdras*. Male-controlled, caste-ridden *brahminical* socio-moral standards provided the basic framework on which the suppression of women's identity rested. Our ancient law-givers prescribed sex-based rules of law. The crime may be the same but the punishment for men and women differed. In case the offender was a man, the 'crime' was not taken seriously but was considered a 'privilege' of man; whereas, in the case the offender was a woman, it was judged an unpardonable crime and drew a more severe punishment, to provide a lesson to other women in society. The male-dominated society of the *Rāmakathās* tried in innumerable ways to make women humble, injure their dignity and self-respect. Humiliating women symbolically confirmed their lower strata in the social hierarchy and reached, in most cases, to the levels of oppression. The highest form of humiliation and oppression is the use of physical violence and rape. A survey of the *Rāmakathās*, in the background of their historical milieu, elucidates the conviction that in every period of its rewritings, women were humiliated, humbled and oppressed by male-dominated social orders.

Law-givers, who sanctioned the social behaviour in various epochs of our ancient history, supported the theology of the subordination of the feminine. According to Manu[10], "even in their own homes, a female, whether she is a child, a young women or an old lady, should never carry out any task independently. As a child, she must remain under her father's control; as a young woman, under her husband's and when her husband is dead, she shall be under her son's care." The codifiers rewrote the 'goddess' theory with a 'husband-worshipping' theology, and *strīdharma* became a synonym with *pativratādharma*. The model was of a woman docile, subdued and subservient to males, a passive instrument to fulfill male requirements. She must be self-denying, self-sacrificing—in fact, she must not have any desire of her own. Manu's injunctions were approved of and reiterated by all law-givers. Narada[11] said that it was independence that ruined women. Brihaspati[12] declared that a woman must be restrained from slightest transgressions by her relations, and day and night she must be watched by her mother-in-law and other wives of the household. Visnu and Vasistha reiterated similar views. Women were not independent, men were their masters. The question arises: what was the need to control women's sexuality? The answer was clearly provided by the law-givers themselves. Manu said that women needed to be controlled in order to maintain the purity of the offspring and, thus, the lineage. This was the central cause for the successful perpetuation of patriarchy. The idea of a 'divine mother', who is source of creation in Vedic times, was discarded to save the patriarchal, caste-oriented stratified social order of the later period, which preponderated the *Rāmakathā* tradition.

Preconceived notions and imperfect assumptions misinterpreted women's nature and provided a biased data for future estimation. Women were condemned as the source of all troubles. Female sexuality was considered an inherent danger for the prevailing social order. 'Silence' was imposed on women so that their behaviour could be regulated. It was believed that women were provocative and lured men. The dominant trend was that women's passion should be regulated by social morality. Their conjugal relations were to be governed by duty over desire. Women's destiny triumphed over her sexuality and women absorbed these restrictions as their own (*swadharma*). Women's *dharma* was sanctioned by socially approved conduct and righteousness. Kunal Chakravarty[13] comments, "*Brahminical* religion displayed a paranoiac fear of the malevolent power of a sexually aroused woman, who has been rejected." Women were portrayed as the creatures of passion, not suited for the spiritual life and as the most powerful obstacle to man's pursuit of it. Men always tried to blame the seductress for their own lack of self-restraint. There was a conflict between legitimate, habitual male aspirations and unrecognised, nonetheless powerful urge of feminine desires, which were given a vicious hue. "It was considered that an insubordinate woman was more cruel and ill-natured than a fierce animal or a murderer[14]." Manu[15] condemned women as the worst kind of human species. He said, "Lechery, fickleness of mind and hard heartedness are innate in them even when they are carefully guarded in this world, they become hostile to their husbands." In the *Anuśāsana Parva* of the *Mahābhārata*[16], Bhisma explained the nature of women to Yudhisthira. He said, "Women are inherently fickle, difficult to manage and, in their very nature, difficult to understand." Similarly, Agastya muni in Valmiki's *Rāmāyana*[17] says to Rama, "Women become attached to the person in affluence but leave him in adversity. In their attachments, they are unstable like lightning; in snapping affection, they are sharp as weapons; and in evil, they are quick as the wind or the winged bird." The Jain *Rāmāyana Paumacariyam*[18] conveys similar views when Rama commented, "Even if a wicked woman dies, she looks at someone else and adores someone else. Who could understand the conduct of a woman? ... She is filled with doubts like the forest and could be controlled with great efforts like the treasures." Even the later composer Tulsidas[19] criticised women in a similar way. *Vidhihun na nāri hridaya gati jāni sakala kapata accha avaguna khāni* (Not even the gods can fathom the ways of a woman's heart, the repository of all deceit, sin and vice). Similar expressions were repeated again and again by Tulsidas. Interestingly, even when natural calamities such as drought occurred, it was attributed to a 'sinful woman'. Krttivasa[20] in his

Bengali *Rāmāyana* said, "Lomapada's kingdom suffered from drought because impure girls resided in it." In the didactic portion of the *Rāmakathās*, many indignities and insults were hurled upon women by men to impose male superiority morally and psychologically, to make women to continue living under oppressive male domination and humiliation. Swami Vivekananda[21] commented, "They were mentioned as insatiated with carnal pleasures, lascivious, immoral, heartless, fickle and inconsistent. Therefore, they were kept under perpetual tutelage throughout their lives and were classed amongst possessions and property." Women were defamed in the worst possible terms and were subjected to most humiliating subservience to men.

Stridharma, as outlined in the *Dharmaśāstras,* gave detailed instructions about the conduct, posture, duty and behaviour of a 'good woman', which was reinforced in the *Rāmakathās* as well. Valmiki's *Rāmāyana* crystallises *strīdharma* with *pativratādharma*, whereby the mindless inculcation of male excellence resulted in conceptualising a character like Sita, whose subjugation and self-sacrifice created a model for future generations. Ideologically, Indian women were presented as stereotypes of the impeccable woman. The ideology of *pativratā* nullified the very individuality of women. She was not permitted to have even her own little pleasures and leisure. She was to eat, drink and dress according to her husband's desires. Manu[22] dictated the path, "Day and night, men should keep their women from acting independently; for attached as they are to sensual pleasures, men should keep them under their control." In fact, women themselves assimilated the social expectations. The *strīdharma* and *pativratādharma*, imposed on them by male-dominated codifiers, were internalised by women themselves, who sustained this inhuman subjugation and advocated in favour of these laws. They executed the job of pleaders and practitioners.

In Valmiki's *Rāmāyana*[23], Sita tells Rama, "She who has been given away as wife, with religious rites, will belong to him even in the next world." In another context she says, "I have never seen another man's face even in my thoughts." She further tells Rama, "A woman can never be happy even with hundred sons, without the husband. Husband is the highest god to a woman." Similarly, "Virtuous women regard their husbands as living gods, be they accomplished or not." Kausalya says to Sita, "The woman who fails to serve her husband in adversity is reckoned as unchaste." Similar views echo through the later *Rāmakathās.* In *Adhyātma Rāmāyana*[24], Anusuya tells Sita, "Following the path of a pious wife, you now follow Rama." Tulsidas[25] was a strong upholder of the *pativratādharma.* He said, "*Vriddha rogvasa jaḍa dhanahīna; andha badhir krodhi ati hīna; aisehu pati kara kiye apamānā; nāri pāva jamapur dukh nānā.* (Women go through pain in the abode of Yama if she insults her husband, who may be old, sick, mentally ill, poor, blind, deaf, bad-tempered or has an immoral character.)" Further, "She who is disloyal to her husband becomes a widow in her early youth, wherever she is born...Though woman is inherently impure, she wins to a happy state by serving her lord."

Patriarchal society helped in inculcating an acceptance of this social inequality. It upheld the system of subordinating women. From birth, a girl was regarded as a burden for her father. There was a marked difference in the way the birth of a girl child and a male child was heralded in society by our ancient lawgivers. Sacred rites such as that of *pumsavana* were prescribed solely for the birth of a son. There was no reference of *mantras* being recited at the birth of a girl child[26]. Her purification with *mantras* was prescribed only during her marriage ceremony[27]. No initiation ceremony, which made a child *dwija* (twice-born), was prescribed by the codifiers for girls; it was a special privilege only for boys. This *śāstric* statement regulated the gender-biased society, in which education and enlightenment were prescribed for a male child and which enforced the marital future of every female, discouraging her to pursue an independent academic life as a spinster. Higher education among girls was very rare although a few incidents were referred to in the later *Rāmakathās*. In *Uttararāmacarita,* Atreyi was seen as a student in Valmiki's *āshram*, studying with Lava and Kusa. Some lady philosophers were known in ancient times as well. They were known as *brahmavādins.* Usually, however, girls did not go for higher education. They were educated in their parental homes by their fathers and brothers. They were known as *sadyodvāha*—those who pursued their studies till they got married. Sita was such a lady. She learned Vedic prayers too. Some determined women confronted these limitations, only because the conditions of their birth, childhood and early maidenhood had provided them a supporting environment and were regarded by their parents, especially their father, as cherished daughters. This was definitely a departure from the usual favouritism of sons and set the tune for their unconventional choices. Only in royal families or in families with sensible, rational principles could some women accomplish their religious and ritualistic trainings. There is an interesting story of Vedvati, the high thinking daughter of Avaidyanath, a *brahmarsi* of illimitable brightness. She was engaged in austere penance[28]. She lived in a cave, in a secluded place, adopting all the outward paraphernalia of asceticism (matted locks, bark robes). She realized the insignificance of the world, the unpredictability of earthly life, and gained confidence by the power of penance. The story is repeated in the later *Rāmakathās* as well, for example, in *Brahmavaivarta Purāṇa*[29] and *Krttivasa Rāmāyana*[30]. A similar, ritualistic training was awarded to Kausalya. We find her uttering *mantras* when Rama visited her before proceeding to the forest[31]. Valmiki insisted that a pure woman should observe religious vows and fasts. Such training was given to maidens of noble families from their early childhood. Sita was quite conversant with these religious rituals. She performed them even during their exile[32]. Similar ideas were preserved in the later versions of the *Rāmakathās*. The *Adhyātma Rāmāyana*[33] describes how Kausalya was trained to do ritualistic *puja* at home. She was worshipping Durga and Laksmi when Rama came to meet her. Tara was another female character, who was trained in ritualistic worship. It is difficult to ascertain to what extent a woman could perform a ritual independently. *Mānava Dharmaśāstra*[34] said categorically, "There is no ritual for woman separate from her husband." A number of *gṛhyasūtras* did allow a wife to offer daily offerings in the domestic fire. Women were active religious practitioners but they had little religious authority. They were invisible religious practitioners because most of their religious rituals were performed within domestic spheres. Sabari, a low-caste woman in Valmiki's *Rāmāyana*, was a rare woman, who attained a high spiritual standard and was, thus, called a *siddhā, tāpasī* and *jaṭilā*[35]. But

Valmiki's *Rāmāyana* stressed that Sabari was a *paricārinī* (maidservant)[36]. It is interesting to note that whenever and wherever Rama met any male ascetic, for example, Muni Bharadwaja, Atri, Sarabhanga and Agastya, during his forest sojourn, he prostrated and clasped the feet of the ascetics. However, when he met the ascetic woman Sabari, she clasped Rama's feet. Sabari's gender, social status and spiritual achievements notwithstanding, this was considered the appropriate decorum. Later, with the effective influence of the *bhakti* movement, caste and gender distinctions were to some extent challenged, and an egalitarian status given to all devotees. The *Adhyātma Rāmāyana*[37] clarified this issue of Sabari when she asked Rama, how she, a woman of lower caste, could receive a favour from Rama. Rama explained that there was no distinction of caste, sex, name or *āśrama* in the path of devotion. Everyone had the same opportunity. Sabari was called the *bhakti mārga viśāradā* in *Ādhyātma Rāmāyana*. Similar expressions can be traced in *Ānanda Rāmāyana*[38], *Padma Rāmāyana*[39], *Bhaṭṭīkāvyam*[40], *Rāmacarita Mānas*[41], etc. Some ascetic women, who embarked on a course of austerities and attained a high standard of penance, figure in Valmiki's *Rāmāyana*[42].

There are, of course, many passages in Valmiki's *Rāmāyana* and other *Rāmakathās*, where we find parents showering their love and care on their daughters. The adoption of a girl child has also been referred to Lomapada was the king of Angadesa. His queen, Varsini, was the elder sister of Kausalya. They did not have any offspring. When Santa was born to Kausalya, she was given away to Lomapada, who adopted her as his own daughter[43]. Similarly, Janaka was not the biological father of Sita. She was found by him and adopted by him. Such adopted daughters were given wholehearted love and care in their parental homes. In *Adhyātma* Rāmāyana[44], Janaka cherished his daughter as the incarnation of Laksmi.

A girl's stay in her parental home has always been a short phase of her life. It was a basic duty of a father to marry his daughter to a suitable groom from a good family. *Manu Smṛti*[45] equates marriage for women with the *upanayana*, or the initiation ceremony, prescribed for men. This duty of a father became a burden because caste was a decisive, regulatory order in marriage strategies. In the persistent patriarchal structure, the marriage of a girl was an essential condition for the happiness of a family. Daughters were a hindrance to the family honour. A father lamented in Valmiki's *Rāmāyana*[46], "To be the father of a daughter is an affliction. For him that seeks after honour and no one knows who will take a maiden to his home, thus it is. The mother's kindred, the father's and they to whom she goes in marriage—three families are brought over into danger by a daughter." Patriarchal families considered "woman as chattel, a moveable property, who can be handed over just like any other inanimate object of dowry[47]." Sita recounted the story of her marriage to Anusuya in the forest. She said[48], "A father may be equal to Indra in every respect, position, power, wealth or honour. Nevertheless, if he has a daughter not yet married, from his equals and from his inferiors, he gets humiliation, censure of the worst kind." This view was repeated again and again in Valmiki's *Rāmāyana*[49]. Sumali (Ravana's maternal grandfather) wanted to get his daughter, Kaikasi, married. He too faced a similar difficulty. He told his daughter, "You are so beautiful, so handsome, so able and so learned. Yet, I am unable to find you a suitable husband. If people have any self-respect, a daughter is sure to ruin it." A father had the duty and right to select the groom. Marriages had to be solemnised by the father or a male member of the family.

Women were unable to disentangle themselves from male dominance because from childhood, the families promoted a persisting cultural and social singularity, which was laden with religious and ethical overtones. Family traditions, dictated by religion, played an important part in forming a gender-aligned, value system. The family, as an institution, reinforced the virtues of compliance and discouraged critical engagement. Maidens, from childhood, were restricted to the domestic sphere, and were submissive to the power and domination of the patriarchal ideology, which they themselves internalised. Their education and training within the family generated and impelled them to develop 'the virtue of the heart, but not so much the power of the intellect'. Compliance, tolerance, adjustment, deference, forgiveness—all these social instincts formed the basic components of the education of a girl child, which was developed at the cost of individuality. Religion was a part of the masculine power structure, within which social relations became gender and class-stratified. Religion never defended female rights. In the patriarchal *brahminical* tradition, women were systematically excluded from Vedic ritualistic religion because they were deemed unclean and, hence, closer to the *śūdras*. Menstrual blood, the delivery period and woman's sexuality were regarded as impure and dangerous for men. Menstruation was considered a mark of woman's sexual hunger and her innate impurity[50].

By *brahminical* norms, which affected most of the higher castes, a woman was not supposed to take any independent decision about herself[51]. Barring a few extraordinary women, conventionally maidens were nurtured and coached for a domestic life, in which free thinking or expressing bold judgment was deemed not a virtue but a vice. A maiden was psychologically restrained from the very beginning of her life. The eventual principle of a feminine birth was to get married and attend to her husband. Man needed a wife to beget children, to perpetuate his *jāti*. Man had to be sure of his paternity; therefore, the freedom of a maiden was not considered acceptable in the larger social context. "The rule was to see a woman as *kṣetra* (site, field), *dharā* (place), a site for men's work, conquest and control[52]." Pre-pubertal marriage "was an effective mode to secure the unpolluted womb of the wife as the sexual property of the husband[53]." The sole purpose of a woman's life was to procreate, eternalise her husband's lineage, bring children up, work day in and day out for the perpetual 'good' of her family. A woman could not even declare any apprehension about the fidelity of her husband. She towed the husband's line. She was her husband's exclusive and uncomplaining maid, and in that lay her sublimity. Men could not trust women. Chastity was the most indispensable quality of a wife. She had to serve her husband faithfully unto death. Women were considered as the fountainhead of danger. Male insecurity and anxiety rested on the presumption that woman had the capacity to disrupt the structure of paternity[54]. Her action, communication, thoughts and vision—everything had to be directed only towards her husband. Any deviation from it was condemned as the greatest sin.

Law-givers had elucidated clear-cut punishment for any marital transgression. Vinita Chandra[55] suggests, "There was a connection between adultery and the *varna* structure." Manu[56] explicitly said that adultery is censured, and punishment was decreed to men, who commit adultery with others' wives because adultery leads to the mixture of *varṇa* among men, from which sin follows and cuts up the roots, causing the downfall of everything. Vinita Chandra further argues that it was "the sustenance and maintenance of the social order," for which "tireless attempts were made" by the codifiers to prevent adultery. Yajnavalkya[57] clarified, "The highest form of pecuniary punishment is the penalty when adultery is committed with a woman of same caste, the second form is the punishment when adultery is committed with a woman of lower caste, and death is the penalty when it is committed with a woman of a higher caste." But a clear gender bias can be observed when we study the comparative degrees of punishment for and social stigma attached to adulterous females. Manu[58] said that a corrupt wife should be confined to one apartment and compelled by her husband to observe penance. Dislodgment from the household formed the punishment for the adulterous wife. Brihaspati[59] was stern about punishing an adulterous woman. Such a woman should be paraded in the street and plunged into water, should be torn to pieces by dogs in public places, her nose, lips and ears having been cut off beforehand for entering a man's house and seducing him. Half of this punishment should be inflicted upon the man.

The *Rāmakathā* composers followed a similar attitude when dealing with Renuka, Ahalya or Surpanakha. They are the true representatives of the prevalent ideology as prescribed by the lawgivers. Unhappy circumstances, unsatisfactory conjugal relations and frustrated sexual requirements of a married woman were not accepted as an excuse even for her momentary lapses. Hardly any support was available to a woman for common human frailties. They needed to be noble in every respect. Her crime was judged by her husband, who articulated her due punishment. Even a king had no jurisdiction over such incidents. Jamadagni, an ascetic, lived with his wife Renuka, a princess, in a forest. She was the mother of

Parasurama and his four brothers. Once she went to bathe in a pond where she saw King Citraratha, entwined in lotuses, playing in the water with his wives. Her heart was seized with a desire for him. As a result of her unfaithful thought, she came back home with a disturbed mind. The ascetic noticed her agitated erratic conduct and condemned her as a sinner. He ordered his sons to kill their mother; stunned by the situation, her sons got bewildered and could not act instantly. Father called on his youngest son, Parasurama, and asked him to slay his sinful mother. Parasurama killed his unfortunate mother with his axe.

In a similar way, another inflexible punishment for a lascivious wife was recorded in Valmiki's *Rāmāyana*[60] in the case of Ahalya. The tragedy of Ahalya took many twists. The *Rāmakathā* composers, who narrated the story, had their own perceptions about it, sometimes putting the blame on Ahalya fully, sometimes relaxing their attitude. In some *Rāmakathās,* it is said that Ahalya flirted with Indra unknowingly. The lustful king of the gods, Indra, took on the guise of her husband Gautama when the hermit went out of his hermitage to take an early morning bath. When Gautama came back and saw Indra emerging from his hut, he suspected him and his own wife. He instantly cursed Indra and Ahalya both. The *Mahābhārata*[61] also recounts this story. Viewing Ahalya's unfaithful behaviour, Gautama *muni* became so furious that he ordered his son Cirakarita to kill his mother. The son, however, thought over the incident with a cool mind, and found his mother innocent because she had been deceived by Indra, who had assumed Gautama's form. So her act was done unknowingly and, therefore, was not worthy of such a harsh punishment. He did not kill his mother and, later, Gautama also realized her innocence and did not curse her. Valmiki's *Rāmāyana* in *Uttarakāṇḍa*[62] as well did not castigate Ahalya because she was the victim of Indra's machination. But the *Bālakāṇda* of Valmiki's *Rāmāyana* held Ahalya responsible for her action. Although Indra entered her cottage in the guise of her husband Gautama *muni,* Valmiki said she did recognise the imposter. She was not actually raped by the deceitful Indra but she encouraged the sexual act. She said to Indra, "O, amorous one, my enchanting beauty does not wait for their monthly course. So you satisfy my desire now." Perverse Ahalya, knowing that it was Indra, who had come in the guise of the ascetic, agreed to his proposal. After enjoyment, Ahalya said to Indra, "My desire has been satisfied; now take me away from this place and protect myself and yourself from the wrath of Gautama." Indra replied, "I have been gratified and now let me go to my place." With these words, Indra left the cottage with hurried steps. Seeing Indra, thus, stealing away from his cottage in the attire of an ascetic, Gautama cursed him in anger, "You have enjoyed my wife assuming my form, you will be sexless." And to Ahalya, he said, "You will live in the hermitage unseen by others (*adṛṣya sarvabhūtānām*) till Rama's arrival; he will redeem you from your present situation." *Kamba Rāmāyana*[63] admonishes Indra for his unscrupulous behaviour. Indra had imitated the sound of a cock, hearing which Gautama thought it was daybreak and left for his morning bath. Indra then entered the cottage in the guise of Gautama and enjoyed Ahalya's sexual company. Ahalya was innocent in the beginning because she did not think of him as anyone else other than her own husband. She only realized later in the middle of the sexual act. But her folly was that she enjoyed the pleasure of sex, though unknowingly. Because of this, she was cursed by her husband. *Brahmavaivarta Purāṇa*[64] refers to Ahalya twice. In the first reference, Indra attempted to seduce her by offering her a position higher than even his wife Saci. Ahalya rejected his proposal and reported this to her husband. In the second incident, Indra took the guise of Gautama and enjoyed her company. Here also, Ahalya was innocent because she had been cheated by the dishonest Indra. *Padma Purāṇa*[65] repeats the story. Here, Gautama's curse turned Ahalya into a skeleton-like appearance, devoid of all her beauty.

Turning Ahalya into a stone figure was a later addition in the *Rāmakathā* tradition. According to *Raghuvanśa*[66], she was turned into a stone figure because of her husband's malediction. *Adhyātma Rāmāyana*[67], which is a part of *Brahmāṇḍa Purāṇa*, says that Gautama cursed Ahalya and said that she would "remain in the *āśrama* fixed on a slab of stone (*śilāyām tiṣṭha*)." Later many *Rāmakathā* stories such as *Kamba Rāmāyana*[68], *Ranganatha Rāmāyana*[69], *Ānanda*

Rāmāyana[70] and *Ramacarita Mānas*[71] spoke of Ahalya being converted to stone. Such was the plight of the helpless young wife of an old ascetic. Her natural sexual urge remained unsatisfied because her husband was mostly occupied in his meditation and *tapa*s. Ahalya slipped in her wifely obligations and committed a mistake, which was considered a heinous crime. Sex in women was constrained by their duty towards her husband. Even if she was cheated by an absconder of society, she was blamed for being a co-conspirator, who enjoyed the sexual act voluntarily. Later, some writers had different views.

Valmiki's *Rāmāyana*[72] recounts the fate of Indra. Indra was punished by Gautama; he was shorn of his testicles, and a thousand *yonis* developed on his body. Similarly, the *Adhyātma Rāmāyana*[73] recounts about the curse of Gautama, "*Yoni lampaṭa duṣṭātman sahasra bhagavanbhava.*" Valmiki's *Rāmāyana*[74] stressed that intercourse with another man's wife was one of the greatest sins a man could commit and he was given the strictest of punishments for this—he became an outcast, went to hell, etc. Jatayu threatened Ravana, "Another's wife should be protected like one's own wife from the (contaminating) touch of any third person[75]." Rama promised to kill Bali only because he was the 'abductor' of Sugriva's wife[76]. Adultery was condemned all through the *Rāmakathās*. Rama's action of killing Bali treacherously became acceptable only because he took the position of the punisher of an adulterous man[77]. Many of the *Rāmāyanas* such as *Brahma Purāṇa*[78], *Padma Purāṇa*[79], *Kamba Rāmāyana*[80], *Ānanda Rāmāyana*[81], *Krttivasa Rāmāyana*[82] and Tulsidas's *Mānas*[83] refer to the curse that Gautama inflicted on Indra. Indra, however, could reduce his punishment soon thereafter because other male gods strove to extricate him from the wrath of the sage. *Kamba Rāmāyana*[84] narrates that all the gods went to appease Gautama and release Indra from the curse. He was pardoned and the thousand *yonis* on his body were converted to a thousand eyes by the mercy of the wise men. *Brahma Purāṇa* says that he was exonerated by the hermit after he took a plunge in the river Gautami. *Brahmavaivarta Purāṇa* says that his curse was condoned after he worshipped the Sun god. And *Krttivasa Rāmāyana* says that Indra's curse was withdrawn after he performed an *Aśvamedha yajña*. This was male justice. Men could be absolved but not women.

Ahalya was to remain in her *asrama* till the advent of Rama. With the *bhakti* movement gaining ground, Rama was accepted as an *avatāra* of Visnu, who had taken birth to save the world. The *Mahābhārata* never referred to Rama at all in connection with the emancipation of Ahalya. But the *Uttarakāṇḍa* of Valmiki's *Rāmāyana*[85] says that Gautama had cursed Ahalya to remain in the *asrama*, unseen, till Rama visited her. When Rama and Laksmana arrived in her cottage, she received them with full devotion and subordination and the young princes touched her feet (*rāghavāu tu tada tasyah pādau jagrihatustadā*). In the later *Rāmakathās*, Ahalya was a stone figure and could only be brought back to life by the touch of Rama's feet (*Kamba Rāmāyana, Ānanda Rāmāyana, Brahmavaivarta Purāṇa, Krttivasa Rāmāyana* and Tulsidas' *Rāmacarita Mānas* refer to this role of Rama).

Infringement in the sexual life of a couple was morally and socially condemned by lawgivers. The *brahminical* male scribes, however, with their expected racial prejudices, highlighted many non-Aryan characters with lower social morality and voluptuous lifestyles. Men of a different racial background such as the *vānaras* or the *rākṣasas* were depicted as habitual exploiters of women's modesty. Ravana's sexual advances towards *apsarās, kinnarīs,* women belonging to the *deva* category and human females were repeated in numerous episodes, reflecting clearly the racial prejudice of *brahmin* composers. Adultery, however, was condemned even in non-Aryan social systems. Mandodari, in the Jain *Rāmāyana Paumacariyam*[86] explicitly said, "In the rule of Jinas, having sexual relations with the wives of others was completely discarded and considered inauspicious." Aryan males could not be excluded from this vice. Ancient literature depicted famous ascetics, fired with lust, who on occasion forgot their celibacy; a classic example of this was Visvamitra who begot Sakuntala by cohabiting with the *apsarā* Menaka. Of interest is the fact that Valmiki's *Rāmāyana*[87] never condemned a sexual act of an ascetic even with an unmarried woman, who may have aimed to get a virtuous son through a conjugal relationship with him. The story of the *brahmin*, Chuli, who was engaged in great religious austerities and a *gandharva* woman called Somada is relevant here. Somada asked the ascetic to grace her with a virtuous son although she was still a maid. *Kāmasūtra*[88] permitted kings to have access to any woman they found attractive. They were advised to employ slave women to lure attractive housewives. They could use force to fetch such innocent women if they resisted. Therefore, an extramarital relationship was only a crime for women; men received lesser or no punishment for similar transgressions. *Dharma*, or the law, was drafted by men and had a pro-male disposition.

Women themselves administered the male-biased laws and rules on their own daughters and daughters-in-law. When a bride arrived in her marital home, she occupied the lowest rung in the family rankings. Her mother and mother-in-law both commanded her to remain subservient, to attend to her elders, husband and brothers-in-law. Women operated in the socially endorsed *dharmic* way and by strictly adhering to their pre-ordained duties and restrictions that would help them create an important position for themselves in the family. The norms preserved in literary texts and traditions indicate that a woman's religion was her family life and that all notions of a woman should be submerged in the ideal of a wife. She was expected to follow the social requirements of marriage, and her religious practice was focussed on the welfare of her husband and sons. A woman's duties confined her to her home and involved home-making and motherhood. Family and society only had these traditional expectations from her. As a housewife and mother, she had to make every family member happy, and as a daughter-in-law she had to fulfill all the demands and expectations of her mother-in-law and sisters-in-law. As a wife, she craved the intimacy and support of her husband, which if unavailable, she must not bemoan. Self-abnegation and self-sacrifice were the decisive aspects of her character. She was the 'stress-absorbent'. She had to carry on with her 'duties' despite the levels of stress in any situation. She was to uphold the family's name and honour within society; this even implied suppressing her personal desires, sexuality or physical needs as a human being. Kum

Kum Roy[89], on the basis of the *brahminical* literature, highlights that through legalised reproduction linked with marriage, women were expected to participate in biological reproduction, but her rights over her children were secondary to those of her husband's. As a mother, she fulfilled the duties of a guardian with maternal aptitude, without any expectations in return. A woman's status in the family rose if she gave birth to a male child. Barrenness was the greatest grief and curse for any woman. The prescribed codes of Manu[90] and Yajnavalkya[91] provided details about which days of the month a husband should cohabit with his wife to beget a son. According to Manu[92], by having sex with the wife on even dates, sons are conceived, and daughters are conceived by having sex on the odd dates; hence, a man who desired to have a son should approach his wife during her fertile period (*ṛtu*) on even dates. Narada's[93] code of law forbade a husband to show love to a barren woman. If a woman gave birth only to girls, the husband should not have intercourse with her. Having girl children in succession was considered to be one of the inadequacies of the wife. All these prescribed laws gave men the option to resort to polygamy. The writers of the *Rāmakathās* accepted and followed this social custom in every rewriting of the epic. To pay respect to one's mother was considered a vital aspect of morality. However, a mother's requests can be overruled by the father's requirements. Mother Kausalya tried to stop Rama from going to exile by saying that a son had duties towards his mother too[94]. Similarly, in *Adhyātma Rāmāyana*[95], she insisted that Rama should obey her as well: "Just as your father is your respectable elder, much more so am I, your mother." In Valmiki's *Rāmāyana*[96], she argued, "Sage Kasyapa attained heaven by serving his mother;" and "You shall suffer for the sin of inflicting agonies on your mother;" "I have reared you up with affection and love and like the king, I am equally loveable to you; how can you leave me then?" But Rama refuted her by arguing that a "father's order is supreme over his mother's request." Rama told Sita to serve his parents during his absence. He even directed her to behave with respect to his younger brother Bharata because he would occupy the throne during his absence. She was asked to be careful not to say a word in praise of Rama to Bharata because it might ignite jealousy in him.

Women had to accept strict monogamy throughout their lives whereas men's polygamy played a vital role in influencing his wife's status in the family. Uma Chakravarty[97] points out that polygamy proved to be the source of anxiety in the king's household, since primogeniture was disputed only because there were sons from multiple wives. Due to the polygamous marital family structure, co-wives clashed with each other and hostility prevailed. There was constant power struggle in the women's quarters. The senior-most wife tried to do her utmost to maintain her power and position whereas the junior wives challenged her deferential status. Having a co-wife is painful for any woman. The story of Asita, as told in Valmiki's *Rāmāyana*[98], showed his two queens trying to administer poison to each other to destroy the foetus each was carrying. Women never tended to cultivate a common class sensibility regarding their exploitation. They very often became collaborators in the abuse of their own sex. Polygamous marriages generated strained relationships among co-wives. The women never faulted their husbands, who had condemned them to such a marital status, but retained their venom for their co-wives and step-children. Antagonism between co-wives was quite natural. In the *Adhyātma Rāmāyana*[99], Manthara warns Kaikeyi that if Rama were anointed king, "You will have to serve Kausalya as her maid-servant all your life (*tvam tu dāsīva kausalyām nityam paricārisyasi*)." That Dasaratha had many wives was recorded in most *Rāmakathās*. In Valmiki's *Rāmāyana*[100], Rama bade farewell to his 350 mothers and step-mothers before going into exile. The Jain *Rāmāyana Paumacariyam* spoke of 500 queens of Dasaratha. The Telugu *Ranganatha Rāmāyana*[101] mentioned 350 wives of Dasaratha. *Ānanda Rāmāyana*[102] and the Assamese *Rāmāyana*[103] enumerated 700 wives of Dasaratha whereas, according to Krttivasa[104], he had 750 wives. Kausalya lamented to Rama that although she was the eldest queen, her position in domestic matters was never supreme. The domination and subordination dynamic is expressed through the medium of sexual relationship in connection with love. Due to the younger queen Kaikeyi, Dasaratha never paid enough attention to Kausalya through her life. Kausalya said to her son that she had never had real peace of mind. She felt insecure[105]. Rama never understood Kausalya's pain. For the patriarchal mind-set that Rama had, his mother's emotions and feelings always took a back seat in his mind. His father needed to have a wife, who could provide him the required emotional support. Even though his favourite wife, Kaikeyi, may have brought such misery on him, Kausalya's role and responsibility would continue to be towards her husband. Rama restrained his mother's emotion by justifying his father's requirements. He said, "In your thoughts, you must not entertain this idea of abandoning your husband. It is the last thing a dutiful wife should think of. It is a cruel thing. While he is alive, your place is beside him[106]." A distressed mother, who had been wronged by her husband due to the polygamous social order muffled her maternal urges. She considered Rama her last hope, and her son, the upholder of righteousness, overruled her dejection with faithful consideration for his egoistic, self-centred father. The *dharma* Rama upholds is the law of male superiority and female inhibition. He stressed, "You must follow your husband. It is only by serving the husband, waiting upon him and attending to his wishes that a woman would reach heaven[107]." Even if a woman neglected her ritualistic religious activities, that would not be considered a sin because her *dharma* is only *pativratādharma*. Here again, for her, no other sacrifice and oblation was greater than serving her husband. The codifier Manu[108] enjoined, "Although destitute of virtue or seeking pleasure elsewhere or devoid of good qualities, yet a husband must be constantly worshipped as a god by a faithful wife. By violating her duty towards her husband, a wife is disgraced in this world. After death, she enters the womb of a jackal and is tormented for punishment of her sin." In *Paumacariyam*[109], Rama said, "Whether a person is weak or virtuous, damsels never betray him even after the time of death." Even if husband was atrocious, incompetent, and injurious to his wife, neglectful of his own duty as a protector of his wife, she must worship him and only then could she be regarded with reverence in the socio-religious-moral yardstick of the *Rāmakathās*.

The story of Anusuya depicts the depth of this perception. In Valmiki's *Rāmāyana*[110], Anusuya was presented as an old woman, living in her husband's hermitage with dignity and esteem; and her husband emphasised her virtues. In *Adhyātma Rāmāyana*[111] too, Atri praised his wife Anusuya for her austerities and asked Sita to go inside the hermitage to see her. Anusuya presented Sita two heavenly ear ornaments made by Visvakarma and also two lovely pieces of silk. She gave Sita a unique paste for bodily application, which would maintain the lustre of the skin. Anusuya's earlier birth is presented in *Mārkaṇḍeya Purāṇa*[112] and *Garuda Purāṇa*[113]. Vidyut Aklujkar[114] in her paper *Anusuya,* analyses the composite character of Anusuya by explaining and coordinating three stories related with this mythical lady. She argues that Anusuya of Valmiki's *Rāmāyana* and *Mārkanḍeya Purāṇa* are the same character referred to in the *Garuda Purāṇa*, wherein Anusuya helped to revive a *brahmin* named Kausika. This *brahmin* Kausika was a leper and his wife was Sandili. Sandili carried her leper husband to prostitutes as instructed by her husband. Once Kausika, by mistake, touched the body of sage Mandava with his foot. The sage got furious and cursed him that he would die as soon as the sun rose. When Sandili heard of this curse, she said, "The sun shall not rise." She had such a great moral strength that sun was unable to come out. All became dark. The gods and men were both got scared. They approached Anusuya, the other *pativratā*, to appease and mollify Sandili. Anusuya pacified Sandili, who allowed the sun to rise. Anusuya had such strength of character that she could give new life to Kausika. The story showed that women of high moral standards appreciated and supported other women of similar qualities. But Anusuya never understood Sandili's sufferings. Neither of the women condemned the leper husband for his unreasonable demand to carry him to prostitutes. They only tried to save his life and cure his ailment. For a woman, her husband's interest and enjoyment was the only thing to strive for. The most powerful tool in the hands of the male-dominated/caste-ridden society was the ideology of *pativratā*, in which women were thoroughly imbued, mentally and psychologically, to uphold the entire edifice of the rigid patriarchal organisation. Shalini Shah[115] comments, "It was an ingenious ideology, which eschewed the necessity of applying physical coercion over women in an oppressive patriarchal household, which would have been more difficult to establish and maintain. Instead, this ideology was used to elicit conformity with the oppressive norms on a psychological plane." The only consolation given to a woman, though handled unjustly by her husband, was her predestination. Most of the damsels in the *Rāmakathās* lacked self-reliance and strength to express their individual minds. Even if they comprehended the principles of legal and moral justice, they were incapable of pursuing this path. Their private feelings and conceptions were suppressed from childhood and trained to approve the wrongdoings of men, if any, as permissible eventualities and to their own destinies. Rama insisted that "Fate cannot be set aside[116]." Women had only duties and no rights. Whether treated well or ill, a wife should never indulge in ire.

Women's chastity was sullied if she were touched by another man. Women's integrity hung on an extremely delicate balance of modesty. In the Telugu *Ranganatha Rāmāyana*[117], Indra condemns Diti for sleeping with her head towards the foot of the bed and keeping her hair untied, declaring her 'impure'. These female-bashing statements of Indra were only a continuation of age-old code of conduct prescribed by *dhārmic* laws, pertaining to different stages of our social history. Manu provided a list of actions that would bring ruin on any woman. These include drinking spirituous liquor, associating with wicked people, separating from her husband, rambling abroad, sleeping in unreasonable hours and dwelling in other man's home. Judging the scale of the Hindu social laws, all the *Rāmakathā* versions have righteously condemned Sita for her abduction by Ravana whereas Rama's decision to sanctify Sita by a fire ordeal after she was rescued was justifiable. Valmiki's *Rāmāyana*[118] tells the story of the *rākṣasa* Viradha, who met Rama, Laksmana and Sita in Dandaka forest. Captivated by Sita's beauty, he took away Sita all of a sudden. Rama became mentally imbalanced by the sudden turn of events. He told Laksmana, "To tell you the truth, I have been more distressed today at the sight of Sita being touched by another man than by the loss of kingdom or by father's death..." In Valmiki's *Rāmāyana*[119], Ravana forcibly abducted Sita. He held her hair with his left hand and with his right, he clasped her thighs... Ravana got on to the chariot with Sita in his embrace. When Jatayu attacked him, he placed Sita on the left side of his lap and struck Jatayu. Sugriva reported to Rama that he saw that Sita writhed like a serpent on Ravana's lap[120]. *Paumacariyam*[121] also recounted

Ravana lifting Sita and carrying her in both his hands. *Bhaṭṭikāvyam*[122] had a similar storyline. Ravana carried Sita, clutching her in his arms, (*bāhupapi maslisya* and in *parigṛhya rāmakāntām*). Gradually, however, the composers of the *Rāmakathās* became more protective about maintaining the unsullied purity of Sita. The *Adhyātma Rāmāyana*[123] said that Ravana dared not touched Sita; he scooped up the ground on which Sita was standing and placing that block of earth in his aerial car, he hastened through the sky. Not only this, the poet initiated the story that Sita, who was carried away by Ravana, was not the real Sita but her substitute. Rama, who was an incarnation of Visnu, asked Sita to hide herself in the fire and produced a duplicate Sita (*tvam tu chhāyā tvadakaram sthapayitvotaje viśa*). Tulsidas also tried to save Sita's reputation from all possible dishonour using the same story of *Adhyātma Rāmāyana*. Tulsidas's[124] Rama advised Sita to hide in fire till he killed Ravana because his purpose of taking birth in this world was to save Earth from the atrocities of the *rākṣasas*. The *Adhyātma Rāmāyana*[125] further added that in the *Asokavana,* Sita stopped Ravana's advances by placing a blade of grass between Ravana and herself so that Ravana could not make her impure by touching her. Later on, when Hanumana came to her with a message from Rama, he offered to carry her to Rama on his shoulders[126]. But Sita refused such a way of rescue because it would have sullied her purity to be touched by a man other than her husband. So she consoled Hanuman by saying that it would be preferable if Rama rescued her by killing Ravana, thereby enhancing his reputation (*Rāmasya kīrtibhavati śāsvatī*).

Women were blamed merely on the basis of suspicion. Their husbands could penalise them for an offense they might not have committed. The classic example of this is provided in Valmiki's *Rāmāyana*[127] in the episode of Sita's fire ordeal. This was the most sadistic and the most inhuman way of ill-treating a woman. After slaying Ravana, Rama sent Vibhisana to fetch Sita from Lankapuri and ordered, "Ask her to bathe and perfume herself. Let her come to me all bejewelled." Sita was perplexed. She was eager to meet her husband as she had lived all that period of separation, bedraggled, tarnished and lamentable. But she had to follow her husband's command. Women were not entitled to exercise any choice. Women's submissiveness and their obedience to their husbands, even if unjustified diktats were imposed on them, were the criteria by which they were evaluated on how they sustained her high moral values. Rama's behaviour at this juncture revealed his male superiority and dominance over his wife. He treated her like a sinner. Rejecting her, he declared, "Remember, I did not do all this for your sake." He did it only to restore his family's and his own reputation. Ravana had challenged his honour and the supremacy of the Iksvaku family and, therefore, Rama's duty was to take revenge and re-establish his own honour. Rama saw the "stain on Sita's character" and asked her to go wherever she liked. He had no more use for her. He commented, "Which man descended from a great family can take back with confidence and with longing a wife who has gone and lived for about a year in another man's house?" Magnanimously, he offered her four possible choices. She could go to Laksmana, Bharata, Sugriva or Vibhisana. "You may fix your affection on any one of these four people. I do not mind. Choose one or the other of these, if you like[128]. This was an extreme case of male high-handedness and it highlighted the deplorable plight of women. Sita was not only slandered but was held accountable for a crime she did not commit.

Rama's rejection of Sita should be seen in comparison with the dictums of the codifiers. The *Dharmaśāstras* vary in their opinion on the question of the treatment to be meted out to women, who were forcibly abducted or raped. Manu and Yajnavalkya remained silent regarding the treatment to be given to the victim while laying down punishment for the wrong doer. But Brihaspati[129] advocated punishment for the victim too. According to him, when a woman has been ravished against her will, she should be kept secluded in the house, be smeared with ashes, made to lie on a low couch, and would receive a nominal maintenance amount. Attri argued that if a woman was abducted or raped by deceit or force, she should remain unaffected by the sin. But if she was violated by a *mleccha*, she should perform penance to purify herself. Thus, even the lawmakers prescribed only temporary exclusion from household activities or penance for such a victimised woman and did not justify her abandonment by her husband. Why, then, did *purushottama* Rama decide to abandon Sita? Initially, after her fire ordeal, Rama accepted Sita as his wife; however, he ultimately sent her away from her home when she was pregnant. He was portrayed as a selfless king, for whom the happiness of his people was more important than his own joy of life. Uma Chakravarty[130] says, "In all the canonical *Rāmāyanas*, beginning with Valmiki's, the *prajā*, a faceless, nameless aggregate, whose social location is fuzzy at best, is the catalyst for Sita's abandonment...Two moves are made through such a portrayal: first, it is the common people who are responsible for Sita's sufferings and, second, Rama is exonerated of blame. In fact, he too is a victim of the cruel expectations of the 'people', who in reality govern the personal lives of the kings and queens." However, this is not a logical or acceptable conclusion because the role of the *prajā* or 'people' was never so significant in such an uncontrolled monarchical state of polity. In fact, it was the *brahminical,* male composers of the *Rāmakathās,* bent on proving male domination over wives, who exaggerated the theory of *pativratā* and purity of wives to its maximum capacity. Wives should accept complete subjugation and subordination to the husband's desire and will. Here, canonical *Rāmakathā* writers have disregarded any sense of justice for women. Rama abandoned Sita to enhance his reputation as a benevolent king. He became a heartless husband, renounced his pregnant wife and showed lack of concern for his own progeny. *Pativratā* ideology overpowered women to such an extent that even wives did not blame their husbands but blamed their own past life deeds (*pūrvakarma*) or present life shortcomings, or their destiny, for any harsh treatment meted out to them.

Rama insulted Sita beyond endurance and renounced her in the presence of others till she was forced to ask Laksmana to prepare the pyre for a fire ordeal so that she could prove her chastity[131]. Sita's *agni parīkṣā*, by which a woman's *satītva* could be proclaimed and sanctified, was a theme of the *Rāmakathā* tradition. Later compositions all dwell on the episode with slight variations of perspective, reflecting the time-space variations of different writers. *Bhaṭṭīkāvya*[132] took a similar view for judging Sita. Rama says to her, "Molested on Ravana's lap, you who have left scars on my heart, fix your mind on Sugriva or enjoy pleasures from Bharata or choose Laksmana..." Rama's suspicion and reservation about the purity of Sita was illuminated by the fire god himself, who rebuked Rama, when He was invoked for the fire ordeal of Sita. This episode was described by most of the *Rāmakathās.* Even in later compositions, such as the Oriya *Rāmāyana*[133], Sita was treated with suspicion by Rama after he killed Ravana. He admitted that he had rescued Sita only to save himself from public criticism (*jana apavāda bānchilu*) and declared that being the scion of the *Raghukula*, he could not accept a sullied woman as wife. Kambas's Rama was equally harsh on Sita. After killing Ravana, Rama summoned her in public, all dressed up and bejewelled. He said with a tone similar as Valmiki described, "I have won you back, having killed the foe. All that could be done by means of valour." But Kambas[134] shuddered at the crude thought that Rama told Sita to live with any other man. Instead, his Rama said, "You may end your life or live a worthy kind of life of your own." Rama, here, is more concerned about Sita's honour. He does not ask her to select some other man. Here is an indication of the approval of the *satī* system in contemporary society. Not only did Kamban suggest that Sita could end her life but he also referred to the fact that 60,000 damsels of Dasaratha had preferred to follow the path of their husband after his demise. The *satī* system of the Middle Ages in north India had equal takers in south India. Ravana himself led a voluptuous life, had many wives. After abducting Sita, he told Mandodari, "You perform my funeral rites. Kill Sita and you immolate yourself in the flames in which my body will burn[135]." *Pativratādharma* supports the *satī* system. But the Jain *Rāmāyana Paumacariyam*[136] did not support the *satī* system, which imbibed the concept of forced killing. It described Ravana's end with its own conviction. After the demise of Ravana, damsels of his inner apartment fainted and lamented but, in the end, they took their bath and performed the purification ceremony. Mandodari, the chief queen, then accepted *sanyāsa*.

The *Vaiṣṇava bhakta Rāmakathās*, of course, tried to absolve Rama from all criticism related with this act of Sita's fire ordeal.

Rama could not be presented as a cruel man, who gave Sita such a harsh treatment. Although the *Adhyātma Rāmāyana*[137] admitted that Rama had addressed Sita with improper words (*avācya vadanbusah prāha tam raghunandana*), it brought out the new story of *Chhāyā* Sita (Duplicate Sita). On the advice of Rama himself, the real Sita had camouflaged herself as fire[138]. Only after the killing of Ravana did she come back to Rama. This indicated that the fire ordeal of Sita was just a *leela (*divine play) of Rama. Through this fire ordeal, he only brought back the Sita who was concealed in the fire. Tulsidas[139] gave the same clarification. In both these scriptures, Rama devotees were made to believe that Sita did not undergo any fire ordeal at all—it was only Rama's *naraleela*. Even Laksmana was not aware of that mystery. Tulsidas's Sita did not even show any anger or defiance when Rama condemned her as impure. Kandli's Assamese *Rāmāyana*[140] presents a more vibrant personality of Sita, who expresses her anger to Rama during her fire ordeal.

Sita proved her purity after the battle in Lanka. She served Rama with love and loyalty after their return to Ayodhya and, subsequently, she became pregnant. Sita again suffered indignity when Rama "her husband decided to abandon her permanently in the forest" because of certain scandals that were talked about in some streets. "In order to obtain *kīrtī* (honour)[141]," Rama sent her away to the forest discreetly. The concept of male prestige and reputation was so strongly embedded in the Indian ethos that male composers of later periods also justified Rama's action of banishing Sita. Kalidasa in his *Raghuvamśa*[142] said, "Having realised that this stain on his image could not be removed by any other means, he opted to abandon his wife." *Paumacariyam*[143] provided a similar justification that because of the loose talk among the people of Ayodhya, Rama was forced to take such an inhuman approach to Sita. Somehow, he convinced Laksmana to take her from the palace and abandon her in the forest. Similar viewpoints were carried through in several *Rāmakathās*. However, the Odisi *Rāmāyana*[144] gives a remodelled version of the episode. Sita with her delightful memories of their *vanavāsa* expressed her desire to pass some time with forest-dwelling ascetic families. Therefore, when Rama was informed of the unfavourable comments of some of his subjects, who doubted Sita's purity, he decided to desert her by sending her away to the forest on the pretext that she herself had desired to go. This, however, was just an excuse; the real reason was his own prestige and reputation (*Jana apavāda nāsa kore sukīrtti; enu kori tahin ki mun karai bhītī; gangā tire balmīkī āśrama pasa; rishi kuti dekhibāku tankara manā; koitobe nei shari asa bahānā*).

The Kashmiri *Rāmāyana*[145] gave a different perspective of the story. Sita was pregnant and had a jealous sister-in-law, who asked her to draw a picture of Ravana. After much hesitation and reluctance, Sita drew a picture of Ravana. The sister-in-law carried it off and showed it to Rama saying that she had seen Sita gazing at it and weeping. Rama believed the story, sent for Laksmana and told him to take Sita away and desert her in the forest. He wanted to have her killed secretly. Later on, when Rama met his sons Lava and Kusa, and felt repentance and remorse, he wanted to bring back Sita home, but only after she performed the fire ordeal once again. Sita turned down the proposal. She wailed that she was born a girl and wondered why she was not poisoned at birth because her fate is like dust[146]. The story of the sister-in-law was not confined to the Kashmiri *Rāmāyana* alone; many other renderings of the *Rāmakathā* such as *Chandrāwatī Rāmāyana* and the Javanese *Rāmāyan*a carry the story. Rama's behaviour in this incident was rather inappropriate because it clearly indicates that he did not abandon Sita under pressure from public opinion but it was a blatant failure on his part of not verifying the facts or the roots of the conflict within the royal household. This surely degrades the evaluation of Rama as a protector and promoter of *dharma*.

The story of *Paumacariyam*[147], in a new revelation, described Rama as having a battle with Lava and Kusa. Narada introduced the father to the sons and the fight stops then. With joy, Rama escorted his sons to Ayodhya, where all the courtiers and royal household rejoiced. However, they felt their celebration was incomplete, in the absence of Sita. Hanumana, Vibhisana and Angada were sent to fetch Sita from her hermitage. Sita said, "Whatever treatment was extended to me by Rama, there is no justification for it. Yet, in case all of you insist, I shall go." She boarded the Puspaka plane and reached the city of Ayodhya. She herself proposed the fire ordeal, to disperse any doubt about her chastity in the public mind. On hearing the words of Sita, the people were delighted but Rama was skeptical. When the heap of firewood started burning, all the queens of Dasaratha along with all the brothers, courtiers and the sons of Rama wept. The people of Ayodhya cried. They said, "Rama is heartless." Sita said, "Oh, Fire, in case my exile is justified, you should burn me completely." Soon the fire turned into a lake and a lotus emerged to take Sita in its lap. Ultimately, Sita was not burnt; she became free from all attachments and adopted *sanyāsa*.

The story of Sita's abandonment is studied by Rangacari[148], on the fundamentals of Bhavabhuti's *Uttararāmacarita*, which overturned the original story. Bhavabhuti added two strong female characters, who moulded the storyline and brought it to a happy ending. One was Arundhati and the other was Kausalya. When Rama asked Sita to go through another fire ordeal before allowing her to come back home with her sons, Janaka, Sita's father, questioned the need for yielding to public opinion. Janaka said[149], "Who is this fire to purify our progeny? Already insulted by Ramabhadra, we are given a fresh insult by these people indulging in such talks." He further lamented "the hard-heartedness of the wicked citizens" and "the rashness of King Rama." Sage Kasyapa's wife, Arundhati believed that Rama abandoned Sita because the poor, common people doubted her sincerity and it is a king's primary duty to protect the wishes of his subject, "Even though the people are beggarly, they have to be protected[150]." Arundhati, however, played a clever and decisive role by involving Laksmana. She questioned him, "What would the people of the cities and villages of Ayodhya think if Rama takes Sita back once again because Sita is absolutely chaste and holy in character?" Her trust in Sita's purity gave a subtle encouragement to Sita, and public opinion suddenly changed. People showed unanimous repentance for their unfounded criticism of Sita. Thus, Bhavabhuti introduced a new turn to the drama of the *Rāmakathā*, in which the reunion took place due to Arundhati's clever manoeuvering. One thing conspicuous here is Arundhati's role; by her cool-headed approach to Sita's tragedy, she was able to propitiate all the characters of the epic. In Bhavabhuti's *Uttararāmacarita*, Kausalya also figured as a spirited woman. She refused to re-enter Ayodhya and participate in the sacrificial rites because the city had deprived the daughter-in-law of the family. She chose to live in Valmiki's penance grove instead. She insisted that she would join the sacrificial ceremony only if Sita were brought back. Thus, she too played a significant role in rehabilitating Sita.

The Bengali *Rāmāyan*a of Krttivasa[151] presented the female voices of objection to Rama's order for the second fire ordeal of Sita. Rama's diktat was so atrocious that even his old mothers shuddered at the thought. They objected to it and said, "*Loiyā porikkhā ek sāgorer pār, ki hetu porikkhā nite cāho ārbār*." For Rama, his own reputation was so important that he replied, "*Porikkhā nānile dibe loke apobād* (If he does not insist on another test, people would blame him)." It can, thus, be seen that in many of the *Rāmakathās*, Rama was deemed a crusader and upholder of male-evaluated righteousness, and very few voices were raised when he acted against feminine dignity. There was very little censure of his act of banishment of Sita in the *Rāmakathās* composed by men.

The worst kind of abuse is physical violence. Valmiki's *Rāmāyana*, following the dictates of the lawgivers, vigorously condemned the execution and slaughter of women in general. Women were considered *aghnya*, that is, one who cannot be assaulted. In the context of Tadaka, Rama and Laksmana expressed similar ideas. Later on, when Laksmana expressed anguish against Kaikeyi and Manthara, he said that hitting a woman was not acceptable to Rama and, therefore, he was restraining himself. The later *Rāmāyanas* upheld these views. In *Kambas Rāmāyana*[159], Satrughna was about to butcher Manthara but Bharata pacified him saying that Vedic scriptures forbade a man to hit a woman. In spite of these injunctions, there are many instances of physical violence against women. The most known example is that of the thrashing of Manthara by Satrughna when he comprehended that she had plotted to incite Kaikeyi. Kaikeyi was presented as a virtuous lady until transformed by Manthara, who was described as the devil incarnate. Manthara, Kaikeyi's nurse maid from her natal family, understood only Kaikeyi's material rights and advantages, along with which her own destiny was connected. She was convinced that the downgrading of Kaikeyi's prominence was inevitable when Rama ascended the throne because Kausalya was bound to take revenge on Kaikeyi, who had been vindictive to her at times. Valmiki portrayed Manthara as evil, as did many other retellings of the *Rāmakathās*. The beating up of Manthara had a comical matrix as well. The story narrated how Kaikeyi fell into Manthara's trap; wanting to reward her, Kaikeyi tries to adorn and make Manthara's hunchback body alluring. Her hump was described by Kaikeyi as the repository of her brain power, propensity, jurisprudence, acumen and alertness. With gratitude to and admiration for Manthara, Kaikeyi adorned her hump with a gold necklace and anointed it with sandalwood. Satrughna dragged the bedecked and bejewelled Manthara across the floor destroying her necklace; Kaikeyi interceded with Bharata to save Manthara. The beating of Manthara remained an interesting part of the episode. *Krttivasa Rāmāyana*[153] described Satrughna as having thrashed Manthara with full venom...so much so, that he broke her legs (*Satrughna kupita hoye dhore tār cūla; cūle dhore kunjire se phele bhūmi tole; aye to kutsit kunji tāi hoilo khorā*). The violence against Manthara clearly pointed to the attitude of the *Rāmakathā* composers, who supported the autocratic behaviour of men over the theoretical injunction that women should not be physically abused.

In some compositions, Manthara is exonerated of her evil characteristics. In the Telugu *Rāmāyana* of Ranganātha[154], Manthara's reason for her anti-Rama attitude was explained. Once, when Rama was playing with a ball in the royal courtyard, Manthara stopped Rama's ball, which annoyed the child so much that he hit her legs and broke it. Manthara rushed to Kaikeyi in pain and narrated about Rama's misbehaviour. This incident stayed in Manthara's mind and she became hostile to Rama. In *Bhuṣuṇḍi Rāmāyana*[155], Manthara was shown merely as an agent of the gods. Saraswati, through the complicity of the gods, influenced Manthara to provoke Kaikeyi so that all acts of the *Rāmleela* could be initiated. In fact, in the *Vaiṣṇava Rāmāyana*, the incidents of Rama's life acquired the additional meaning of being 'preordained', wherein every character was serving and promoting the 'purpose of gods'; thus, Kaikeyi, instigated by Manthara, only sets in motion the whole series of events that were mandatory for achieving the justification of Rama's birth. This interpretation is given in *Adhyātma Rāmāyana*[156] as well. Rama took birth only to extinguish evil-doers. Therefore, the drama of his exile was preordained. To obstruct his ascendency on the throne, the gods sent Saraswati to possess Manthara, and then, Kaikeyi, to achieve their purpose through them.

The racial portrayal of non-Aryan women supported the act of physical violence against them. Race had an obvious and pronounced ongoing influence over legal decision-making. Assaulting or killing a woman of the *rākṣasa* race was considered a lesser (if any) evil that attracted little or no punishment. The *Rāmakathā* is a story of monarchical ascendancy and expansion of imperial jurisdiction over tribal communities of not-so-developed forest-dwellers. The main motive of the politics of domination was the crusade for authority, for which identity was invoked as a means of mobilization. The social identity of any human being served as a cohesive compulsion to achieve internal solidarity. The north Indian Aryans, identified themselves—racially, culturally and religion-wise—as superior to southern tribal communities, who belonged to different races and were designated as *rākṣasas,* an all-inclusive terminology. The female *raksasis* were mentioned in Valmiki's *Rāmāyana*[157] as having terrifying and fiendish countenances. The poet considered it to be the duty of a north Indian king, the defender and promoter of *brahminical* religion and social order, to punish, execute and annihilate the existence of such unknown classes of beings from the surface of Earth. Racial status was highlighted during the cases of mutilation of *rākṣasis*. The women in Ravana's harem were sometimes described as erotically charged beauties; they were mainly, however, given grotesque features and described as consuming such food that sometimes creates revulsion. *Bhaṭṭīkāvyam*[158] portrayed the women in Ravana's harem as always enthusiastic about the acts of sexual enjoyment, who seduced young men by intoxicating them, to fulfill their own purpose (of sexual enjoyment). The non-brahmin *Rāmāyanas*, on the other hand, gave a more sober resume of Ravana's palace. The Jain *Rāmāyana Paumacariyam*[159] described it as a place where "damsels with tender limbs reside and Mandodari was more graceful than Laksmi." The whole description of Ravana's harem in the north Indian *Rāmakathās* was based on racial hatred of any non-Aryan tribe. The racial bias of physical violence against women was an intrinsic feature of any imperial rule. Religion served as a powerful means of mobilisation. The killing of Tadaka by Laksmana is one such example. Influenced by Aryan ideology that forbade the killing of women, Rama and Laksmana hesitated to kill this *rākṣasi.* But their guru, Visvamitra, explicitly approved the killing of the *rākṣasi,* who did spoil religious rituals (*yajñas*) of Aryan ascetics. In Valmiki's *Rāmāyana*[160], Visvamitra told to Rama, "Destroy the terrible *rākṣas*i Tadaka for the welfare of the *brahmins* and the cows…nor should you hesitate from killing her in the interest of the four orders of castes, simply for the consideration that she is woman…" Further, Visvamitra clarified his stand by giving numerous examples to Rama about how *rākṣasi* women were killed in the days of yore. For example, Indra killed Virocana's daughter Manthara and Visnu slew Kavya's mother, the devoted wife of saint Bhrigu, when, at the request of the *asuras,* she desired the destruction of Indra. Gods and princes have killed many wicked women in Valmiki's *Rāmāyana*[161] such as Ayomukhi, a *rākṣasi,* of ridiculous shape and unashamed of sexual urge. She approached Laksmana with an offer to dally in amorous sports. Laksmana, disgusted with her behaviour, cut off her ears, nose and breasts. In *Adhyātma Rāmāyana*[162], Visvamitra told Rama, "Kill Tadaka without any hesitation because she is a *kāmarūpinī rākṣasi.*" This contradicted another of his comments, in the same text when Ravana described Tadaka as having bashfulness and timidity as her ornaments (*lajyā bhaya vibhūṣanā*) and condemned Rama's act of killing her. Hanumana killed a *rākṣasi* on his way to Lanka, according to *Bhaṭṭīkāvyam*[163]. Kamba in his *Irāmvatāram*[164] endorsed a similar action. There, Visvamitra advised Rama, "You should treat Tadaka as a wicked person. Killing an evil woman is supported; Indra killed Kumati because she killed and ate all types of creatures…what I am asking you is an eternal *dharma."* The *Vaiṣṇava Rāmāyana* tried to absolve Rama from this heinous act of killing

Tadaka by saying that Rama had, in fact, given her salvation by killing her. Tulsidas[165] said, "*Ekahi bān prān hari linhā, dīn jānahin tehi nija pada dīnha.*" Similar expressions can be traced in the *Adhyātma Rāmāyana* as well.

Non-Aryan women were given different characteristics. They were not only provocative but also had strong physical attributes. The *Adhyātma Rāmāyana*[166] presented strong women characters such as Surasa and Simhita, who could even challenge Hanumana. Surasa was a damsel of the Naga family whereas Simhita was a *raksasi*[167]. An amusing episode dealt with Surpanakha. She was an unconstrained woman of different racial and social milieu. Seized by passion, she approached Rama to marry her. This forthrightness in a woman was incomprehensible for *brahmin* composers[168], who considered the proposition an absurd perversity and an amorous courtship of an ugly woman, and did not rate it as a befitting action. The *Paumacariyam*[169] provided a pertinent argument in favour of Surpanakha. According to it, Surpanakha wanted to take revenge on Laksmana, who had, by accident, killed her son Sambuka. When she saw the comely Rama, however, she was enchanted by him and approached him. Rama and Laksmana made fun of the woman, teased her and subsequently mutilated her when she threatened Sita. The story was a fascinating part of every *Rāmakathā* retelling. In *Narasimha Purāṇa*[170], Surpanakha says about herself, "*Atīva nipunā cāham ratikarmāni.*" Such shameless advances by a woman to a man were condemned by all composers, more so, if she belonged to a different race, whose cultural primitiveness and barbarous disregard of *brahminical dharma* were highlighted as in the Surpanakha incident. The disfiguring of an immodest woman was regarded as a just punishment. The story takes various forms in the later *Rāmakathās*. In some of these, for example, *Kamba Rāmāyana*[171] and *Ānanda Rāmāyana*[172], Laksmana cut off her breasts as well; *Ramkien*[173] elaborated the story by saying that Laksmana cut off her nose, hands, ears and feet. The Jain *Rāmāyana Paumacariyam*[174] said Surpanakha was burning with passion when she approached Rama and Laksmana. She tried to conceal her identity by adopting the form of a beautiful maid. As soon as Laksmana discovered her identity, he threatened to kill her. She then scratched herself with her sharp nails and blood started flowing from her breasts. Here, Laksmana, in fact, did not mutilate her. It was the work of that wily woman herself, which her co-wives, that is, other queens of Khara Dusana, immediately comprehended. The same source tells the story of Lankasundari[175]. When Hanumana was on his way to Lanka with a message from Rama to Sita, Lankasundari saw him. She was so attracted to him that she proposed. The *Rāmakathās* composed outside the *brahminical* restrictions show a permissive disposition to women's sexual urge, especially when narrating stories related to non-Aryan maidens. Orthodox principles laid down the rules that women's sexuality was to be channellised and needed to be restricted within patriarchal family norms. The unconstrained and forthright nature of a woman was not acceptable in the male-dominated social ideology.

Man's candid expression of his sexual demand, on the other hand, was not a matter of mockery. Ravana did similar heinous deeds. He captured, molested and raped many maidens of different racial backgrounds. The poets of the *Rāmakathā* tradition criticized him as voluptuous, unrestrained and haughty but he was not an object of ridicule. The *Rāmakathās* outside the ambit of *brahminical* influence, like the Jain *Rāmāyana Paumacariyam*, evaluated Ravana with much compassion. Ravana is presented here as a pleasant character, a great hero, reputed for his knowledge, physical strength and his wealth. The male guardians of maidens considered him as the best sought-after choice as a groom. Maya and Marica brought Mandodari to marry her to Ravana, the best possible groom they could trace[176]. Gandharva women, being struck by arrows of passion, themselves entreated Ravana to marry them. The socio-religious criterion was re-evaluated, to some extent, in the later versions of the *Rāmakathās*, composed beyond the limits of *brahminical* strictures. In south Indian *Rāmāyanas*, women characters were more open-minded, had robust personalities, and communicated their sentiments boldly. Chandranakha (Surpanakha), Ravana's sister, was abducted by Khara Dusana. When Ravana came to know that, he rushed to punish the miscreant. But his intelligent wife, Mandodari, had the courage and an unprejudiced lenient perspective of the matter in hand. She said to her husband, "Whether she be daughter or sister, she never belonged to the parents. Leave the idea of war; send your courtiers and get them married[177]." Would such a plainspoken attitude of a queen be written about by a north Indian *brahmin* composer? Similarly, Kambad's Sita, imprisoned by Ravana, may be intimidated and dismayed by Ravana's approach but she had the courage of rebuking him. "I am not the kind of woman for you. I am another's wife. Think of *dharma* and set your conduct right. The wives of the others deserve protection as much as your own. Confine your sports to your own wife." Kambad[178] presents his women characters as courageous ladies, who had individuality and moral fortitude. They had dignity in their detached comments and expressions. This sort of straightforwardness was absolutely unthinkable in the context of north-Indian *brahminical Rāmāyanas.* There, a woman selecting her own husband and approaching him with a proposal was taboo. Women were mentally subjugated by their menfolk. Although the women in the Jain *Rāmāyana*[179], show more strength of character, more self-determination and self-reliance, courage to express their sexual urges; to some extent, the *brahminical* ideology of subordination had penetrated there as well. Mandodari, wife of Ravana, was praised by the *Rāmakathā* poets for her chastity, virtue and devotion to her husband. Ravana after abducting Sita wanted to entice her. But he was unable to do so because Sita denounced him. Ravana commanded Mandodari to go to Sita as his messenger. On this occasion, Mandodari made a very significant statement. She said, "I shall have to do according to your command, because for the sake of the husband even the immoral act becomes moral." This is the *pativratādharma* of the orthodox tradition which directed even the southern composers.

Hindu codifiers regarded a husband as the protector, guardian and benefactor of his wife. The word for 'husband' is *bhartṛ* and wife is *bhāryā,* that is, the one 'who supports' and the 'one requiring support'. A husband was also called *pati* or *nātha*; all these terms express the concept of the husband as the dominant partner. Sita considered Rama as her protector. She proclaimed her confidence in Rama's ability to protect her in the forest. Rama failed to protect Sita, however, against Ravana or Viradha; however, the *Rāmakathās* do not comment or criticise Rama for his failure. With her marriage, a woman loses the benefit of her father's custody. There are many examples in the *Rāmakathās*, which highlighted the failure of men's dependability and protection. A neglected, rejected and deserted woman could not take shelter in her parental home or with her kin group. Protection was only accorded to an obedient wife whom society considered flawless. In fact, Sita lost the protection of Rama because she had spent a long period in Ravana's household. In people's minds, if a married woman wanted to take refuge in her father's home, she could not be entertained. This idea remained prevalent throughout the *Rāmakathā* tradition. As recent as Krttivasa's time, the poet said, "*Pitri grihe yuvākayā sobhā nāhi pāye*[180]." Even in adversity, she would not be welcomed; she would be denounced in her parental home, if she left her marital abode alone. Even if her husband turns out to be unworthy, treacherous or a wife-basher, there was no going back to her father's protection. This *brahminical* perspective was preserved even in the Jain *Rāmāyana*. *Paumacariyam*[181] tells the story of Pavananjaya, a Vidyadhara. He married Anjana, a Vidyadhari, and left her for 12 years after she conceived. Her mother-in-law suspected her chastity and turned her out of their home. Anjana hesitated to go back to her own parents because she knew that she would not be welcome. One of her girlfriends tried to help her and took her to her brother Prasanna Kirti. As soon as the brother heard that she had come alone, was pregnant and grief-stricken, he also thought of her as a wicked lady. He closed the door on her face. That was the tragic fate of any woman abandoned by her husband. Her father or brother would not provide her shelter. The unfortunate Anjana had to deliver her son in the forest, just as it happened with Sita.

The social structure, in the context of the *Rāmakathās*, did not evince any interest about women's access to property. No economic protection can be detected in the underlying social fabric. Women's wealth, or *streedhana*, as enumerated in the legal framework of Manu, Narada, etc., was accepted in the *Rāmakathās* as well. However, *streedhana* was carefully defined in terms of moveable goods and a bride's ornaments, which were part of her dowry. An overarching survey of the *Rāmakathās* clarifies that the parents of the bride were socially obliged to deck-up their daughters with ornaments of gold and precious stones as much as they could possibly afford. Women had an absolute right over this but none of these belongings could have been directly utilised for profitable output. Bhattacharya[182] stresses that "through access to such resources, women's access to economic empowerment was never comprehended. In fact, limiting women's rights on *streedhana*, her access to other kinds of property had become restricted." Similarly, Shalini Shah suggests that "for women, patrilocal residence is virtually akin to disappearance at marriage from her lineage...In fact, the term used for bride (*vadhu*) means one who has been carted away. The bride is an alien in a lineage that she joins through marriage. Women are thereby itemized and their subjection is more easily guaranteed. In a marriage like this, the alienation of woman from her own family is so complete that she is unable to turn to them at any point of her life." Women's role in economic activeness, her direct participation or control over productive enterprise was not an issue in the social context of the *Rāmakathās*. Naturally, a rejected or abandoned wife had no provision for dignified survival.

Male-dominated, socio-religious principles prevailed in the *Rāmakathās* that were largely composed by the orthodox brahmins of north India. Another set of *Rāmakathās* were those that were dominated by the *bhakti* cult of the mediaeval period. With the rise of the *bhakti* ideology, Rama was raised from being a mortal king of Valmiki's *Rāmāyana* to an incarnation of Visnu. All Rama's flaws as a human character were absolved by these later *Rāmāyanas*. Rama's actions were given a mythological and philosophical hue of 'divine play'. There was a larger design in his being born as Dasaratha's son. He was born to save Earth from the atrocities of the *rākṣasa*s. Therefore, everything was preordained and there existed a hidden motive of supernatural power, which steered and determined all the events of Rama's temporal life. He was only the earthly instrument of the all-powerful god, Visnu. An atmosphere of divine play (*leela*) pervaded such *Rāmakathās*. Rama was called *puruṣottama*. He was considered the ideal son, brother and king. But that he was an ideal husband cannot be accepted beyond a point. The only point in favour of proclaiming him as an ideal husband may be that he remained monogamous in the earliest versions of the *Rāmāyana*, but so were all his brothers, which thereby diminished the claim that he was an ideal husband. Whereas Sita's life was solely about being an ideal wife. Therefore, that role models generated by Rama and Sita were structured on gender specifications is a fact.

A significant departure from the dominant patriarchal ethos can be seen in *Śakti Tāntric* philosophy, which was outside mainstream Hinduism and in the retelling of the *Rāmakathās* through folk songs and folk tales, which were mostly composed by women poetesses. *Tāntric* textual sources codified and rewrote the goddess theology, where woman power, identified as *Śakti,* acquired an independent cult status, which was mythologised in the *Devī Mahātmya*. Durga or Kali, the *Devī,* was portrayed as a woman not submissive and subordinate to males, but an independent and autonomous *devī,* who played a male role. She is the power of creation and destruction, both simultaneous, representing the highest principle of the cosmos. This new trend brought a significant diversion in the rewriting of the *Rāmakathās*. In such *Rāmakathā* stories, Sita was depicted as tougher than Rama. She had the sturdiness and courage to dislodge and slaughter the thousand-headed Ravana. The story was originally referred in the *Adbhuta Rāmāyana*[184]. It is said that "Rama was fighting with the thousand-headed Ravana when Ravana was able to pierce Rama's chest with a razor-edged arrow, which passed through the earth and entered hell." The *munis* then go to Sita for salvation. She "grasps Rama's bow and arrow and acquires the terrible form of *Devī,* ravenous, hollow-eyed, with a swirling look, long-legged, shouting loudly, wearing a garland of skulls, anklets made of bones, dreadful in speed and might, harsh-voiced, four-armed...lolling tongue, matted hair...She dismounts from the chariot armed with a sword and shield and like a hawk pounces upon Ravana...In an instant, she butchered off his thousand heads." *Adbhuta Rāmāyana* influenced later provincial *Rāmāyanas* as well, for example, the Bengali *Rāmāyana* of Krttivasa, the Oriya *Rāmāyana* known as *Vilanka Rāmāyana*, and *Ānanda Rāmāyana*. A complete deviation in Sita's characterisation was implicit in these *Rāmakathās*. She was not a scared, petrified woman captured by Ravana and saved by the grace of Rama but a courageous woman who could fend for herself and even helped her husband.

Folk tales and folk songs contribute to a new dimension and cater to a new analysis in the endless *Rāmakathā* tradition. More than propagating the exemplary deeds of Rama, these tales and songs highlight the meritorious qualities of Sita and other women of the *Rāmakathās*. In many cases, the story of Rama drifted from the sanctified classical tradition and portrayed him as a down-to-earth, unremarkable man. Sita, although projected as an unpretentious, village girl or the daughter of an ordinary village chieftain, manifested in her character an inherent firmness and fortitude, and a strong will power and resoluteness. A comprehensive study of these folk tales and folk songs is presented by V.B. Singh[185]. He studied the popular stories of Rama, particularly those composed in the Hindi-speaking belt. Similarly, K.S. Singh[186] provides us a glimpse of the *Rāmakathās* that have been re-adapted and recreated "in terms of the local milieu and ethos of the Munda tribals." K.D. Upadhyaya[187] studied the Avadhi and Bhojpuri folk songs, and D. Ramaraju[188] examined the *Rāmāyana* stories preserved in Telugu folk literature. Saraswati Benugopal[189] provides us some references to the Tamil folk tales of the *Rāmakathās*. A detailed study of the 'women's oral tradition' was done by Paula Richman[190], and Noboneeta Dev Sen[191] provided a glimpse of the Bengali folk songs compiled by D.C. Sen[192] in his Bengali *Rāmāyana*. These folk tales and folk songs provide an alternative evaluation of the women characters of the classical *Rāmāyana*, which echo through their own local cultures.

Women composers of rural India disturbed the male-oriented tendencies of the *Rāmakathā* tradition. They conveyed a female-focused narrative sequence. They highlighted episodes of the ignored women characters of the *Rāmakathās* such as Kausalya, Sumitra and Urmilla. They wrote about the melancholic condition of Urmilla, the unsung heroine, whose sacrifice and desolation was beyond the capacity of comprehension of male writers. They sympathised with Sita's anguish, the solitude she suffered as a kidnapped woman, the disgrace she faced as an abandoned, pregnant woman. These relatively new trends in the *Rāmakathās* have challenged the prevailing male bias. Women composers of folk songs and folk tales were much more enterprising, progressive, dynamic when expressing Sita's feelings. Sita was portrayed as a common village girl in Hindi folk songs. The pre-marital encounter of Sita with Rama crossed the confines of bashfulness. She went to a garden and ran into the young prince, Rama. He held her by her arms. Sita objected but succumbed to the feelings of her own love-torn heart. When she went back home, her face reflected her heightened emotions, which her mother noticed. Mother and daughter had a frank exchange of aspirations and dreams. She confided to her mother, "Mother, punish me as you like; admonish me, beat me as you will. I happened to meet Rama in the garden. He held me by my arm and would not leave me." Her mother supported her by saying, "I will get you married to Rama." There is a class difference between the description of folk-tale composers and classical writers of the *Rāmakathās*. In *brahminical* versions, Sita's mother, who perceived Rama in the *dhanurbhanga sabhā*, admired him and wished for his success in breaking the bow but was worried because Rama was so delicate looking and did not appear to have the strength to break the bow. She had no courage to ask her husband to abandon his pledge and allow Sita to marry Rama.

The male-oriented *Rāmakathās* present the image of a domineering father and an accommodating mother, whereas the folk tales show a strong-willed, self-confident mother, who could take independent decisions to make her daughter happy, without even thinking how the menfolk of the family would react. Folk songs and folk tales of the *Rāmakathās* promote the empowerment of women. In them, Sita was presented as having a strong character, independent decision-making mind and remarkable physical strength. Janaka's pledge of marrying of his daughter to a person who could break the *Śivadhanuṣ* was not because of an arbitrary, egocentric wish of a commanding father. He had been surprised to discover Sita's physical strength; she could lift the *Śivadhanuṣ* with her left hand, which he himself could not even move. In Telugu folk songs, Sita spoke about it to Rama, whom she saw as a *bālayogī*; after being convinced that the *bālayogī* would be able to break the bow, she herself requested her father, "Get me married to Rama[193]." There was no hesitation, no timidity, no societal barriers of modesty for the Sita of the folk songs. She was as liberated, self-reliant, unconventional, blunt and bold as any down-to-earth folk woman might be. All the women characters of the folk tales represented sturdy personalities because the composers were most likely women themselves. V.N. Rao[194] says, "The women who sing these songs have not sought to overthrow the male-dominated family structure, they would rather work within it. They have no interest in direct confrontation with authority. Their interest, rather, is making room for themselves. It is this internal freedom that these songs seem to cherish." The woman's role in every field of social undertaking was dominant. Women composers felt the pain of Kausalya, Sumitra, Kaikeyi, Sita and Urmilla. They sang on their behalf, expressing their own feelings, which epitomised the sentiments of the feminine world.

Kausalya realised Dasaratha's distress of being progeny-less. The disgrace of barrenness, which had defiled her name, was so painful that she was compelled to take the desperate decision herself. She made Dasaratha undergo two more marriages. She brought Sumitra, her own sister, and Kaikeyi, of an unmentioned family, as her co-wives so that they could beget a son for Dasaratha. For a woman, a son was so desirable that she could bear the pain and agony of having co-wives. The male-oriented *Rāmakathās* showed Kausalya as a dejected queen, whose husband married without consulting her. He was described as dilly-dallying with the youngest queen, leaving Kausalya to pass her time as an isolated, uncared-for woman. In folk literature, however, she was a dominating chief queen, who supervised all the family functions and directed her husband to marry again. Only in the women's *Rāmāyan*a do we find the description of Kausalya in labour, expressively speaking of the pain associated with it[195]. Mother Kausalya worried about the tonsuring ceremony of her child Rama. She pointed out its necessity to her husband Dasaratha. Her anxiety about the marriage of her son was portrayed in a natural description of a village woman in Hindi folk songs[196]. As a typical village mother-in-law, she tried to keep a tight bridle on the newly wedded couple. A woman was a very important personality in all family functions. She took the initiative herself and advocated her husband. Men were just speculative masters whereas the real power rested with the housewives. Man was a minor performer in women's *Rāmakathās*.

Women composers understood the pain of rejected and discarded wives. Sumitra and Urmilla hardly existed in the classical *Rāmāyanas*. Urmilla's sacrifice was consigned to oblivion. Women composers, however, venerated the memory of Urmilla in their songs, recognised her contribution in the saga of Rama's story. Laksmana, in his absolute obedience to his elder brother, was insensitive to the fate of his bride. In the Telugu folk songs, the tragic condition of Urmilla was remembered with pathos and sorrow. Although Sita suffered during her forest stay, she enjoyed the company of her dear husband whereas Urmilla suffered the agony of enforced isolation. The lady went into a somnolent state and lingered like that for 14 years till her husband came back. The women's *Rāmakathās* depicted Sita as a person of strong disposition. After return to Ayodhya, Rama was coronated. Laksmana got involved in court duties. Nobody, except Sita, recollected the fate of Urmilla. Men lacked sensitivity. Neither Rama nor Laksmana had any concern for the unremembered princess. It was Sita who ultimately reminded Rama, "Now, at least, relieve Laksmana and allow him to meet his dear one[197]."

Similarly, in the sixteenth century *Chandrāwatī Rāmāyana* too, Rama was immaterial except when he was mentioned in relation to Sita. It is a depiction of Sita's story, narrated by Sita as a character. *Chandrāwatī* related Sita's supernatural birth, her childhood and marriage, her anguish and her ordeal as an abducted woman, her pregnancy, her distress during her exile, and her entry into Earth. "*Rāmāyana* is a misnomer for this narrative. It should have been called *Sitāyana*[198]."

Women writers condemned Rama on many accounts, especially when he sent away his pregnant wife merely on some suspicion. Folk tales concocted many versions of this event. Some blamed Rama's elder sister Santa, who due to the typical jealousy of a sister-in-law (*nanadinī*), brought discord between Rama and Sita[199]. Some invented the story of Kakua, the daughter of Kaikeyi, who falsely alleged that Sita was secretly painting Ravana's face[200]; some of the Tamil folk songs put the blame on Ravana's sister, Surpanakha, who had not forgotten her attraction for Rama and wanted to retaliate.[201]

To sum up, *Rāmāyana* was originally composed by Valmiki and was later recreated and reframed through different periods of Indian history in every region and language. It had basically designed a male-dominated social fabric, in which women were subjugated and maltreated in every walk of life. The main story adopted some additional episodes to align it with the socio-religious understanding of the later writers; the *Rāmakathās* written by men bore a similar outlook, wherein woman was subordinate, inferior and served man's needs. Obedience, service to one's husband (*patisuśṛuṣānām*) is the primary religious duty of a wife. She should serve her husband without any regard for her own life like Sita did. When Sita saw her husband and brother-in-law Laksmana being carried off by a powerful demon, she begged the demon to release them and take her away instead[202]. It is only through the *Tantra*-influenced retelling of the *Rāmāyana* and the women folk singers that gave the women in *Rāmāyana* their due honour. Although these *Rāmakathās* are numerically so few, they remained mostly unheard of.

References

1. Ranganathananda, Swami, 1992:6–7.

2. Manu, *Dharmaśāstra*, III:56, 57, 58.

3. *Adhyātma Rāmāyana*: II:2:9.

4. *Mānas, Bāla Kāṇḍa, dohā* 3, *chaupai* 7.

5. Meillassoux, Claude, 1986:15–21.

6. Andre Bettaille, 1983:7–8

7. Manu, *Dharmaśāstra*, IX:18; V.139; XII.3.9; *Mahābhārata*. XIII.120.9.

8. *Śatapatha Brāhmaṇa* XIV.1.1.31.

9. Baudhāyana, I.5.11.7; Manu, IX.18.

10. Manu, *Dharmaśāstra*, V:147–150.

11. Narada, XIII.30.

12. Brihaspati, XXIV.2.

13. Chakrabarti, Kunal, 1999:72–73.

14. *Ibid.*

15. Manu, *Dharmaśāstra*, IX:15.

16. *MBH*, XIII:38–39.

17. Valmiki *Rāmāyana*, III:13:5.

18. *Paumacariyam, Uttara Kāṇḍa*, 81:5.

19. *Manās, Ayodhyā Kāṇḍa, dohā* 161, *chaupai* 2; *Ayodhya Kanda, dohā* 46, *chaupai* 4; *dohā,* 160, *chaupai* 3.

20. Krttivasa *Rāmāyana*, I:81–82, 87.

21. Vivekananda, Sw, 1948, *Poona Orientalists*, XIII.3–4, 64–67; 1949, *Poona Orientalists*, XIV:85–88.

22. Manu, *Dharmaśāstra*, IX:2.

23. Valmiki *Rāmāyana*, II:27:4–5; II:29:17–18; II:25:14–15; II:29:7; II:29:16; II:39:20.

24. *Adhyātma Rāmāyana*, II:9:90.

25. *Manās, Araṇya Kāṇḍa, doha,* 4, *chaupai* 4–5 & 10; *sopana* 1:1.

26. Yajnavalkya, I:2–13; Visnu, XXVII:13.

27. Visnu, XXVII:14; Yajnavalkya, I:2–13.

28. Valmiki *Rāmāyana*, VII:17:7–10.

29. *Brahmavaivarta Purāṇa, Prakriti Kāṇḍa, adhyāya* 14.

30. Krttivasa *Rāmāyana*, VII:170.

31. Valmiki *Rāmāyana*, II:20:16–17.

32. ——, III:8:3–4.

33. *Adhyātma Rāmāyana*, II:2:41–43.

34. Manu, V:155.

35. Valmiki *Rāmāyana*, III:74:9–33.

36. ——., III:73:26.

37. *Adhyātma Rāmāyana*, III:10:18–20.

38. *Ānanda Rāmāyana*, I:7:160–166.

39. *Padma Purāṇa*, VI:265–269.

40. *Bhaṭṭikāvyam*, VI:60–71.

41. *Mānas, Araṇya Kanda, doha* 34–36.

42. Valmiki *Rāmāyana*, I:1:46.

43. Valmiki *Rāmāyana*, I:9:12–18.

44. *Adhyātma Rāmāyana*, I:6:59, 65–67.

45. Manu, II:67.

46. Valmiki *Rāmāyana*, VII:9:10–11; V:15:48.

47. Mies, Maria, 1980:36–103.

48. Valmiki *Rāmāyana*, II:118: 34–36.

49. ——, VII:9:7–10.

50. Gupta, Samjukta Gombrich, 2000:90–91.

51. Rangacari, Devika, 2009:274.

52. Singh, P and Jaidev, 1999:4.

53. Chakravarti, Uma, 2003:7–74.

54. Roy, Kumkum, 1999b:18–37.

55. Chandra, Vinita, 2010:104–105.

56. Manu, *Dharmaśāstra*, VIII:352–353.

57. Yajnavalkya, II:24:286.
58. Manu, *Dharmaśāstra*, XI:177.
59. Brihaspati, XXIII:15–16.
60. Valmiki *Rāmāyana*, I:48:26–32.
61. *Mahābhārata*, *Śānti Parva*, 258:46.
62. Valmiki *Rāmāyana*, VII:30:37–45.
63. *Kamba Rāmāyana*, I:9:544–545.
64. *Brahmavaivarta Purāṇa*, *Krishna Janma Kāṇḍa*, *adhyāya* 47 and 61.
65. *Padma Purāṇa*, *Sriṣṭi Khāṇḍa*, V:51:28–33.
66. Kalidas, *Raghuvamśa*, II:34.
67. *Adhyātma Rāmāyana*, I:5:27.
68. *Kamba Rāmāyana*, I:9:548.
69. *Ranganātha Rāmāyana*, I:29.
70. *Ānanda Rāmāyana*, I:3:16–20.
71. *Mānas*, *Bāla Kāṇḍa*, *dohā* 210.
72. Valmiki *Rāmāyana*, I:48:27.
73. *Adhyātma Rāmāyana*, I:5:26.
74. Valmiki *Rāmāyana*, III:38:29–30.
75. ——, III:50:6–7.
76. ——, IV:5:25.
77. *Bhaṭṭi Rāmāyana*, VI:138.
78. *Brahma Purāṇa*, 87:59.
79. *Padma Purāṇa*, V:51:28.
80. Kamba *Rāmāyana*, I:9:547.
81. *Ānanda Rāmāyana*, I:3:19.

82. Krttivasa *Rāmāyana*, I:59:0.

83. *Mānas, Bāla Kāṇḍa, dohā* 210.

84. Kamba *Rāmāyana*, I:9:540–550.

85. Valmiki *Rāmāyana*, VII:30:43.

86. *Paumacariyam, Ayodhyā Kāṇḍa*, 41:6.

87. Valmiki *Rāmāyana*, I:30.

88. Vatsyayana, *Kamasutra*, V:5:11–21, 26.

89. Roy, Kumkum, 1999:20.

90. Manu, III:45–47; II:67.

91. Yagnavalkya, I:3:79.

92. Manu, III:48.

93. Narada, XII:94.

94. Valmiki *Rāmāyana*, II:21:52.

95. *Adhyātma Rāmāyana*, II:4:12–13.

96. Valmiki *Rāmāyana*, II:21.

97. Chakravarti, Uma, 2006:232–233.

98. Valmiki *Rāmāyana*, I:70:30.

99. *Adhyātma Rāmāyana*, II:2:63.

100. Valmiki *Rāmāyana*, II:18.

101. Ranganatha *Rāmāyana*, I:250.

102. *Ānanda Rāmāyana*, I:1:72.

103. Kandli, Madhav, *Sāta Kāṇḍa Rāmāyana*, I:11:63.

104. Krttivasa *Rāmāyana*, I:29.

105. Valmiki *Rāmāyana*, II:21:27; II:20:36, 37, 38, 42.

106. ———, II:24:11–13.

107. ———, 24:25–30.

108. Manu, *Dharmaśāstra*, V:154, 164.

109. *Paumacariyam*, *Uttara Kāṇḍa*, 83:8.

110. Valmiki *Rāmāyana*, II:117; II:118.

111. *Adhyātma Rāmāyana*, II:9:84–89.

112. *Mārkaṇḍeya Purāṇa*, XVI:51–63.

113. *Garuḍa Purāṇa*, I:42.

114. Aklujkar, Vidyut, 2000:56–68.

115. Shah, Shalini, 1995:82.

116. Valmiki *Rāmāyana*, II:24:32–33.

117. Ranganatha *Rāmāyana*, *Bāla Kāṇḍa*, 1410.

118. Valmiki *Rāmāyana*, III:2:17 21.

119. ———, III:20, 25.

120. ———, IV:6.

121. *Paumacariyam*, *Ayodhyā Kaṇḍa*, 38:12.

122. *Bhaṭṭīkāvyam*, V:94, 95; V:108.

123. *Adhyātma Rāmāyana*, III:7:51–52.

124. *Mānas*, *Araṇya Kāṇḍa*, *doha* 23, *chaupai* 1–2.

125. *Adhyātma Rāmāyana*, V:2:31.

126. ———, V:5:68.

127. Valmiki *Rāmāyana*, VI:117:21.

128. Valmiki *Rāmāyana*, VI:117:22–23.

129. Brihaspati, XXIII:13–14.

130. Chakravarti, Uma, 2006:241.

131. Valmiki *Rāmāyana*, VI:118:18.

132. *Bhaṭṭīkāvyam*, XX:21–25.

133. *Vichitra Rāmāyana*, VI:74:2.

134. Kamba *Rāmāyana*, II:4:602; VI:37: 3960; VI:36:3889.

135. *Adhyātma Rāmāyana*, VI:10:43.

136. *Paumacariyam*, *Uttara Kāṇḍa*, 77:18–20.

137. *Adhyātma Rāmāyana*, VI:12:77.

138. ——, III:7:1–3; VI:12:68.

139. *Manas*, *Aranya Kāṇḍa*, *doha* 23; *chaupai*, 1–2.

140. Kandli, Madhav, *Sātkāṇḍa Rāmāyana*, VI:50, 55.

141. Valmiki *Rāmāyana*, VII:45:13–14.

142. *Raghuvamśa*, 14:35.

143. *Paumacariyam*, *Uttara Kāṇḍa*, 81:3, 4, 8.

144. *Vichitra Rāmāyana*, VI:74:2; VII:16:1–9.

145. *Kashmiri Rāmāyana*, XLIII:285; XLVIII:164–66. (see Grierson, G.A., *Bulletin SOAS*, Vol. V) .

146. ——, XLVII:1585–1617.

147. *Paumacariyam*, *Uttara Kāṇḍa*, 83:3–17.

148. Rangacari, Devika, 2009:304–305.

149. *Uttararāmacarita*: IV:11.

150. ——, IV:24.

151. Krttivasa *Rāmāyana*, *Uttara Kāṇḍa*, *Sitā Debir Pātāl Prabesh*, 8:10.

152. Kamba *Rāmāyana*, II:11:993–994.

153. Krttivasa *Rāmāyana*, *Ayodhyā Kāṇḍa*, 53–54.

154. *Ranganatha Rāmāyana*, *Bāla Kāṇḍa*, 591–600.

155. Singh, B.P., 1980:500–504 .

156. *Adhyātma Rāmāyana*, II:2:44–46.

157. Valmiki *Rāmāyana*, V:23; V:24.

158. *Bhaṭṭīkāvyam*, VIII:46–49.

159. *Paumacariyam*, *Yuddha Kāṇḍa*, 72:7; *Ayodhyā Kāṇḍa*, 41:4.

160. Valmiki *Rāmāyana*, I:25;

161. ——, III:69.

162. *Adhyātma Rāmāyana*: I:4:27; V:40.

163. *Bhaṭṭīkāvyam*, VIII:5.

164. Kamba *Rāmāyana*, I:7:394–400.

165. *Mānas, Bāla Kāṇḍa*, *dohā* 208, *chaupai* 3.

166. *Adhyātma Rāmāyana*, I:4.

167. ——, V:1:12–13, V:1:34–42.

168. ——, III:17–18.

169. *Paumacariyam*, *Ayodhyā Kāṇḍa*, 36:6–11.

170. *Narasimha Purāṇa*, *adhyāya* 49.

171. Kamba *Rāmāyana*, III:5:314.

172. *Ānanda Rāmāyana*, I:7:55.

173. *Ramkien*, chapter X.

174. *Paumacariyam*, *Ayodhyā Kāṇḍa*, XXXVII:3–7.

175. ——, *Sunder Kāṇḍa*, XLVIII:12–13.

176. ——, *Vidyādhara Kāṇḍa*, X:5.

177. ——, *Vidyadhara Kāṇḍa*, XII:3–4.

178. Kamba *Rāmāyana*, V:3:444–450.

179. *Paumacariyam*, *Ayodhyā Kāṇḍa*, XLI:9.

180. Krttivasa *Rāmāyana*, *Uttara Kāṇḍa*, *Sitār apovād*, 3–9.

181. *Paumacariyam*, *Vidyādhara Kāṇḍa*, XVIII:3–10; XIX:2.

182. Bhattacharji, Sukumari, 1999:196–228.

183. Shah, Shalini, 1995:24.

184. *Adbhuta Rāmāyana*: *sarga* XXII-XXIII (see Grierson. G.A., *Bulletin SOAS*, IV:11–26)

185. Singh, V.B., 1991:xxxiii–lxiii .

186. Singh, K.S., 1993a:49–66.

187. Upadhyaya, K.D., 1993:67–68.

188. Rama Raju, D., 1993:79–99.

189. Venugopal, Saraswathi, 1993:100–109.

190. Richman, Paula, 1991a:3–21.

191. Sen, Nabaneeta Dev, 2000:183–191.

192. Sen, D.C., 1920 (Reprint 1987).

193. Rama Raju, D., 1993:79–99.

194. Rao, V.N., 1991:133.

195. Valmiki *Rāmāyana*, 119.

196. Singh, V.B., 1991:40–43.

197. Singh, K.S., 1993:86.

198. Sen, Nabaneeta Dev, 2000:188.

199. Singh, V.B., 1991:6.

200. Sen, Nabaneeta Dev, 2000:188.

201. Rao, V.N., 1991:126; Venugopal, S., 1993:104.

202. Valmiki *Rāmāyana*, III:4.3.

4

Female Subordination and Gender-Based Division of Labour

Men and women are regarded as distinct and respond differently at the biological and psychological levels. In patriarchal societies, social disparity and exploitative narratives are inherent. The reproductive labour process of women is not considered as 'work'; it is accepted as the 'function' of their biology, or 'nature'. Child-bearing and giving birth to a child may necessitate stupendous labour but that is considered as part of their physiology, and is compared with that of the animal world, where the female gives birth with inborn tendency. It is argued that giving birth to a child is an activity of nature because the child-bearing faculty is provided through the female uterus only. Even 'child-care' activities such as breast-feeding children, providing food to older children, taking care of them with love and affection, and doing all other related domestic chores are not considered 'work'. These are all considered an extension of their physiology. The assumption is that woman, by nature, is born to be a housewife only. For male-oriented sociologists, 'work' is that which is done by the appliance of 'hand' and 'head' but never by the 'womb' or 'breast' of a woman. Society has demarcated the 'work' on the basis of sex, where 'hand' and 'head' transact work and 'womb' and 'breast' are purely 'natural instruments' and not a 'working means of production'. This biological concept of work is the basis for feminine exploitation. The concept of 'labour' is usually reserved for the constructive work of men, who create things of surplus value for society. Women's activities, confined within the domestic compass, are not considered 'work'.

The life of women remained restrained to the four walls of her home. She looked after the family and household without her activities getting any recognition as 'work'. The *Rāmakathās* followed this all-pervading notion throughout its many retellings. From the very beginning of the *Rāmakathā* tradition, we see ordinary women confined within the premises of their household. During festive occasions, they would clad themselves in their fineries and best apparel but were 'bound' to their homes; they could only observe the processions of merrymakers from their windows and roof-tops. When Rama returned after marrying Sita or when he passed through a town with his wife and brother Laksmana during his exile, the ordinary village women could not come out of their homes to either express their joy or sorrow. They rejoiced or lamented "standing at their windows." The women of the palace were not allowed out of their homes even in extreme situations of grief. They "cried standing on the roof of the palace." Women were born, lived and died within the confines of their homes. Royal women were not to be exposed to 'vulgar looks' and had to be protected by *purdah* (veil), otherwise the king's absolute sexual rights were encroached upon.

When Sita accompanied Rama for his exile, she came out of her secluded palace for the first time. On this occasion, Valmiki[1] says, "Every passer-by today beheld Sita, who had not so far been seen even by the birds of the sky. Summer heat, winter chill and rains will soon mar the beauty of her body, now adorned with sandal paste."

The later *Rāmakathās* followed the same ideology. The *Adhyātma Rāmāyana*[2] says, "Sita, a beauty without peer anywhere in the world, had hitherto been living in seclusion, without being seen by any man outside the circle of her kith and kin." The poet laments, "She was now walking barefoot along the crowded public road without even a veil covering her face." The *Adhyātma Rāmāyana*[3] speaks of a similar situation for the ordinary women of the town. Women's seclusion was an accepted rule even in these compositions. Tulsidas[4], who was influenced by the *purdāh* system of the Mughal rulers, wrote of the townswomen of Videha looking through curtained windows (*jharokhā*). During Sita's marriage ceremony, a separate enclosure was built to keep the women out of the sight of men onlookers[5]. Similarly, *Ranganatha Rāmāyana*[6] says when Rama returned from Lanka with his wife and brother, the townswomen threw flowers from their rooftops and windows. Some *Rāmakathā* references offer a liberal attitude. In Valmiki's *Rāmāyana*[7], the appearance of women in public is not condemned in times of adversity, conflict, during the selection of a husband, at a sacrificial performance, or at the nuptial ceremony. Later on, in the Assamese and Bengali *Rāmāyanas*, we see women running out of their homes in joy or grief, expressing their emotions freely. Probably, this reflects the liberal attitudes of eastern India. The *Rāmāyanas* such as that of Krttivasa, Raghunandana or Ramamohan Bandopadhyaya were composed in the 17th–18th centuries. By that time, the *Adbhuta Rāmāyana*, written in Sanskrit, had become very popular in Bengal; it incorporated many new stories and interpretations to Valmiki's original story. Not only this, the *Vaisnava* sect, especially the Krsna cult, had penetrated the Bengali literary world. As a result, the influence of the *Bhāgavata Purāṇa* was very dominant. The description of Maithili women, assembled to behold Rama entering their city to marry Sita, is almost exactly what we read in the *Bhāgavata* about the gathering of the *gopis* to see Krsna. In fact, "Bengali life is portrayed with all its light and shade in the description of this *Rāmāyana* incident[8]. When recasting and remodelling a tale told with such superb effect in the original, Bengali poets almost rejected the restrictions and limitations imposed on ordinary women and presented them as women who came out of their houses freely to express their feelings of joy.

Situations leading to unfair ascendancy in social hierarchy are created when non-producers own and regulate producers and their products. The social atmosphere in the *Rāmakathā* tradition manifests such a state of affairs. Men own their women (the 'machinery' for production) and their children (the 'products') as well. Child-bearing, child-rearing and the domestic work were all controlled and commanded by men. Women remained enslaved workers without any rights over their body, the machine of reproduction, or over their children, its product. Like all ancient societies, the *Rāmakathā* composers interpreted these feminine activities as physiological operations, and control over this source of labour as an inbred, unavoidable human activity. Ancient Indian ideology further argued that woman is equivalent to a *kṣetra* (field) wherein men sow 'seeds' (semen). Because the 'seeds' determine the quality of the product, the owners of the seed, that is, the men, are rightful owners of the product, that is, the children, and not the women, that is the owners of the *kṣetra*. Man's right over his wife and children was accepted by all sects of Hindu ideologues. This was part and parcel of the sanctioned patriarchal proprietorship of rights over land, cattle and women[9]. Gender discrimination, thus, became the root factor of class composition. Males were distinguished from the female class. Labour outside the designated sphere of artisans, agricultural labourers and unskilled labourers was not accepted as 'workers'. All the classified sectors of industry were male-dominated. Of the sexual division of labour, the prescribed cultural prototype was based on differences in physical vigorousness and the pronounced diversity of men. Murdoch and Provost[10] explain, "The occurrence of the strictly masculine tasks on the basis of the greater physical strength of males and their superior quality of mobilising it in brief bursts of excessive energy." Although women undertook some work such as gathering fruit and roots, processing vegetable food, cooking, washing, cleaning household things, rearing domestic animals, milking cows, serving all family members and guests—these constructive and creative activities remain associated with private household domains and, therefore, labelled as 'no work'. Such was the despotism of the household, clearly visible in the *Rāmakathās* of all ages. Because women did not produce non-domestic items on a large scale, which went beyond individual household subsistence needs, their 'labour' was not recognised as 'work'.

Women had no economic ascendency over the management of products of their own labour beyond the household sphere. Therefore, any item they produced remained within the domestic range and they were economically subordinated. A wife's ordained roles were more defined, and her duties were more precise than those of her husband's; she had to stick to the set model of conduct laid down for her. The *Rāmakathās*, following the dictates of the *Dharmaśāstras*, are full of references to a wife's duties and obligations. Her complete devotion and obedience to her husband was expected, avoiding all social stigma thereby creating little likelihood of marital disagreement. Man was considered the 'protector' and the 'provider'. He was the bread-earner of the family. And, thus, women spent their lives within the protected atmosphere of their homes, and were not required to work outside. They only performed some rudimentary household chores, which was the manifestation of their motherly instincts. Ideally, therefore, there was no room for conflict.

Did women have any property rights? Women were often equated with wealth. The *Rāmakathās* refer to a woman as Laksmi, the goddess of wealth. Women are exchanged on the occasion of marriage between patrilineal clans. They were 'given' by their parents or male relatives to the groom and his family along with many objects of dowry. All the *Rāmakathās* refer to the dowry given to Sita by her father. The dowry included, according to Valmiki's *Rāmāyana*[11], cows, fine blankets, silken clothes, well-adorned elephants, horses, infantry as guards of honour, gold, silver, pearls, rubies, coral, hundreds of servants and maids of honour. According to the *Adhyātma Rāmāyana*[12] Sita's dowry included gold coins, chariots, horses, elephants, foot soldiers, female attendants besides Sita's valuable clothes and jewellery. Tulsidas description of Sita's dowry includes blankets, clothes, precious jewellery, elephants, chariots, horses, cows, and male and female slaves. Of a woman's dowry articles, the things of productive utility were controlled by her in-laws. The bride was basically a vehicle for passing heirlooms from her own group to those of her husband's. The multi-generational dominance along patriarchal lines gave an important role to the mother-in-law, who allotted the household ruling plans and controlled the precious gifts given to a bride by her parental home. Women had some ownership rights on the dowry articles of personal use such as jewellery, clothes and precious stones; however, as far as the dowry objects of productive value such as animals, male and female slaves, and land were concerned, it was not the bride but her husband and his family that enjoyed its benefits. We see Kausalya gifting her jewellery to her favourites maids and religious recluses. Similarly, Kaikeyi gifted her precious jewellery to her maid Manthara, when she was thrilled by her wisdom. It was Rama who suggested that Sita bestow their valuable gifts, both hers and his, to brahmins and their dependents when, following his exile, they were leaving the city of Ayodhya[13]. Again, it was Dasaratha who asked Sita to carry some of her own clothes and ornaments with her when she decided to go with Rama to the forest[14]. Rama took special care to protect Sita's jewellery when they were living in forest. And later, Rama saw Sita's personal ornaments scattered on the ground when she was abducted by Ravana and was flown through sky in Puspakayana towards Lanka[15]. A woman's right over things of her personal use was more or less accepted. But there is no reference of any woman using any article of productive value given to her as dowry. Renee Hirschen[16] argues, "Wealth is that which may be 'detachable' from the person but it is never 'alienated'. Women and things are exchanged as inalienable gifts but not as disposable property. This quality of 'detachability' is what makes woman a wealth item...and appear as objects."

A woman's right to property was a controversial subject in the ancient literary sources. The *Dharmaśāstras* upheld disputable attitudes. Baudhayana[17] says, "Women are considered to be devoid of strength and are not to inherit property." And again, "Daughters should take their mother's jewellery and anything else customarily given to her. It is not possible for women to act independently." Apastambha[18], however, shows a slightly liberal attitude. He says in his *Dharmasūtras*, "There is no division of property between a husband and a wife because from the time of their marriage they are linked together in performing religious rites....While husband is away people do not consider it a theft for the wife to make a gift when the occasion demands ." This view is supported in Valmiki's *Rāmāyana*. There is an interesting remark by Vasistha when he addresses Kaikeyi, "Sita cannot go to forest. She will occupy the throne in Rama's place for the wife is the better half of a man. So Sita will rule over the earth being the half of Rama's self[19]." The suggestion, however, was not acceptable to Sita herself. Women refused to enjoy the property rights in place of their husbands; yet Vaśistha's suggestion itself was revolutionary. It may have been only a sympathetic outburst when he saw Sita clad in a bark robe, ready to accompany Rama in exile. In another episode, Valmiki expresses his view about a woman's right over her property. Laksmana was very confident of Kausalya when he decided to join Rama in his forest sojourn. He did not worry about his own mother Sumitra because he knew that she would be fully supported by Kausalya herself. He argued with Rama, "Kausalya who has made grants of a number of villages to her servants can maintain thousands like us and will have enough to maintain herself and my mother[20]." Women in the *Rāmakathā* tradition, however, did not control their cash or landed property even if it was a part of their dowry or was a personal gift from her husband. They usually assented to its appropriation by men. The framing of the household group and the organism of its functions had a straightforward bearing on the degree of independence that a woman may have had within it. She may have enjoyed considerable authority in the allocation of resources, as is clear from the reference of Laksmana's argument; but within residential groups, the main factor is gender relations, and women preferred to surrender their property rights in favour of male members of the family (like in Sita's case, who did not think it appropriate to enjoy the throne while her husband passed his long period of exile in the forest).

Assets are a decisive index of the balance of power between men and women. Gender is very relevant when deciding the ownership of assets. When women were considered 'wealth', 'Lakshmi' or 'property', and their offspring too were a father's property, the relationship between men and women was structured accordingly. Although land, in a kin-based society, provides livelihoods for all by virtue of their kinship affiliations, inequalities do exist. The ideology of male superiority predominates, and each conjugal household is accorded autonomy under its male master. Marriage only regulated the socially recognised form through which women's reproductive activities and subsequent work were considered a subordinate natural activity, without any economic value. Marriage regulated women's capacity to reproduce, conserve and process this capability. Only men, however, enjoyed the right over this valued asset.

The system of polygamy was a widely accepted norm in the *Rāmakathā* stories. Polygamy contributed to the augmentation of wealth within patrilineal societies. Societies where a man has more than one wife, each of them bring their respective dowry, thereby enhancing family wealth. . Moreover, women had no control over the allotment or distribution of products of their own wealth, received as dowry from their kin-group, beyond the domestic sphere. Women had no jurisdiction over wealth or property, income and its distribution. A women's contribution in household jobs was seldom acknowledged or valued. This is because a woman's energy was considered to be spent not on productive work but on survival tasks such as cooking, fetching firewood and water and looking after the domestic animals. It had no value in the market and, therefore, household chores, which kept her occupied all day long, were not categorised as 'work'. In the Jain *Rāmāyana Paumacariyam*[21], a vivid description is found of the regular working life of an ordinary housewife. During their exile in the forest, Rama and Sita saw many *janapadas* (settlements). They saw housewives churning milk with churning rods, looking after their young ones, placing them on swings, and singing lullabies to them to put them to sleep.

Contrary to the image projected by general survey of the *Rāmakathā* tradition, in which women primarily fulfilled domestic and child-rearing roles, there are some clear references of those women, who were obliged to seek an income outside their homes due to poverty and deprivation. For example, *Paumacariyam*[22] refers to women water-carriers too. The *Rāmakathā* describes the environmental background of the royal families of Ayodhya, Mithila, Kiskindha and Lanka. In these royal families, there were a number of working class women, who were involved in the informal sector, and can be classified as a part of the 'hidden', or 'shadow', economy. When women were required to work as helpers in a family unit, their inputs were not recognised as 'work'. Women themselves undervalued their economic activities. They did not, possibly, earn any fixed salaries or wages. The royal women capitalised on the labour of working class women, who were engaged in the king's *antaḥpura* (inner apartment). These women belonged to the common people. They were poor, and not in a position themselves to exploit the labour of other women. The myth of the 'protector-provider' men was contradicted by the fact that sometimes women's labour was crucial and was, sometimes, the primary source of family subsistence.

These non-formal women workers were engaged in multiple occupations such as that of domestic help, midwives, beauticians, tutors and peons. By and large, women of poor families accepted the role of *dāsis* in the royal households. But some women, who were knowledgeable, sophisticated, and accomplished as singers, musicians and artists, joined the royal entourage as the companions of queens and princesses. As mentioned, women remained in the peripheral areas. They were refused access to the very texts that prescribed their boundaries and limitations in the family and society at large; and defiance, if any was expressed or displayed about their imposed destinies never entered the scriptures or written texts. Therefore, while re-examining their status as a mode of production, in relation to a patriarchal constitution of society, the picture remains obscure and dark. The common women usually followed upper-caste norms and were an integral part of the royal household. These palace women remained largely hidden from view. They represented the principle of seclusion and sex segregation. The women's quarters were separated from the outer sector of the palace. On the basis of the *Arthaśāstra*[23], Kum Kum Roy[24] shows that *strīniveśa*, or the women's quarters, in the palace were ideally situated in the farthest interior. This was enclosed by pleasure gardens. Queens may have had some male servants, especially as guards or messengers, but they used to be men over eighty. Women maids were employed too with the similar duties in the queen's quarters but they were expected to be elderly women, aged above fifty[25]. The Jain *Rāmāyana Paumacariyam*[26] supports this statement. It is said that women workers in the royal household were quite old in age. It was king's duty to guard his women wards in the palace carefully, especially when they were potentially of the productive age[27].

The *Rāmakathās* provide a vivid picture of the king's palace. The palace was built in a distinguished area of the town. Describing the palace of Janaka in Mithila, *Kamba Rāmāyana*[28] says, "There was a huge moat surrounding the palace. There was an orchard nearby, in which damsels arrive to pluck flowers...The moat surrounded the golden palace of King Janaka. Sita had a separate palace of her own." The poet refers to the tradition, according to which, a girl is accommodated in a separate house till she gets married. This place was called the 'palace of the girl'. Each queen occupied separate enclosures. Kausalya, Kaikeyi, and Sita's quarters (*antaḥpuras*) were different units. There are very clear allusions of these separate living places in the *Rāmakathā* stories. When Rama's coronation and then exile was decided by Dasaratha, Rama went from his own section of palace to that of his father's and then to his mother's, to inform them about all the changes. Dasaratha was called by Kaikeyi, on the advice of Manthara, to her apartment. And when Rama left for his forest sojourn, Dasaratha retired to Kausalya's section of the palace. The whole palace complex was, of course, within a boundary wall, within which each queen lived in a separate section. It was the duty of the male and female slaves or maids to maintain the sanctity of each section of the *antaḥpuras*. They shuttled with messages, information and news from one section to the other. When the king moved from one enclosure to other, slave girls accompanied him[29].

The royal household maintained various types of working women. They can be classified as those who were trained and those who were only fit for menial jobs. *Sakhis* were the first category of workers. *Sakhis* were female companions of queens and princesses, who were of noble blood. They came probably from the friendly associates of royal family. They were not paid servants; it is possible, however, that they or their families received special favours from the king. They were the sweet-tongued, clear-headed associates of the queens and the princesses. They represented a combination of beauty and artistic aptitudes. *Sakhis* became a prominent element in the later *Rāmakathās*. They performed various activities in the royal household. *Sakhis* worked as beauticians at the time of Sita's *svayamvara*. They washed Sita's face with rose water, they applied sandal paste on her body, made decorative designs on her forehead, tied her hair, dressed her in silken clothes and put on her jewellery[30]. In this work, they were assisted by *dāsis*[31]. The poet Tulsidas witnessed the luxurious lives of contemporary Mughal kings, when the women companions of queens and princesses had many roles to play in the king's harem. He, thus, described the *sakhis* in the royal palace of Mithila and Ayodhya, who became a part and parcel of the queen's entourage. They seemed to have equal ranking with the princesses because they teased her and won the confidence of the royal women. They even made Sita playful suggestions such as, "One *sakhi* grasped Sita's hand and said 'Meditate on Girija another time, why not look now at the princes?'[32]" *Sakhis* escorted Sita to the marriage arena[33], singing songs in charming tunes[34]. Tulsidas refers to many rituals and ceremonies when Rama was growing up. In each ceremony, the queens were accompanied by the *sakhis* and *dāsīs* of the royal family. These ceremonies such as *jāta karma*[35] (performed on the birth of a child), *nāmakaran* (naming the child ceremony), *cuḍākaran* (tonsure ceremony)[36], *yagnapavıta*[37] (sacred thread ceremony), and *karṇa-bheda*[38] (piercing the ear ceremony) were some of the manifold activities performed by royal women, and their *sakhis* participated in all of these functions.

Sakhis shared the worries and agonies of the queens. Sita's mother could express her anxiety to her *sakhis*[39]. These wise women would console her too[40]. In fact, they were the confidants of the royal women[41]. A similar conception of *sakhis* continued in all the later *Rāmakathās*. *Sakhis* in the Bengali *Rāmāyana* of Krttivasa dress the bride Sita and accompany her up to the marriage hall[42]. He refers to 700 *sakhis* of Kausalya[43]. Kamba's *Rāmāyana*[44] describes the *sakhis* of Sita as panicky and worried and critical of Janaka's vow because their sole concern was Sita's happiness, and they knew that in case Rama failed to break the bow, Sita would be devastated. *Sakhis* sometimes played very important roles too. In *Paumacariyam*, the role of Vasantamala, a *sakhi* of Anjana, was very significant. Anjana was impregnated by Pavananjaya, her husband, but soon after that Pavananjaya had to leave for a battle. Anjana expressed her anguish and fear to her *sakhi*, Vasantamala. Anjana's mother-in-law did not accept her story that she was pregnant with Pavananjaya's child, and threw her out of home, suspecting her character. Even Anjana's parents did not trust her and refused to give her shelter. Only Vasantamala stood by Anjana, accompanied her when she was thrown out, helped her give birth to Hanuman and stayed with her till Pavananjaya came back and was reunited with his son and wife. Such trustworthy companionship was expected of a *sakhi* and, in all the *Rāmakathās*, *sakhis* fulfilled their expected roles. *Paumacariyam*[45] refers to a similar role of a *sakhi* in the story of Uparambha and her female friend Citramala. Uparambha, wife of Nala Kubera, heard about the glory of Ravana and felt attracted to him. She told her *sakhi* Citramala, "This youthfulness of mine should be the glory of the family of Ravana. In case you unite me with him, my life will be successful." On hearing this, Citramala said, "Nothing is impossible. Command me." She became the messenger, who went to Ravana's palace to convey the message. *Sakhis* came from the cultured, higher ranks of society and although they did various types of work in the royal household, they were not paid for their work as such and, therefore, they did not fall in the category of female workers.

There was another set of female workers known as *dāsīs*. The status of the *dāsīs* in the royal household was inferior to that of the *sakhis*. The *dāsīs* entered the palace through diverse ways. They often belonged to socially deprived classes or poor families, whose parents had sent them to tend for themselves, or they were captured along with male slaves as war booties or were given as maidens-in-waiting with the dowry. *Paumacariyam*[46] clearly says, "*Dāsīs* were captured from defeated kings. The victorious king took away many damsels, who were employed and kept in his palace as menial workers." A daughter of a *dasi* inherited her mother's profession and served as a *dasi* herself. The custom of sending *dāsīs* as part of the dowry was prevalent in all the *Rāmakathās*. Valmiki[47] refers to them as dowry gifts given by Janaka to his daughter and all his nieces. Similar references occur in the *Adhyātma Rāmāyana*[48]. Tulsidas says that *dāsīs*, given as dowry, served the princesses as *paricārikās*, that is, personal attendants[49]. The female attendants, who accompanied Sita to Ayodhya, were her 'trusted' and 'favourite' hand-maids[50]. In

Kamba Rāmāyana[51], we find *dāsīs* serving Sita all the time. They moved along with her, spreading flowers over the ground to prevent her feet from getting hurt. The love-torn Sita felt miserable and, finding her in such a condition, her *dāsīs* became miserable[52]; they fanned her standing nearby[53], applied fragrant sandal paste over her body to cool her[54], and as soon as the old flower petals withered, they replaced them with fresh flowers[55]. *Kamba Rāmāyana*[56] says that there were dwarfish damsels of the sizes from three to four feet, besides hunchbacks. A group of *dāsīs* kept bowing to the feet of Sita and accompanied her all the time. They moved fly whisks, and held a gem-studded umbrella over Sita's head. During Sita's marriage, they brought a pedestal of emeralds for her comfort[57]. Queens had many *dāsīs*. Kamba[58] refers to the thousand maids of Kaikeyi and the thousand *dāsīs* of Kausalya, who accompanied their mistresses wherever they went to serve them in every situation. The main duties of the *dāsīs* were to beautify the princesses, adorn their bodies with flowers[59] and dress her up with silken garments and ornaments[60]. Whether the job of dressing up the men of the royal household was entrusted to female attendants is not specified. Probably the *dāsīs* were excused from this duty. Women servants were, of course, used as personal attendants of the male members of the royalty. Valmiki's *Rāmāyana*[61] refers to the *dāsīs* in Rama's bed-chamber, fanning him when he is in bed. In Ravana's harem, similar duties were assigned to *dāsīs*. Mandodari's legs were messaged and fly-whiskers moved the fans over her head[62]. In Ravana's household, *dāsīs* carried the royal symbols such as the square flower *maṇḍapa,* fly-whisks, fans and other things for Ravana[63]. The duty of a *chaurī* (fly whisk) bearer and betel bearer was not always considered degrading. It symbolised nearness and dearness. The favourite wife carried the fly whisk and also carried the betel dish for her husband. Valmiki[64] presents Sita, standing by Rama's side, holding a *chaurī* in her hand. Similarly, *Paumacariyam*[65] refers to wives as betel bearers and describes them as adorning their husbands with auspicious applications.

Food was prepared by male cooks[66]. In Valmiki's *Rāmāyana,* male servants alone served the royal guests and fed them. Female attendants are not mentioned in such occasions. In Tulsidas's *Manas*[67], queens inspect the royal kitchen and, at these times, *dāsīs* accompanied the queens and helped them in the kitchen work. In *Paumacariyam*[68], damsels of the Kubera country cooked and served food to Laksmana themselves. The kitchen duties of the *dāsīs* were common. *Dāsīs* served food to the queens[69]. One of the major duties of *dāsīs* was to look after the royal children. They also worked as mid-wives. Mid-wives did many things to ward off the evil eye. They burnt a lamp of *ghee* (purified butter), sprinkled water with flowers, adored the family deity and gave away gold in charity to those well-versed in the *Vedas*, to protect their wards from the evil eye[70]. The story of King Sagara is quite illuminating in this context[71]. King Sagara had 60,000 sons. They were solely looked after by woman attendants. They looked after the babies cautiously, keeping them in *ajyabhāṇḍa* (pots of purified butter). *Dāsīs* acted as nursing maids and were a substitute for biological mothers. In the queen's apartments, *dāsīs* assisted queens in looking after the young princes. Although Kausalya enjoyed bathing and dressing up Rama, dangling him on her knees, and rocking him in the cradle[72], housemaids were employed to help the queen in all these activities[73]. The *dāsīs* served as messengers inside the royal household. When children were born to the three queens of king Dasaratha, *dāsīs* from each of the separate apartments of the queens rushed to communicate to the king the happy news of the new arrivals[74]. Similar duties were performed by the *dāsīs* in *Rāmacarita Mānas* too[75]. The duties of a messenger were not only limited within *dāsīs*. Sometimes, even a queen was treated like a messenger by an arrogant king. *Paumacariyam*[76] says that Ravana ill-treated Mandodari so much that he asked her to go to Sita as his messenger and persuade Sita to marry him. It was a disgraceful act by Ravana but his subdued wife had no choice. She accepted this shameful job assigned to her by her husband and said, "I shall have to do according to your command, because for the sake of husband even the immoral act becomes moral." Professional female messengers were quite trained. They knew the court intrigues and worked as informers and spies[77].

The violence against women was unlimited. *Dāsīs*, who formed the informal sector of workers, had the lowest position in society. They were economically dependent on the royal household. Violence was accepted as a means to regulate disputes. The royalty enjoyed the politics of domination over the oppressed and marginalized groups, from where the *dāsīs* originated. Physical violence was an ingrained trait of imperial rule. Plurality of wives, that is supposed to reinforce man's domination over women, created unfavourable family complexities for men. It generated many conflicts, suspicion, and struggle for female power in order to usurp and achieve supremacy over the household. The *Rāmakathās* portray some maids (*dāsīs*) as playing crucial roles in *harem* conspiracies and becoming the prime movers behind the plots. They were the scheming non-royal women, who made accurate assessments of the king's character and encouraged their own favourite mistresses to act as the unofficial authority behind the throne. Manthara was one of such character, whose rise happened due to her display of intelligence, presence of mind and her refusal to be cowed down by the disapproval of Kaikeyi. She ultimately ended in a miserable state, thrashed by the physically dominating males.

The *śāstric* theory that the rule of primogeniture is normal, advisable and admirable to other modes of succession was challenged by Manthara. She instigated Kaikeyi to foster and accomplish the ambition of her son Bharat against the logical heir Rāma. In royalty, where polygamy was normative, the senior wife was projected usually as the exemplary and amiable whereas the younger wife was presented as aggressive. Significantly, the issue of loyalty among attendants resolved itself into a situation of women versus women, ranging round a man's sexual attention. The involvement of attendants in *harem* intrigues is not clear. It could have been a desire for adventure or prompted by resentment towards the other queen or with a view to gain royal favour. In Manthara's case, the last reason seems to be the primary reason that motivated her to intrigue against Rama. Manthara made a pragmatic survey of the realities of her position. She was a *dasi* of Kaikeyi, who had accompanied her from her natal family. She had worked as her nurse maid. For her to retain the eminence and honour of her own mistress was the only solution for the continuation of her own survival. The announcement of Rama's coronation date set the ball rolling. She interpreted it as outmanoeuvring by a conniving Dasaratha. Valmiki's *Rāmāyana* accepts that at the time of marriage with Kaikeyi, Dasaratha had given assurance to Kaikeyi's father that her son would inherit his kingdom, and nobody else. Therefore, according to Manthara, who knew all these arrangements, Rama's succession was a wrong move by King Dasaratha, who needed to be stopped in time. Manthara was possessive about Kaikeyi, whom she regarded as her ward. She could shout at her[78]. She aroused hostile feelings for Rama in Kaikeyi[79]. She advised her to plot against Rama. She told Kaikeyi, "You are under my refuge. Why should I leave this place? I shall not back out from explaining whatever is beneficial for you." She considered herself a well-wisher of Kaikeyi and her son Bharat. She reprimanded Kaikeyi and with her fiery eyes, she looked at Kaikeyi and abused her, removed her facial make-up and cried aloud[80]. She said, "You are a fool and mad. Now be prepared for facing misfortune for a long time with your son. I will not be able to tolerate your becoming the slave girl (*dāsī*) of your co-wife[81].

According to Tulsidas's *Rāmacarita Mānas*[82], she was a typical representative of a physically handicapped *dāsī* of low origin. He described her as *kāne, khore, kubre, kuṭil, kuchālī*. Manthara was indebted to Kaikeyi—so she was her well-wisher. She claimed, "*Khaia pahiriā rāj tumhāre, satya kahen nahin dosu hamāre*." But for Tulsidas, the whole story of *Rāmāyana* was pre-ordained and, therefore, Manthara's character was needed for the story to proceed to its natural consequences. Manthara was only an instrument in Saraswati's ultimate planning because Rama was destined to leave Ayodhya to fulfil his purpose as an *avatāra* of Visnu and to kill the demon king Ravana[83]. The story goes that the gods persuaded Saraswati, the goddess of learning and speech, to influence Manthara's bitter tongue so that she would think and utter such mischevious words to mould Kaikeyi against Rama. Valmiki did not fabricate any such story. For him, Manthara only showed the meanness of her own low nature. Being a maid from Kaikeyi's paternal home, her only interest was to safeguard Kaikeyi's future. In *Rāmopakhyāna* of the *Mahābhārata*[84], Manthara is described as incarnation of Dundubhi, who was a nymph, born as a wretched *dasi* due to a curse in her previous birth. Kamba[85] gives a very childish explanation for Manthara's disapproval of Rama. He says, "In earlier times, Sri Rama used to attack her with clay balls shot from a small bow. She was reminded of it and was filled with rage" when Dasaratha decided to coronate Rama. Similarly *Agni Purāṇa* says that Manthara hated Rama because she had been dragged by her feet by Rama in his childhood.

Conniving Manthara was able to play a crucial role in harem politics. Kaikeyi was soon moulded according to her plans. Kaikeyi embraced Manthara and showered her with precious jewellery and words of praise for her intelligent understanding of the forthcoming situation. Kaikeyi presented her with lots of wealth, gold, gem-studded necklaces—all from her own collection, given to her by her parents in dowry or by her husband, as the gifts of love. Valmiki[87] says, "Manthara wore royal robes, besmeared her limbs with sandal paste and adorned her body with ornaments, having put on a girdle around her waist, when Bharat and Satrughna saw her, on return from their maternal uncle's home." Thus, we see that *dāsīs* played crucial roles, sometimes even dictated plans, to formulate palace intrigues. Lonely queens, who thought they were losing their sole authority and primary position in the family, in the many wives of a king could swing their fortune away from them, depended much on these *dāsīs,* who had accompanied them from their parental homes. Yet a *dāsī's* position was quite vulnerable in such royal households. The male members of the royal family had full right to thrash them physically. Valmiki's *Rāmāyana*[88] further says, "Satrughna took the hunchback Manthara by force and the house began to resound with her piteous cries….Satrughna dragged her and all her ornaments fell from her body. He tortured her physically and abused her in harsh words." Kaikeyi was greatly alarmed at this and sought the protection of Bharata. Women, whether *dāsī* or queen, could become the object of male violence if men lost their temper because women were physically not strong enough to resist it. Valmiki accepted the *sastric* ideology that women should not be 'killed'. Bharat says, "A women should not be killed, so forgive her. I would have killed Kaikeyi but Rama would despise me as the murderer of my mother. So if you kill this hunchbacked woman, he would not speak to us." At these words of Bharat, Satrughna desisted from the reproachful act and let Manthara off.

Female workers were employed as guards and warriors as well in the royal household of Ayodhya, Kiskindha and Lanka. Valmiki's *Rāmāyana*[89] says that Sita's guards in Lanka were instructed to bring her to reason by recourse to intimidation and persuasion. They were posted in the Asokavana, and tried to coax her to accept Ravana's proposal. They questioned Sita when they saw her talking to Hanuman and, being suspicious, they quickly reported this to Ravana. Their reporting was prompt; Ravana sent male guards to Asokavana to imprison Hanuman[90]. Women guards also accomplished important wartime duties. Sita's guards were given the duty of taking Sita to the battleground and showing her the plight of the two scions of Raghu, Rama and Laksmana, bound by Indrajit in a network of arrows. The guards, headed by Trijata, accordingly took Sita in the aerial car, Puspaka, and showed her the two princes lying unconscious and motionless on the ground. However, Trijata reassured Sita, on the strength of the good omens, and cheered her up when they returned to the Asokavana[91].

Among the female characters in the *Rāmakathās*, Tara, wife of Bali and later of Sugriva, stood out as a remarkable woman because of her learning, wisdom and bravery. Valmiki's *Rāmāyana*[92] says that Tara was a learned woman, who performed *swastāyana* rites (scattering boiled rice on the ground and invoking blessing by the repetition of certain *mantras*) and was conversant with the sacred texts. Tara was extremely clever in discerning the most profound matters as well as in deciphering the meaning of portents of various kinds. Bali advises Sugriva on his deathbed that whatever Tara recommended should be unhesitatingly followed by Sugriva[93]. *Kamba Rāmāyana*[94] refers to Tara's women guards. They were strong enough to form a military-like barricade for their wise and powerful queen. When Laksmana arrived in Kiskindha, Tara along with her guards went ahead to meet the angry prince, whom she consoled through her sweet diplomatic words; she was strongly guarded by her female attendants, and in case she was challenged, they could protect her.

The Jain *Rāmāyana Paumacariyam*[95] also refers to the female guards of Sita. It describes the female spies engaged in battle. During Rama's exile, he entered the city of Ksemanjali[96], where the princess of the country was quite valorous and could destroy an enormous army. In the southern states, women warriors were enumerated on many occasions. *Paumacariyam*[97] refers to the woman warrior Lanka Sundari, who with a bow in her hand, started raining arrows and fought with Hanuman. Kamba[98] says that Ravana was accompanied by many female guards as powerful as Tadaka, who held swords, shields, *paraśus*, iron clubs, tridents, goads, clubs with thorns, shields of wood besides other weapons, which were carried by them on their heads. The female guards were duty-bound to follow the orders of the king, whether they liked it or not. Sita understood their compulsion when in the *Asokavana* in Lanka. Female guards, who had threatened Sita and had spoken inappropriate words to her, were only following Ravana's commands. Sita assured them that they would not be harmed by Hanuman or any other winning commander of Rama's army[99]. The study of the *Rāmakathā* tradition, thus, clarifies that women were not only engaged in lower category menial works but were also allotted jobs of strength and valour. Looking after the welfare of these female attendants was strongly recommended. Valmiki's *Rāmāyana* stresses that it is a sacred duty of the king to protect the women in his kingdom. Similarly, Tulsidas says that when Rama was leaving for the forest, he instructed Vasistha especially to take care of the women maids of the royal household[100].

The *Rāmakathās* that come to us in the form of folk songs were mainly composed by women themselves. These songs show that women were engaged in many other works as well. These songs comprise a very dissimilar Rāmāyana than that told by Valmiki or other poets of literary renderings. The Telugu folk songs recount Kausalya in labour assisted by her mid-wife in the royal chamber[101]. Further on, these folk songs relate a sensitive situation in which Sita is obstructed from going to bed because she had work to finish in the household. The *Rāmakathās* composed by ordinary women of any region present the royal households of Ayodhya and Mithila as simple families; there is no mention of *dāsīs* working to assist the queens or princesses but here Sita, her mother and mother-in-law all work themselves. Folk tales and folk songs opened up new perspectives of interpretation of Valmiki's *Rāmāyana*. In many cases, folk songs side-tracked from the venerated classical tradition and described the story in terms of the ordinary man's everyday life. In the Hindi folk songs[102], Sita was depicted as an ordinary, poor man's daughter, whose father Janaka says to Dasaratha, "I am sending Sita to your home. She will serve you by cleansing your royal abode with cow-dung." This was, of course, a conventional way of expressing submission by a father of a bride. In reply, Dasaratha gave an obligatory courteous reply, "Sita is like a daughter to us and also our daughter-in-law....She will preside over the royal kitchen and see to it that people are served food to their entire satisfaction[103]." Folk songs constantly present Sita as a typical bride in a joint family, in which the mother-in-law presides and daughter-in-law "sweeps the house and throws garbage in the back lane[104]." In the *Rāmakathā* version in Munda lore, the story is almost tribalised. Ayodhya is portrayed as a village, Sita a tribal girl and Janaka no more than a peasant[105]. In Avadhi and Bhojpuri folk songs, Sita was described as a milkmaid, who prepares food for Rama and Laksmana[106].

Kumkum Sangari[107] argues about the condition of working women. "Women from labouring classes who broadly speaking are not in a position to exploit the labour of other individuals or classes, are subject to different patriarchal systems, though some aspects of these are structurally related to the patriarchal practices and ideologies of upper strata, their 'consent' is nuanced differently, often even centred on the facts of their wide-ranging social subordination. Tied to the family unit in the economy of survival, subject to the coercive patriarchal practices of their own class, as well as the exploitation of their labour and sexuality by upper strata, women's 'acceptance' is poised at the nodes where at least two contradictions are there most acute; that between the economic and ideological dimensions of the family as well as that between the myth of the responsible male protector-provider which men are either unable or unwilling to live up to and the reality of women's labour as being an indispensable and sometimes primary source of the family subsistence."

In the patriarchal social order, several regulations were introduced to restrict women from expressing their inherent biological or sexual urges that are generated naturally by the reproductive glands. It is because of this biological process that women were commonly perceived as sex symbols. Women were, therefore, sex symbols. Enslaved women *(dāsīs)* were meant for the sexual enjoyment of their masters. It was not that the *dāsīs* were of loose moral character; rather, they were employed by their masters either as domestic help or as bed-mates—the choice was never theirs. The king's favourite *dāsīs*, young and comely ladies, were one step above the other working women of the royal household, who did menial jobs. The king's bed-mate *dāsīs* were known as *bhūjīṣyās* (concubines). The birth of a son could raise the status of a concubine. This was possible only when the paternity of the child was certain.

In the didactic portion of the *Rāmakathās*, many indignities and insults were imposed on women. They were described as possessing insatiable carnal pleasures, as being lascivious, immoral, heartless and fickle. Rape was considered a means of punishing women, and sometimes it was a part of a ceremony. There was a peculiar contradiction regarding the status of women in the various *Rāmakathās*. On the one hand, they were objects of honour, devotion and considered equivalent to goddesses; on the other hand, they were regarded as the root of all sin and evil. The *Adhyātma Rāmāyana*[108] says that virgins were required to be stationed at the main gate of the palace as a good omen. But it also says that dancing girls and concubines are essential elements of any palace. In one statement, Valmiki says that it was obligatory for the king to protect all the women throughout his kingdom; on the other hand, however, there are numerous references of how women, especially of the lower class, were controlled by force, thrashed or mutilated by the male-dominant society. Naturally, there were similar contradictions in women, whose primary job was to entertain men. Cultural primitiveness and a barbarous disregard of the *brahminic dharma* were most common among those social classes of women from where the sex workers were generally drawn. Dancing, singing, entertaining men, either in the cities or in royal palaces, was a work assigned to females. Valmiki's

Rāmāyana[109] refers to cities enriched by troupes of female dancers (*vadhu nāṭaka samghaisca samyukta sarvatah purim*), who entertained the townspeople. The king's palace employed these women in the court too. They worked both as entertainers and courtesans. They were called *bhūjīṣyā*, or *vaisyā,* the king's concubines. Although *vaiśyas* were considered auspicious, whose presence in every important court activity was welcomed, they were, in fact, the king's 'domestic cattle', kept for satisfying the sexual urge of royal men, or their favourite courtiers, or even the priests, who served the royalty. According to Kamba[110], entertainers accompanied Dasaratha and his courtiers when they proceeded to Mithila as part of the groom's party. These women sexually satisfied the large number of men on the way to Mithila.

The most visible sign of masculine energy was a man's sexual capability. Concubines bolstered the ruler's prestige. In every royal harem, besides queens, who were the wedded wives, there were numerous 'kept' women, either abducted, won in war, received as dowry, or paid entertainers, sex workers and concubines. In Ravana's harem, there were many *deva-gandharvas* and *nāga-kanyās*, who were erotically charged beauties; their very purpose of staying in the harem was to satisfy the king's sexual demands. Valmiki's *Rāmāyana* presents a vivid description of Ravana's women attendants and entertainers, who besides performing dance, music, etc., for recreation of the royal household were used as sex workers. Women attendants in Lanka applied sandalwood paste on the bodies of *rākṣasas*; they made love, appeased and teased them to keep them in good humour. In Valmiki's *Rāmāyana*[111], sometimes the women entertainers in a king's palace were called *patni,* especially because they were characterised as *pādmūlgatā* (lying at his soles). Skilled women dancers and musicians, who found a place in the arms and lap of Ravana, wore precious jewels and were called *yoṣitā*, and not *patnī.* They were concubines attached to the king's sleeping chamber. These women *(yoṣitā)* were "languid with intoxication and amorous dalliance." These bedroom companions of the king were referred to as *bhāminī, kāminī, nāri,* etc. They were the king's companions but not his wives *(patnī)*[112]. They were presented with good clothes, jewellery, intoxicating drinks, musical instruments, etc., so that the king may enjoy their company, and they provided sexual gratification to the king in exchange. Hanuman saw thousands of such women asleep at night, under the influence of drink, having retired after sport, when he entered Ravana's harem in search of Sita. The erotic life in Ravana's palace even attracted the well-to-do women from better family backgrounds. Valmiki's *Rāmāyana*[114] says that "Fallen a pray to lust, unmarried daughters of royal sages, *brahmānas, rākṣasas* and *gandharvas* had chosen to become Ravana's wives."

Women entertainers and concubines were an essential part of all royal households. In the forest, when searching for Sita, Laksmana visited the monkey king Sugriva's palace. He heard the melodious songs sung to the accompaniment of *veena*, and saw numerous ladies, who were decked with the best of ornaments, attending to Sugriva. The jingling of their anklets and tinkling of their ornaments created an erotic atmosphere to please the monkey (tribal) ruler of the forest[115].

A courtesan's profession passed from mother to daughter. They were at the lowest rung of the hierarchy, and their exit from an occupation of sexual exploitation was not easy, till they turned old and became incapable of instigating a man's sexual urge. They were absorbed in the royal household to do menial jobs, or were employed in the granary, storeroom or kitchen, as the *Arthaśāstra*[116] suggests. The other way of uplifting the social status of a concubine was if she gave birth to a son, provided the paternity of the child could be ascertained. The dangerous potential of female sexuality remained an unchanged motif throughout the *Rāmakathā* tradition. As late as Kandli's *Assamese Rāmāyana*[117], the role of women as dancers and actresses was despised by people in general. Kandli's society, which was in many aspects liberal, compared to the older versions of the *Rāmakathā* tradition, refers to women dancers, entertainers, actresses, etc. It appears, however, that their art did not have a respectable position in society. In Kandli's work, when Rama declines to take Sita back and tells her to go to Vibhisana or Laksmana, Sita replies scornfully that he "was putting her in the same position as a lowly wife of a dancer' (*naṭera naṭini yena amuka bilaha*)." (This is rendered from the original Sanskrit '*sailusaiva mām parebhyo dātum icchasi*').

The status of women entertainers, dancers and singers got mixed up with that of the sex workers. *Kamba Rāmāyana*[118] depicts women singing sweet music and dancing on specially built platforms, where *makaraveena* and drums were played as accompaniments. These public women were shown consuming intoxicating beverages. The poet classified them as whores, who enjoy the company of different men, and also receive money in exchange. Well-decorated whores played dice and engaged in gambling.

The Jain *Rāmāyana Paumacariyam*[119] describes the women entertainers as whores, who were enjoyed by the powerful kings during water sports. An amorous description of Sahasra Kirana's palace, which Ravana visited, revealed that thousands of passionate damsels spent time in love games in the palace pools of Sahasra Kirana. They ultimately ended up as his bed companions in his inner apartment.

Courtesans were sometimes used as king's envoys. Valmiki's *Rāmāyana*[120] refers to the courtesans sent to seduce Muni Rsyasrnga. To please the king and carry out his instructions, they tried to lure the saint with their physical attractions. They carried out the mission and brought him to King Lomapada's (or Romapada's) kingdom. The story features in *Kamba Rāmāyana*[121] too; the courtesans of King Lomapada's court were sent to entice Muni Rsyasrnga, whose presence in the kingdom was required to get rid of consistent drought. The story was an integral part of the *Rāmakathās* and even the thirteenth century Telugu poet, Ranganathan, recounts the incident[122].

Housemaids *(dāsīs)*, entertainers and courtesans in the royal household were not paid fixed salaries. Kings and queens, when pleased with their work, presented them cash, ornaments, precious clothes, etc., as gifts. Kausalya, Kaikeyi, Sita or kings such as Dasaratha, Janaka and Ravana showered their grace on their dependants. And because they were live-in servants, all their expenses and maintenance were covered by the royal household.

Even in the forest hermitages, women were allotted similar roles. Valmiki's *Rāmāyana*[123] describes the forest hermitage of Maharishi Bharadwaj. When Bharat and his companions reached his place, the saint invoked deities and *apsarās* (nymphs) through *mantras*, to entertain Bharata. At that time, 20,000 women were sent by Prajapati and another 20,000 by Kuber. Adorned with pearls and gems, they appeared on the scene to entertain Bharata. Valmiki's *Rāmāyana*[123] refers to the forest dwellings of Sage Mandakarni, who did penance for a long period. The gods engaged five nymphs to distract the hermit. The sage fell prey to his passion and the women became his 'kept' women. The sage was sporting with them when Rama visited his forest hermitage. Further on, the poet says that there was a forest hermitage of Sapta Janas, near Kiskindha. When Rama, Laksmana and Sugriva were passing through that area "they heard the jingling sound of the ornaments of the nymphs and their sweet notes of song[124]." Following the same trend, revealing the existence of women entertainers in the forest dwellings of the great sage Bharadwaj, *Bhaṭṭikāvyam*[125] introduces Tilottama. Poet Bhatti says that although Sage Bharadwaj himself followed an austere lifestyle, there lived damsels like Tilottama and her companions, who sang to melodious music and danced to entertain the members of the hermitage. The sum and substance is that men, whether a king, a commoner, a tribal, or even a hermit, regarded women as objects of enjoyment, born to satisfy and fulfil man's requirement.

References

1. Valmiki *Rāmāyana*, II:42:19–20.
2. *Adhyātma Rāmāyana*, II:5:23–25.
3. ———., VI:27–28.
4. Tulsidas, *Mānas*, I:219:2.
5. ———, I:224:3–4.
6. Ranganatha *Rāmāyana*, I:2420.
7. Valmiki *Rāmāyana*, VI:114:28.
8. Sen, D.C., 1920 (reprint 1987):83.
9. Mies, Maria, 1986:45–57.

10. Murdoch and Provost, 1973:302–330.

11. Valmiki *Rāmāyana*, I:74:3–5.

12. *Adhyātma Rāmāyana*, I:6:76–78.

13. Valmiki *Rāmāyana*, II:30:43–45.

14. ——, II:39:15–16.

15. ——, III:64:39.

16. Hirschen, Renee, 1984:3–7.

17. Baudhayana, II:3:43–46.

18. Apastambha, II:14:16–20.

19. Valmiki *Rāmāyana*, II:37:22–24.

20. ——, II:31:20–23.

21. *Paumacariyam, Ayodhyā Kāṇḍa, sandhi* 24:13.

22. ——, *Ayodhyā Kāṇḍa, sandhi* 24:1.

23. *Arthaśāstra*, I:20:10.

24. Roy, Kumkum, 1999b:21–22.

25. *Arthaśāstra*, I:20:21.

26. *Paumacariyam, Ayodhyā Kāṇḍa, sandhi* 22:2.

27. *Arthaśāstra*, V:6:42.

28. Kamba *Rāmāyana*, I:10:576–578.

29. ——, II:3:187.

30. Ranganatha *Rāmāyana*, I:1910.

31. ——, I:2220.

32. *Mānās*, I:233:1.

33. ——, I:246.

34. ——, I:247.

35. ——, I:193:1–3.

36. ——, I:202:2.

37. ——, II:9:3.

38. ——, II:9:3.

39. ——, I:255:1–3.

40. ——, I:256:1.

41. ——, I:256:1–2.

42. Krttivasa *Rāmāyana*. I:147, 148.

43. ——, II:58.

44. Kamba *Rāmāyana*. I:12:769–772.

45. *Paumacariyam, Vidyādhara Kāṇḍa, sandhi* 15:11–12.

46. ——., *Sundara Kāṇḍa, sandhi* 43:3.

47. ——., I:74:3–5.

48. *Adhyātma Rāmāyana*, I:6:8.

49. *Mānās*, I:325:1–2.

50. ——., I:338:1.

51. Kamba *Rāmāyana*. I:10:580–586.

52. ——, I:10:606.

53. ——, I:10:607.

54. Kamba *Rāmāyana.* I:10:635.

55. ——, I:10:636.

56. ——, I:20:1216–1218.

57. ——, I:20:1263.

58. ——, I:10:871–873.

59. ——, I:20.

60. ——, I:20:1196, 1204, 1206, 1210.

61. Valmiki *Rāmāyana*, II:16:20.

62. Kamba *Rāmāyana,* V:2:292.

63. ——, V:3:408–409.

64. Valmiki *Rāmāyana*, II:16:10.

65. *Paumacariyam, Sundara Kāṇḍa, sandhi,* 56:3; *Yudha Kāṇḍa, sandhi*, 59:3:6.

66. ——, I:14:12–16; *Mānas*, I:328.

67. *Mānas*, I:200:2.

68. *Paumacariyam*, *Ayodhyā Kāṇḍa, sandhi* 26:12; 26:16.

69. ——, *Sundara Kāṇḍa, sandhi* 50:11.

70. Kamba *Rāmāyana*, I:20:1211.

71. Ranganatha *Rāmāyana*, I:1131.

72. *Mānas*, I:192:1; I:198:5; I:199:4.

73. ——, I:202:1.

74. Kamba *Rāmāyana*, I:5:288.

75. *Mānas*, I:193.

76. *Paumacariyam, Ayodhyā Kāṇḍa, sandhi* 41:8–9.

77. ——, *Sundara Kāṇḍa, sandhi* 45:9–10.

78. Kamba *Rāmāyana,* II.2.151.

79. ——, II:2:148–185.

80. ——, II. 2. 150.

81. ——, II. 2 . 151.

82. *Mānas*, II:13:1–2; II:14:3; II:18:2.

83. ——, II:12.

84. *Mahābhārata, Rāmopākhyāna.* III:260:9–15; see Raghavan,V., 1973:17; Brocklington, J.L., 1984:227; Sukthankar, B.M., 1941:422–88.

85. Kamba *Rāmāyana.* II.2.138.

86. *Agni Purāṇa*, 6:8; see Aiyangar, Krishna. 1965: 9–17.; Brocklington, J. L., 1984:239.

87. Valmiki *Rāmāyana*, II:78:5–6.

88. ——, II:78:10–15.

89. ——, V:23:1–19.

90. ——, V:42:4–6; 11; 22–29.

91. ——, VI:47:10–15; VI:48:23.

92. ——, IV:16:12.

93. ——, IV:22:13–14.

94. Kamba *Rāmāyana*, IV:10:594–596.

95. *Paumacariyam, Ayodhyā Kāṇḍa, sandhi* 21:8:6; 30:3.

96. ——, *Ayodhyā Kāṇḍa, sandhi* 31:4–5.

97. *Paumacariyam, Ayodhyā Kāṇḍa, sandhi.* 48:8.

98. Kamba *Rāmāyana*, V:3:424.

99. ——, VII:37:3926.

100. *Mānas*, II:79:3.

101. *Paula Richman*, 1991b:119–121.

102. Singh, V.B., 1991:xlvii.

103. ——, xlvii.

104. ——, xlviii.

105. Singh, K.S., 1993b:49.

106. Upadhyaya, K.D., 1993:67–68.

107. Sangari, Kumkum, 1993a:869.

108. *Adhyātma Rāmāyana*, II:2:9, 13.

109. Valmiki *Rāmāyana*, I:5:12.

110. Kamba *Rāmāyana*, I:13:816–843.

111. Valmiki *Rāmāyana*, V:10:30.

112. ——, V:10:35–49.

113. ——, V:9:33–34; 44–67.

114. ——, V:9:68.

115. ——, IV:33:21–26.

116. *Arthaśāstra*, II:27–8.

117. Kandli *Rāmāyana*, 6:50:55. etc.

118. Kamba *Rāmāyana*, I:10:562–563; I:10:569; I:10:571; I:10:573.

119. *Paumacariyam, Vidyādhara Kāṇḍa, sandhi* 14:7–8.

120. Valmiki *Rāmāyana*, I:10:5–6, 11, 28.

121. Kamba *Rāmāyana*. I:5:217, 218.

122. Ranganatha *Rāmāyana,* I:309–310.

123. Valmiki *Rāmāyana*, II:91:16–18, 26.

124. Valmiki *Rāmāyana*, IV:13:18–22.

125. *Bhaṭṭīkāvyam*, III:41–44.

Bibliography

Adams, Charles J. 1965, (ed) *Reader's guide to the great religions.* New York, Free Press.

Adhyātma Rāmāyana: Spiritual version of the Rama Saga. Sw. Tapasyananda,1985, (tr. English), Madras, Sri Ramakrishna Mission.

Agarwal, P.K. 1983, *Goddesses in ancient India.* NJ, Atlantic Highlands, Humanities Press.

Agarwal, R.P. 1966, *Valmiki aur Tulsi, Sahityik Mulyankan.* Meerut, Prakashan Pratisthan.

Agni Purāṇa, see, Dutta Shastri, M.N.1967.

Agni Purāṇa, see, Hazra,R.C.,1936. *IHQ,* XII.

Agni Purāṇa, Gangadharan,G.(Translated and annotated), Ancient Indian Tradition and Mythology Series 27, 30. Bhatt,G. (ed). Delhi, Motilal Banarasidass Publishers.

Agni Purāṇa, see. Aiyangar, Krishna, A.N.1965 : 9-17; Brocklington, 1984: 239; see Hazra, R.C.1936.

Aitareya Brāhmaṇa, Agashe, R. R. 1979, (Pt. I, 3rd. ed.) Poona, Anandasrama.

Aitareya Brāhmaṇa, Agashe, R. R., 1977, (Pt.II, 3rd. ed.) Poona, Anandasrama.

Aiyangar Krishna, A.N. 1965, Agni *Purāṇa* and the *Rāmāyana. Bharatiya Vidya.* XXV: 9-17.

Aklujkar, Vidyut, 2000, Anusuya- a Pativrata, with Panache. See. Bose, Mandakranta, 2000: 56-68. *Faces of the feminine in ancient, mediaeval and modern India.* New Delhi, OUP.

Aktor, Mikael, 2000, Untouchables - women and territories: Rituals of Lordship in the *Parashar Smriti.* see Leslie Julia and Mary McGee, 2000,133-156. *Invented Identities (Interplay of gender, religions and politics in India).* New Delhi, OUP.

Altekar, A.S. 1953, Ideal and position of Indian women in social life. see Sw. Madhavananda and Majumdar, R.C., 1953. (ed), *Great Women of India.* Mayavati, Almora, Advaita Asram.

Altekar, A.S. 1987, *Position of Women in Hindu Civilisation.* Delhi, Motilal Banarasidass.

Ānanda Rāmāyana, Ramtej Pandeya, 1986, (ed. & tr.), Delhi, Chaukhamba Sanskrit Pratishthan.

Apastambha *Gṛhyasūtra,* Oldenberg, H. 1892 (ed.). (reprint 1967, Delhi, Motilal Banarasidass Publishers).

Apastambha *Dharmasūtra,* see. Buhler, 1879, *SBE.* (reprint 1965.a)

Arthaśāstra of Kautilya. Tr by Kangle, R.P. 1986, Delhi, Motilal Banarasidass.

Assamese (Asamiya) *Saptakāṇḍa Rāmāyana,* Kanak Chandra Sbarma.1940, (ed.), Calcutta.

Assamese *Saptakāṇḍa Rāmāyana,* Madhava Kandli Bardoloi, 1899, (ed). Calcutta.

Atharvaveda Samhitā, Whitney, W.D. 1869, (tr.) 2v. Harvard Oriental Series 7&8; (reprint 1905, London, Cambridge: Harvard University Press). (Revised edition Joshi,K.L. 2000, 3 vols. Delhi, Parimal Publications)

Atharvaveda, see Devi Chand, 1982.

Bader, C.1925, *Women in ancient India: Moral and literary studies,* Trubner's Oriental Series 6. London, Routledge.

Bailey, G.M.1992, *Bhakti studies*. New Delhi, Sterling Publications.

Bandem, I.M. 1992, Sources of delight and ethical precepts in Bali. see Vyas, L.P. 1992: 59-71.

Basu, Aparna and Anup Taneja 2002, *Breaking out of invisibility: Women in Indian history*. ICHR. New Delhi, Northern Book Centre.

Basu, N.K. and Sinha, S.N. 1929, *History of Prostitution in India*. Calcutta, Bengal Social Hygiene Association.

Baudhayana's *Dharmasūtra,* see Sastri, 1934; Buhler, 1882,*SBE*. (reprint, 1965 b.)

Baudhayana's *Gṛhyasūtra,* (ed.) Shamsastry, 1927, Mysore.

Belvalkar, S.K.1915, *Uttararāmcarita,* Harvard Oriental Series. Vol. 21. Cambridge, Mass.

Bettaille, Andre, (1983), *The Idea of Natural Inequality and Other Essays*. New Delhi, OUP.

Bhāgavata Purāṇa, see, Hazra, R.C. 1938.

Bhāgavata Purāṇa, see Satyavrata, 2005: 226-231.

Bhāgavata Purāṇa, see Burnouf, E. and others, 1840-98, (trs), 5v. Paris; Tagare, G.V. (tr. annotated) Ancient Indian Tradition and Mythology Series, 7-11. Delhi, Motilal Banarasidass Publishers.

Bhandarkar, R.G. 1928, *Vaisnavisni, Saivism and Other Minor Religious Sects*. Pune Bhandarkar Oriental Research Institute. (reprint 1969).

Bhatt, Yasoda, 1993, (ed.) *Images of Women in Indian Literature*. Delhi, B.R. Publishers.

Bhattacharji, Sukumari, 1999, Prostitution in ancient India, see Roy, Kumkum, 1999 a. 196-228. *Women in Early Indian Societies*. New Delhi, Manohar.

Bhattacharji, Sukumari, 2002, Revaluation of Valmiki *Rāmāyana*. *Social Scientist, Vol.*30 (1\2), Jan-Feb. 36.

Bhattacharya, Sabyasachi, 2011, (ed.) *Approaches to History: Essays in Indian Historiography.* ICHR. New Delhi, Primus Books.

Bhattacharya, N.N. 1999, Property rights of women in ancient India, see Roy, Kumkum, 1999 a. 113–122. *Women in Early Indian Societies.* New Delhi, Manohar.

Bhaṭṭīkāvyam, Maheshwar Anant Karandikar and Shailaja Karandikar. 1982, (ed. and tr.). Delhi, Motilal Banarasidass.

Bhavabhuti, *Mahāvīracarita,* Quoted by Bulcke, C.1962 : 205.

Bhavabhuti, *Uttararāmacarita,* see, Belvalkar, S.K. 1915, *Uttararamacarita.* Harvard Oriental Series, Vol. 21, Cambridge. Mass.

Bhuṣuṇḍi Rāmāyana, Bhagvati Prasad Singh, 1964, 1975, (ed.) 2v. Varanasi, Visvavidyalaya Prakasan.

Bose, Mandakranta, 2000, (ed). *Faces of the Feminine in Ancient, Mediaeval and Modern India.* New Delhi, OUP.

Boserup, Ester. 1970, *Women's Role in Economic Development.* New York, St. Martins Press.

Brahma Purāṇa,(tr.and annotated) A Board of Scholars. 1983-86, Ancient Indian Tradition and Mythology Series. 33-36. (reprint 1999), Delhi, Motilal Banarasidass.

Brahmāṇḍa Purāṇa,(tr. & annotated) Tagare, G.V. 1999, Ancient Indian Tradition and Mythology Series, 22-26. Delhi, Motilal Banarasidass.

Bṛhadāraṇyaka Upaniṣada, Maxmuller, F. 1969. (tr) *The Upanisads,* Vol.2 (reprint), Delhi, Motilal Banarasidass.

Bṛhadāraṇyaka Upaniṣada, Vasu, S.C. 1933,(ed.and tr.), Allahabad, The Panini Office.

*Bṛhaspati Smṛti,*see Jolly,J,1889. *The Minor Law Books.* pt. I. Narada and Brhaspati, *SBE,* XXXIII.

Brocklington, J.L. 1984, *Righteous Rama.* Delhi, OUP.

Brown, C. Mackanzie, 1990, *Triumph of the Goddess: The canonical models and theological visions of the Devī Bhāgavata Purāṇa.* NY, Albany State University.

Buhler, G. 1879, *Sacred Laws of the Aryas,* Vol. II. pt. I: Apastambha and Gautama, London, Clarendon Press. (reprint 1965, a, Delhi, Motilal Banarasidass.)

Buhler, G. 1882, *Sacred Laws of the Aryas,* Pt. II, pt. 2 : Vasistha and Baudhayana, London, Clarendon Press. (reprint 1965, b., Delhi, Motilal Banarasidass.)

Buhler, G. 1886, *Laws of Manu.* Sacred Book of the East, Vol. 25.(reprint 1988, Delhi, Motilal Banarasidass).

Bulcke, Fr. Camille, 1955-56. Genesis of the Valmiki *Rāmāyana. Journal of Oriental Institute,* Vol. 66- 94. Baroda.

Bulcke, Fr. Camille, 1962, 1971 (eds.), *Rāmakathā Utpattī aur Vikas.* (reprint 1993) Allahabad, Prayag University.

Chakrabarti, Kunal, 1999, Divine family and world maintenance: Ganesa in the Bengal Purāṇas, see Sangari, Kumkum and Uma Chakravarti, 1999, 56-83. *From myths to markets: Essays on gender.* Shimla, IIAS.

Chakravarti, Uma, 1983, a. Development of Sita myth: A case Study of women in mythical literature. *Samya Sakti,* Vol. 1(1). July. 67-75.

Chakravarti, Uma, 1983, b. Myth of golden age of equality, women slaves in ancient India. *Manushi,* Vol. 3, 8-15.

Chakravarti, Uma, 1993, Conceptualizing Brahmanical patriarchy in early India: Gender, caste, class and state. *Economic and Political Weekly,* Vol. 27, 579-85.

Chakravarti, Uma, 1999, Beyond the Altekarian paradigm:Towards a new understanding of gender relations in early Indian history. see Kumkum Roy, 1999 a: article 2. *Women in early Indian Societies.* New Delhi, Manohar.

Chakravarti, Uma. 2003, Gendering caste: Through feminist lenses, see Krishnaraj Maithreyi, 2003 : 7-74.

Chakravarti, Uma, 2006, *Everyday lives, everyday histories: Beyond the kings and Brāhmaṇas of ancient India.* New Delhi, Tulika.

Chand, H. 1928, Valmiki *Rāmāyana,* Eastern Recension. *Indian Historical Quarterly,* IV, 790, Calcutta.

Chhāndogya Upanisad, Max Muller, F. 1969, (tr), *The Upaniṣadas,* Vol. I, II,(reprint) Delhi, Motilal Banarasidass.

Chandra, Vinita, 2010, *Gender relations in early India.* Jaipur, Rawat Publications.

Chandrāwatī Rāmāyana, see Sen, D.C. 1920 (reprint 1987). *Bengali Rāmāyanas,* ch.vii: 197-204; Influence of Jain Rāmāyana on Bengali poems. 204-212.

Chandrāwatī Rāmāyana, see Sen, Nabaneeta Dev, 2000 *Chandrawati Rāmāyana:* Femenising the Rama Tale. in Bose, Mandakranta, 2000,183-191. *Faces offeminine in Ancient, Mediaeval and Modern India.* New Delhi, OUP.

Chattopadhyaya, D.P. 1992, *Anthropology and Historiography of Science.* Delhi, Motilal Banarasidass.

*Chhāndogya Upaniṣada,*Sw. Gambhirananda, 1983 (ed. and tr). Calcutta, Advaita Ashram.

Coburn, Thomas B. 1984, (reprint 1988), *Devi Mahatmya: The Crystallization of Goddess Tradition.* Delhi, Motilal Banarasidass.

Conkey, Margaret W. (in collaboration with Sarah H. Williams) 1991, Original narratives: Political economy of gender, 102-39 see Micaela di Leonardo (ed.) 1991, *Gender in the crossroads of knowledge: Feminist anthropology in the post modern era.* Berkeley, University of California Press.

Connell, R.W. 1987, *Gender and Power in Society: The Person and Sexual Politics.* Cambridge, Polity Press.

Coontz, Stephnie and Handerson, Peta, 1986, (ed), *Women's Work, Men's Property: The origin of Gender and Class.* London, Verso.

Das, R.M. 1962, *Women in Manu and His Seven Commentators.* Varanasi, Kanchan Publications.

Deshpande, M.N. 1981, *Hutatma. Visnu, Ganesh, Sankara Vyakhyayanmala.* Nagpur, Vidarbha Samsodhana Mala.

Devī Bhāgavata Purāṇa, see, Brown, C. Mackanzie,1990.

Devī Bhāgavata Purāṇa see Hazra, R.C (1975). *JOR.* XXl. 49-79; see Bulcke, Fr. C. 1962 : 294.

Devi Chand 1982, (ed) *Atharvaveda.* New Delhi. Munshiram Manoharlal.

Dikshit, Ratnamayidevi, 1964, *Women in Sanskrit Dramas.* Delhi, Meharchand Laksmandas.

Dillistone, F. W. 1966 (ed), *Myth and Symbol.* London, SPCK.

Doniger, Wendy, 2000, *Splitting the Difference: Gender and Myth in Ancient Greece and India.* New Delhi, OUP.

Dube,Leela 1978. The seed and the field symbolism of human reproduction in India.Paper read at the Xth International Conference of Anthropological and Ethnological Sciences, New Delhi.

Dube, Leela, Eleanor Leacock and Shirley Ardener, 1986 a. (ed) *Visibility and power: (Essays on women in society and development).* Delhi, OUP.

Dube, Leela 1986 b. Seed and earth: The symbolism of biological reproduction and sexual relations of production. see, Dube, Leela, Eleanor Leacock and Shirley Ardener, 1986, 22-39. *Visibility and Power (Essays on women and society and development).* Delhi, OUP.

Dube, Leela 1988. On the construction of gender: Hindu girls in patriarchal India. *Economic and Political Weekly.*Vol. *23.11-19.*

Duby, G and Michelle Perrot, 1994. Writing the history of women, see Pantel, Pauline Schmitt, 1994, ix-xiii. *History of Women in the West.* Boston, Harvard University.

Dunge, S. A.1988, *Encyclopaedia of Puranic Beliefs and Practices.* 4, vols., Navrang. New Delhi.

Dutt, M.N. 1889-91. *Valmiki Rāmāyana* (tr. English). Calcutta.

Dutta Sastri, M.N.1967,(tr.) *Agni Purāṇam,* Varanasi. Chowkhamba Sanskrit Studies No. 54.

Eggeling,.J.1882, *Śatapatha Brāhmaṇa,* pt.I and II (tr.) Sacred Book of the East. Vol XII. Motilal Banarasidass, Delhi.

Eliad, Mircea and Kitagawa, J.M.,1959. *History of Religions: Essays in Mythology.* Chicago, University of Chicago Press.

Eliade, Mircea 1960, *Myths, Dreams and Mysteries.* London, Harvill Press.

Eliade, Mircea, 1964, *Myths and reality: World Perspective,* London, George Allen and Unwin.

Eliad, Mircea and Kitagawa, T.M. 1959, (eds.). A *History of Religious Ideas: Essays in Methodology.* Chicago, University of Chicago. (tr.frorn French by Trask, W.R. 1979. London, Collins.)

Erndl, Kathleen M, 1991, The Mutilation of Srpanakha. see Richman Paula, (ed). 1991 :67—88. *Many Rāmāyanas: Diversity of a Narrative Tradition in South Asia.* Delhi,OUP.

Ganguly, K.K, 1983, *Art and Culture.* Vol. I. Calcutta.

Garuḍa Purāṇa (tr. and annotated by) A Board of Scholars. Ancient Indian Tradition and Mythology Series. 12-14. (reprint 1978, Delhi. Motilal Banarasidass).

Gatwood, Lynn E. 1985, *Devi and the Spouse Goddess: Women, Sexuality and Marriage within India.* Riverdale Company, Maryland.

Gautama *Dharmaśāstra,* Buhler, G. 1879. (tr.) *Sacred Laws of the Aryas.* Vol. II, pt. 1. Apastambha and Gautama. *Sacred Book of the East.* London, Clarendon Press. (reprint 1965 a. Delhi, Motilal Banarasidass).

Ghadially, Rehana, 1988. (ed) *Women in Indian society; a reader.* Delhi, Sage Publication.

Ghurye, G.S. 1979. *Legacy of the Rāmāyana.* Bombay, Popular Prakashan.

Gill, S. D. 1982. *Beyond the primitive: The religion of non-literate people.* New Jersey, Prentice Hall.

Goldman, R.P. 2000. Ravana's kitchen, a testimony of desire and the other. See Richman, Paula, 2000 :105-114.

Goldman, R.P. 2000, a.,Language, gender and power: the sexual politics of language and language acquisition in traditional India. See. Leslie, Julia and Mary McGee, 2000 : 84-98. *Invented Identities : the Interplay of Gender, Religion and Politics in India,* New Delhi, OUP.

Goldman, Sally and Sutherland, J. 2000 b. Speaking gender: *Vac* and the *Vedic* construction of the feminine, see Leslie, Julia and Mary McGee, 2000. 57-83. *Invented Identities; the Interplay of Gender, Religion and Politics in India.* New Delhi, OUP.

Goldman, R. P. and Goldman, Sally (tr). 1985-2000. *Rāmāyana of Valmiki : an Epic of Ancient India.* 5 vols. (reprint, 1996, Princeton. Princeton University Press)

Gonda, J. 1969, *Ancient Indian Kingship from the Religious Point of View.* Leiden, Brill.

Goody, Jack and Tambiah, S.J. 1973, *Bride, wealth and dowry.* Cambridge, University Press.

Goswami, Indira, 1996. *Rāmāyana from Ganga to Brahmaputra: a comparative study of Tulsidasa's Rāmacarita Mānas and Rāmāyana* of *Madhav Kandli.* Delhi, B.R. Publishing Corporation.

Gṛhyasūtra (tr) Oldenberg, H.(reprint) 1964,1967, Vols. I,II. (pt.I. Sankhyayana, Asvalayana, Paraskar, *Gṛhyasūtras* ; pt. II. Apastambha, Gobhila,Hiranyakesin *Gṛhyasūtrasi.* Delhi, Motilal Banarasidass.

Grierson, G.A.1921: 422 ff.. Sita's parentage. *Journal Royal Asiatic Society,* London.

Grierson, G.A. 1926, On the *Adbhut Rāmāyana. Bulletin School of Oriental and African Studies,* Vol. 4: 11.

Grierson, G.A. 1928, Sita forlorn - a specimen of Kashmiri *Rāmāyana. Bulletin School of Oriental and African Studies,* Vol. 5: 285.

Grierson, G. A. 1930, *The Kashmiri Rāmāyana.* Bibliotheca Indica. Calcutta. Asiatic Society of Bengal.

Growse, F.S. 1966, *Rāmāyana of Tulsidasa,* 8th ed. Allahabad, Ram Narainlal Beniprasad.

Gupta, Chitralekha, 1988, Rural urban dichotomy, see Tripathi, L.K. 1988, 188-196.

Gupta, Samjukta Gombrich, 2000. Goddess, women and their rituals in Hinduism see Bose, Mandakranta, 2000, *Faces of the feminine in ancient, mediaeval and modern India.* Delhi, OUP.

Harlan, Lindsey, 2000, Heroes alone and heroes at home: Gender and inter-sexuality in two narratives, see Leslie, Julia and Mary McGee, 2000, 231-251. *Invented Identities: the interplay of gender, religion and politics.* New Delhi, OUP.

Hazra, R.C. 1938, *The Bhāgvata Purāṇa. New Indian Antiquary,* I. (8) : 522 -528.

Hazra, R.C. 1940, *Studies in the Puranic Records of Hindu Rites and Customs.* Dacca. (reprint 1975, Delhi, Motilal Banarasidass.)

Hazra, R.C., 1936, Our present *Agni Purāṇa. IHQ,* XII.683ff.

Hazra, R.C., 1952, The *Maha Bhāgavata Purāṇa, IHQ,* XXVIII,17-28.

Hazra, R.C., 1975, *The Devī Bhāgavata, JOR,* XXI, 47ff.

Hirschen, Renee 1984, (ed.). *Women and Property, Women as Property.* London, Croom Helm.

Hopkins, E.W. 1920, *Great Epic of India: Its Character and Origin.* (reprint). New Haven, Yale University Press.

Hopkins, E.W. 1930, Allusion to the Rama stories in the *Mahabharata. Journal of American Oriental Society.* Vol. 50 : 85-103.

Horner, L.B. 1999, Women under primitive Buddhism: Laymen and also women, see Roy, Kumkum 1999, 82-112.(ed.) *Women in Early Indian Societies.* New Delhi, Manohar.

Inden, Ronald B. 1990, *Imagining India.* Oxford, Blackwell.

Jacobi, H.1893. *Das Rāmāyanas.* Bonn, (English tr. Ghoshal, S. N. 1960, *The Rāmāyana*). Baroda, Oriental Institute.

Jaiminīya Brāhmaṇa, Raghu Vira and Lokesh Chandra, ed. 1954, Nagpur, Saraswati Vihar.

Jain, Devaki and Nirmala Banerjee, 1985 (eds.), *Tyranny of the Household: Investigative Essays on Women's Work.* Ghaziabad, Shakti Books.

Jaiswal, Suvira 1993, Historical evolution of the Ram legend. *Social Scientists,* Vol. 21, 3-4 May, April.

Jamison, Stephnie W. 1996, *Sacrificed Wife / Sacrificer's Wife. (Women, Ritual and Hospitality in Ancient India).* Oxford, OUP.

Jamison, Stephnie W. 2002, Giver or Given? Some marriages in Kalidasa, see, Patton Laurie, L. (ed.), 2002.69-83, *Jewels of Authority; Women and Textual Tradition in Hindu India.* New Delhi, OUP.

Jayal, Shakambhari 1966, *Status of Women in the Epics.* Delhi, Motilal Banarasidass.

Jolly, J. 1889 (tr.), *Minor Law Books* pt. I.Narada and Brhaspati Sacred Books of the East, vol. XXXIII (ed.) Max Muller,F. Oxford,Clarendon Press. (reprint, 1965, Delhi, Motilal Banarasidass.)

Jolly, J. 1880, (tr.) *The Institute of Visnu.* Sacred Books of the East. Vol. VII. ed. Max Muller, F, Oxford,Claredon Press. (reprint,1965, Delhi, Motilal Banarasidass.)

Jong,.J.W. de 1993, Story of Rama in Tibet, see Krishnamoorthy, K. 1993-39. *Critical inventory of Rāmāyana Studies in the World.* Vol. 2. New Delhi, Sahitya Akademy.

Kabeer, Naila, 2010, *Gender and social protection -strategies in the informal economy.* Delhi, Routledge.

Kakar, Sudhir 1978, *The inner world - A psychoanalytical study of childhood and society in India.* New Delhi, OUP.

Kalidas Granthāvali,(ed) Chaturvedi,S.R. 1950, Banaras.

Kāmasūtra of Vatsyayana, (tr.) Upadhyaya, S.C.,1961, Bombay.

Kamba's *Rāmāyana–Irāmavatāram.* Shanti Lal Nagar, 2008, (tr. English), 2 vols., Delhi, Parimal Publications.

Kandli's *Sapta Kāṇḍa Rāmāyana,* Baruah, Hari Narayana Dutta, 1968, (eds.), Gauhati, Dutta Baruah and Co.

Kandli, Bardoloi Madhav, 1899, (ed). *Asamiya Sapta Kāṇḍa Rāmāyana,* Calcutta.

Kane, P.V. 1930 -1941. *History of the Dharmaśāstras.* Poona, Bhandarkar Oriental Research Institute. (reprint 1971, Delhi, Motilal Banarasidass)

Kashmiri Rāmāyana of Divakara Prakash Bhatta, see Grierson, G.E. 1930, *Kashmiri Dictionary,* Pt 2, Calcutta, Asiatic Society of Bengal.

Kathak Saṁhitā, see, Bulcke, C.1962 : 13-15.

Kathak Gṛhyasūtra, Dayananda Mahavidyalaya Sanskrit Granthamala, 9.

Kathāsaritsāgara of Somadeva. Tawney, C.H. 1880-84 (tr.) *The Ocean of Story.* 10 vols. (reprint 1968, Delhi, Motilal Banaraidass)

Kautilya's *Arthaśāstra.* Srinivasa, M.S.1961, (tr. 7th ed), Mysore, Mysore Printing and Publishing House.

Keith, A.B. 1924. *Sanskrit Drama in its Origin, Development and Practice.* Oxford. (reprint, 1992, Delhi, Motilal Banarasidass.)

Keith, A.B., 1915, The age of the *Rāmāyana. JRAS,* 1915: 218-228. London.

Kern, Otto, 1927. *Die Grierchischen Mysterien der Klassischen Zeit.* Berlin.

Khanna, Madhu, 2000, Goddess women equation in *Śākta Tantra.* see Bose, Mandakranta, 2000 (ed.) *Faces of the feminine in the ancient, mediaeval and modern India.* Delhi,OUP.

Kinsley, David. 1988, *Hindu Goddesses: Vision of the feminism in the Hindu religious traditions.* Berkley, University of California Press.

Krttivasi Rāmāyana, Nand Kumar Avasthi, 1989 (tr.v. I) by Prabodh Majumdar, 1989, (tr.v.2), Navarun Verma, 1983-84.(tr. v.3). Lucknow, Bhuvan Vani Trust.

Krttivasi Rāmāyana, Majumdar, Subodh Chandra 1968 (new ed. 1970) Calcutta, Dev Sahitya Kutir.

Knox, John, 1964, (new ed.) 1966, *Myth and Truth: an Essay on the Language of Faith,* London, Care.

Krishnamoorthy K. 1991 (ed.), *Critical Survey of Rāmāyana Studies in the World.* Vol.l. Delhi, Sahitya Akademy.

Krishnamoorthy, K. 1993, *Critical Inventory of Rāmāyana Studies in the world.* Vol. 2. Delhi, Sahitya Academy.

Krishnamoorthy, K. 1993 b, Images of women in Sanskrit literature. see Bhatt, Yasoda, 1993 (ed.) *Images of Women in Indian Literature.* Delhi, B.R. Publishing.

Krishnaraj, Maithreyi 1998, (ed.) *Gender, Population and Development.* Delhi, OUP.

Krishnaraj, Maithreyi, 2003, (ed.), *Theorizing feminism,* Calcutta, Stree.

Kuhn Annette and Ann Marie Wolpe, 1978, (ed), *Feminism and materialism - women and modes of production.* London, Routledge and Kegan Paul.

Kumardasa, *Jānakīharan, BSOS,* 1926, Vol. IV : 285. (see Bulcke, C. 1962 : 193-194.)

Kūrma Purāṇa (tr. and annotated)Tagare, G.V. Ancient Indian Tradition and Mythology. Vols. 20, 21. Delhi. Motilal Banarasidass.

Lang, A,1993, *Myth, Ritual and Religion.* Vol.II, (reprint), New Delhi, Aryan Books International.

Laquer, Thomas 1990, *Making Sex: Body and Gender from the Greeks to Freud.* Cambridge, Mass, Harvard University Press.

Leacock, Eleanor 1986, Women, power and authority. see Dube, Leela, E.Leacock and S. Ardener (eds) 1986. 107-135. *Visibility and Power: Essays on Women and Society and Development.* New Delhi, OUP.

Leibowitz, Lila 1986, In the beginning-the origin of the sexual division of labor and the development of first human societies, see Coontz Stephnie and Peta Henderson, 1986: 43-75. *Women's Work, Men's Property- the Origin of Gender and Class.* London. Verso.

Lerner, Gerda, 1986, *Creation of Patriarchy.* New York, OUP.

Lerner, Gerda, 1993, *Creation ofFeminist Consciousness: From the Middle Ages to Eighteenth Seventy.* New York, OUP.

Leslie, Julia 1989. *Perfect wife: The Orthodox Hindu Women According to Stridharmapaddhati of Tryarnbakayajvan.* Delhi, OUP.

Leslie, Julia (ed) 1996. *Myth and Myth Making.* London. Curzon Press.

Leslie, Julia and Mary McGee 2000 (ed) *Invented Identities (Interplay of gender, religion and politics in India).* SOAS Studies in South Asia Understandings and Perspectives. New Delhi, OUP.

Lincoln, B,1986, *Myths, Cosmos and Society.* Cambridge,Mass. And London. Harvard University Press.

Lutgendorf, P. 1992. *The Life of a Text. : Performing the Rāmcarita Mānas of Tulsidas.* University of California Press.

Lutgendorf, P. 2000. Dining out at lake Pampa :The Sabari episode in multiple *Rāmāyanas.* In Richman Paula 2000: 119-136, *Questioning Rāmāyanas* : *South Asian Tradition.* Delhi OUP.

Madhavananda, Sw. and Majumdar R.C. (eds.) 1953, *Great women of India* (The Holy Mother Birth Centenary Memorial) (reprint 2001), Kolkata, Advaita Ashram.

Mahābhāgavata Purāṇa Gujarat Printing Press, 1913. (see Hazra, R.C. 1952. The *Mahabhāgavata Purāṇa. IHQ.* XXVIII : 1 7)

Mahābhārata (tr.) P.C. Roy, 2nd ed. 1919-35. Calcutta.

Mahābhārata, Rāmopākhyāna, (see Sukhthankar, B.M.1941)

Maitrāyanī Samhitā, see, Bulcke, C. 1962 : 13.

Majumdar, R.C. 1943 (ed.), *History of Bengal,* Vol. 1. Dacca, Dacca University.

Mānava Śrautasutra, 1961-63, Van Gelder, J.M. (ed. and . tr.) 2 Vol. New Delhi.

Manjushree, 1990, *Position of Women in the Yajñavalkya Smṛti.* New Delhi, Prachi Publishers.

Mānas, see Tulsidas, *Rāmcharita Mānas.*

Manu, Smṛti, Buhler, G.1886 (tr.) *Laws of Manu.* Sacred Books of the East, Vol. 25. Oxford. (reprint,1964, Delhi, Motilal Banarasidass).

Mārkaṇḍya Purāṇa. (tr. and ed.) Pargiter, F.E. 1904. Calcutta, Asiatic Society of Bengal.

Matsya Purāṇa. Ancient Indian Tradition and Mythology Series.

Maxwell, T.S. 1997, *Gods of Asia: Image, Text and Meaning.* Delhi, OUP.

McDonell, A.A. 1919, Ramaism in *Rāmāyana.* see *Encyclopaedia of Religion and Ethics,* Vol. X :574. New York, Scribner.

McGee, Mary, 2000, Introduction, see Leslie, Julia and Mary McGee. 2000, 1-56. *Invented identities, (The Interplay of Gender, Religion and Politics in India).* New Delhi, OUP.

McKim, Marriott, 1955, Village India: Studies in the little community. *American Anthropologist,* Vol. 57, 71-222. Chicago.

Meillassoux, Claude 1986. The Pregnant male. see Dube, Leela and Eleanor Leacock, (ed). 1986 b, 15-21. *Visibility and Power.* New Delhi, OUP.

Mies, Maria 1980, *Indian Women and Patriarchy.* New Delhi, Concept Publishing.

Mies, Maria 1981. The social origin of the sexual division of labor. *ISS Occasional Papers No.* 55. The Hague, Institute of Social Studies.

Mies, Maria 1986, *Patriarchy and Accumulation on a World Scale.(Women in the International Division of Labour).* New Jersey, Zed Books.

Minor Law Books. see Jolly, J (tr.), 1889, (reprint 1965), Delhi, Motilal Banarsidass.

Misra, K.C.1992, Rāmāyana tradition in Nepal. see Vyas, L.P., 1992: 44-49. *Rāmāyana its Universal Appeal and Global Role.* Kolkata, Ananda Publications.

Moi, Toril, 1999, *What is a Woman and Other Essays?* New York, OUP.

Mollā Rāmāyana. see Tharu, S and Lalitha,K. 1991. *Women's Writings in India.* New York. Feminist Press.

Monier- Williams, M.1956, *A Sanskrit -English Dictionary,* First published 1899, Oxford, Clarendon Press.

Mookerjee, A. 1988, *Kāli the Feminine Force.* London, Thames and Hudson.

Moti Chandra,1973, *World of Courtesans.* New Delhi, Vikas.

Mukund, Kanaklatha 1999, Turmeric land: Women's property rights in Tamil society since early mediaeval times, see Roy, Kumkum, 1999, 123—140. *Women in Early Indian Societies.* New Delhi, Manohar.

Murdock, G.P. and C. Provost, 1973, Subsistence economy and supportive practices: Cross cultural codes. *Ethnology,* Vol. 60, 302-30.

Nārada Smrti. (tr). See Jolly, J. 1889, *The Minor Law Books,* pt. l. Narada, Brhaspati. Sacred Books of the East Series. (reprint 1965) Delhi. Motilal Banarasidass.

Narang, Bhim Sain, 1990, *Concept of Stridhana in Ancient India.* Delhi, Parimal Publications.

O'Brien, Mary, 1981, *Politics of Reproduction.* Boston. Routledge and Kegan Paul.

Ortncr, Sherry, B. 1986, Gender and sexuality in hierarchical societies, see Ortner, Sherry, B. 1986: 359-409. *Sexual Meanings-Cultural Construction of Gender and Sexuality.* Cambridge, CUP.

Ortner, Sherry, B and Harriet, Whitehead, 1986, *SexualMeanings—. Cultural Constructions of Gender and Sexuality.* Cambridge, CUP.

Otis, Leah L 1987, *Prostitution in Mediaeval society: History of an Urban Institution in Langue doe.* Chicago, University of Chicago.

Padma Purāṇa, Uttara khaṇḍa. (tr.) Deshpande, N.A. Ancient Indian Tradition and Mythology Series. Vols. 45-48. Delhi. Motilal Banarasidass.

Patton, Laurie L 2002, *Jewels of Authority: Women and Textual Tradition in Hindu India.* New Delhi, OUP.

Paumacariyam, Jain Rāmāyana, tr by Shantilal Nagar, 2002, Delhi, B.R. Publishing House.

Pollock, S,1991,(tr) *The Rāmāyana of Valmiki,* vols. I, II, III, Princeton, Princeton University Press. (reprint, 2007, Delhi, Motilal Banarasidass).

Pou, S, 1977, Le traits Bouddhique, Etudes Sur le *Ramakerti. BEFEO.* Vol.. Ill : 51-96.

Raghavan,V. 1973, *The Great Rāmāyanas,* Varanasi.

Raghavan, V. 1980, ed. *Rāmāyana Tradition in Asia.* New Delhi, Sahitya Akademy.

Raghuvamśa of Kalidasa, see *Kalidasa Granthavali* (tr. Hindi).

Rama Raju, D 1993, Versions of *Rāmāyana:* Stories in Telugu folk literature, see Singh, K.S.1993: 79-99. *Rāmakathā in Tribal and Folk Tradition in India.* Calcutta, Seagull Books.

Rāmacarita Mānas, (The Holy Lake of the Acts of Rama) by Goswami Tulsidas, ed and tr by Prasad, R.C. 1990, Delhi, Motilal Banarasidass.

Ramaswami, Vijaya 1999, Aspects of women and work in early South India, see Roy, Kumkum 1999, 150-174. *Women in Early Indian Societies.* New Delhi, Manohar.

Ramkien (see) Schwizgut. P., 1951. *Etudes sur la literature Siamese.* Paris.

Ranade, E 1975, Indian womanhood through the ages, *Vivekananda Kendra Patrika.* Vol. 4 (2). Madras.

Rangachari, Devika 2009, *Invisible women Visible Histories (Gender Society and Polity in North India, 7th to 12th century A.D.).* New Delhi, Manohar.

Ranganathananda (Sw.), 1992, *The Indian Vision of God as Mother.* Calcutta, Advaita Ashrama.

Ranganatha Rāmāyana of Gonabuddha Reddy. (tr. from) Telugu to Hindi by Bhimsen 'Nirmal'. 1978-79, Lucknow, Bhuvan Vani Trust, Bihar Rashtra Bhasha Parisad.

Rao, V. N. 1991, Rāmāyana of their own: Women's oral tradition in Telugu, see Richman, Paula, 1991: 114-136. *Many Rāmāyanas -the Diversity of a Narrative Tradition in South Asia.* Delhi, OUP.

Rao, V. N. 2000, Politics of Telugu Rāmāyana, see Richman, Paula 2000 : 1 59. *Questioning Rāmāyana; a South Asian tradition.* Delhi, OUP.

Rice, E.P. 1921. *Kanarese Literature.* Calcutta. Association Press.

Richman, Paula, 1991 a. *Many Rāmāyanas : The Diversity of a Narrative Tradition in South Asia.* Delhi OUP.

Richman, Paula, 1991, A *Rāmāyana* of their own. see Richman, Paula 1991 a : 119-121. *Many Rāmāyanas: The Diversity of a Narrative Tradition in South Asia.* Delhi, OUP.

Richman, Paula, 1991, Many *Rāmāyanas* : The Diversity of Rāmāyana Tradition. See. Richman, Paula, 1991 a, 3-21. *Many Rāmāyanas: Diversity of a Narrative Tradition in South Asia.* Delhi, OUP.

Richman, Paula, 2000, (ed.). *Questioning Rāmāyanas - A South Asian Tradition* Delhi, OUP.

Ṛgvedic Brāhmaṇas, (tr.) by Keith, A.B. 1920, Cambridge, Harvard University Press.

Ṛgvedic Saṁhitā, (tr.) by Wilson, II.II, 1851. London, (revised edition Raviprakash Arya and Joshi K.L. 1997. Delhi,Parimal Publications).

Rosalo, M.Z. and Lamphere, L 1974,(ed.) *Women's Role in Economic Development.* California, Stanford University Press.

Roy, Kumkum, 1994 a. *Emergence of monarchy in North India as reflected in the Brahmanical traditions, c. 8th to 4th century B.C.* New Delhi, OUP.

Roy, Kumkum, 1994 b. Defining the household: Some aspects of prescription and practice in early *India Social Scientists.* Vol, XX : 3-18.

Roy, Kurnkum 1999 a (ed.) *Women in Early Indian Societies.* New Delhi, Manohar.

Roy, Kumkum, 1999 b, King's household - structure and space in the Sastric traditions, see Sangari, Kumkum and Uma Chakravarty, 1999,18-37. *From Myths to Markets: Essays on Gender.* Shimla, IIAS.

Sanday, Peggy Reeves 1981, *Female Power and Male Dominance; On the Origin of Sexual Equality.* Cambridge, OUP.

Sangari, Kumkum, 1993 a, Consent, agency and rhetoric of incitement, see. *Economic and Political Weekly.* Vol..28(18): 867-82.

Sangari, Kumkum and Uma Chakravarty, 1999 a. (eds.) *From Myths to Markets: Essays on Gender.* Shimla, IIAS,New Delhi, Manohar Publishers.

Sangari, Kumkum, 1999 b, *Politics of the Possible: Essays on Gender- History, Narratives of Colonial English.* New Delhi, Tulika.

Sangari, Kumkum and Uma Chakravarty 1999 b. Desperate women: Transitory contexts, persistent structures. see Kumkum Sangari and Uma Chakravarty,1999 a. Intro. : xii-xxiii. *From Myths to Market: Essays on Gender.* Shimla, IIAS.

Sankalia, H.D 1982, *Rāmāyana in Historical Perspective.* Delhi, Macmillan.

Sānkhyāyana Śrautasūtra,(tr.)Caland,W. (revised tr. and ed.)Lokesh Chandra 1953, Delhi, Motilal Banarasidass.

Saraswathi, Venugopal. 1993, Rāmāyana episodes in South Indian folk literature, (see) Singh, K.S. 1993 : 100-109, *Rāmkathā in Tribal and Folk Tradition in India.* Calcutta, Seagull Books.

Sarma, C.R. and Raghavan,V. 1980, Rāmāyana in Telugu literature, see Raghavan, V. 1980, *Rāmāyana tradition in Asia.* New Delhi, Sahitya Akademy.

Śatapatha Brāhmaṇa, Eggling, J. (tr.),1882, pt.I. Bks. 1 and 2, *SBE,* V vols., Oxford, Clarendon Press. (reprint 1963) Delhi, Motilal Banarasidass.

Śatapatha Brāhmaṇa, Weber, A. tr. 1964, Varanasi, Chaukhamba.

Satyavrata, 2005, Rama story in *the Bhāgavat Purāṇa.* see *Vishveshvarananda Indological Journal,* v. 43. Pts. I, II, 226-231.

Schwizgut,P.1951. *Etudes sur la Literature Siamese.* Paris.

Sen, Dinesh C.1920, *Bengali Rāmāyanas.* Calcutta, Calcutta University. (Reprint 1987, Delhi, Amar Prakashan).

Sen, Dinesh,1911. *History of Bengali Language and Literature.* Calcutta. Calcutta University.

Sen, Nabaneeta Dev 2000, *Chandrāwatī Rāmāyana* -ferninizing the Rama tale see Bose, Mandakranta, 2000,183-191. *Faces of the Feminine in Ancient, Mediaeval and Modern India.* New Delhi, OUP.

Shah, K.K 2001, *Problems of Identity: Women in Early Indian Inscriptions.* Delhi, OUP.

Shah, Shalini, 1995, *Making of Womanhood - Gender Relations in the Mahabharata.* New Delhi, Manohar.

Shahid, Ayesha, 2010, *Silent Voices; Untold Stories.* Karachi, OUP.

Sharma, R.S. 1983, *Perspectives in Social and Economic History of Early India.* New Delhi, Munshiram Manoharlal.

Sharma, U.M., 1980, *Women, Work and Property in North West India.* London, Tavistock Press.

Shastri, Shakuntala,Rao, 1953, *Women in the Sacred Laws.* Bombay, Bharatiya Vidya Bhavan.

Shulman, David, 2000, Bhavabhuti on cruelty and compassion, see Richman, Paula, ed. 2000, 49-82. *Questioning Rāmāyanas,* Delhi, OUP.

Singh, Bhagavati Prasad, 1980, *Bhuṣuṇdī Rāmāyana* and its influence on the mediaeval *Rāmāyana* literature, see Raghavan,V.

ed. 1980, 475-504. *Rāmāyana Tradition in Asia.* New Delhi, Sahitya Akademy.

Singh, K.S., and Dutta, B.N. 1993 a.(ed.). *Rāmakathā in Tribal and Folk Tradition in India:* Proceedings of a Seminar, Anthropological Survey of India. Calcutta, Seagull Books.

Singh, K.S. 1993 b, Tribal version of the *Rāmakathā,* see Singh, K.S. and Dutta, B.N. ed. 1993, a. 49— *66. Rāmakathā in Tribal and Folk Tradition in India.* Calcutta, Seagull Books.

Singh, Pankaj and Jaidev, 1999, Descanting a patriarchal myth: Bhisam Sahani's Madhavi, see Sangari, Kumkum and Uma Chakravarty, 1999, 3-5. *From Myths to Markets: Essays on Gender.* Shimla, IIAS.

Singh, Vidya Bhusan, 1991, Study of *Rāmāyana;* its significance in Indian folk literature, (see) Krishnamoorthy, K.(ed). 1991 : pp. XXXIII-LXIII. *Critical Survey of the Rāmāyana Studies in the World.* Vol.1. Delhi, Sahitya Akademy.

Sircar, D.C. 1953-54. *Epigraphic India,* No. 30: 287.

Sisurang Poolthupya, 1992, Character of Rama in Thai *Rāmāyana.* see, Vyas, L.P. ed. 1992: 26-30. *Rāmāyana, its Universal Appeal and Global Role.* Kolkata, Ananda Publications.

Sitanatharaman, 2009, *Women in India: A social and cultural history.* Vol. 1, California, ABC CLIO.

Sitaramiah, V, 1980, *Rāmāyana* tradition in Kannada, see Raghavan, V. ed., 1980: 184. *The Rāmāyana Tradition in Asia.* New Delhi, Sahitya Akademy.

Skanda Purāṇa (tr. and annotated), Tagare,G.V. Ancient Indian Tradition and Mythology Series.49-58.

Srinivasa, M.N.1966, *Social Changes in Modern India.* Barkley, University of California Press.

Srinivasan, K.S. 1993, Rama tradition in South East Asia, see Krishnamoorthy, K. ed. 1993: 55-59. *Critical inventory of Rāmāyana studies in the world.* Vol. 2. New Delhi, Sahitya Akademy.

Srinivasan, K.S. 1994, *Rāmāyana as Told by Valmiki and Kamban.* New Delhi, Abhinav Publications.

Stutterheim, Williem 1989, *Rama Legend and Rama Reliefs in Indonesia.* New Delhi, Abhinav Publications.

Subbarayachar, U. K. 1967, 50. *Rāmāyana Theme in Kannada Literature.* Thirupati, Rāmāyana Samhita.

Sukthankar,B.M.1941 : 422-88. *The Rama Episode (Rāmopakhyāna) and the Rāmāyana,* Poona, *Kane Commemorative Volume.*

Sundararajan, K.V. 1981, *Cave temples of the Deccan.* Archaeological Survey of India.

Taittirīya Āraṇyaka, Upaniṣada of Kṛṣṇa Yajurveda (tr) Sastry, A.M. 2004, Delhi, Bharatiya Kala Prakashan.(see Bulcke, C. 1962 :13).

Taittrīya Brāhmaṇa of Kṛṣṇa Yajurveda. With the commentary of Sayana (ed.)Mitra,R.L. 3 vols.1859-1870.

Taittrīya Saṁhitā,Keith, A.B.(tr.}, 1914, 2 vols. Cambridge: Harvard University Press.

Taittrīya Saṁhitā,. Dharmadhikari,T. N.(ed.), 1981, 2 vols. Poona, Vaidik Samsodhan Mandala.

Thapar, Romila 2000, *Cultural Past.* New Delhi, OUP.

Tharu, Susie and K. Lalita, (ed.), 1991, *Women Writings in India: 600 B.C to the Present.* New York, Feminist Press. (reprint 1995, Delhi OUP)

Telugu Rāmāyana of Budhraj, (see) Richman, Paula 1991 : *The Many Rāmāyanas : Diversity of a Narrative Tradition in South Asia,* Delhi, OUP.

Thomas, F.W. 1929, *Rāmāyana* story in Tibetan from Chinese Turkistan. *Indian Studies; Lanman Commemorative Volume,* 1929, 193-212.

Thomas,Laquer,1990. Making Sex, Body and Gender from the Greeks to Freud. Cambridge.Mass,Harvard University Press.

Torwe Rāmāyana. (see) Rice, E. P. 1921. *Kanarese Literature*. Calcutta ; (see Bulcke, C. 1962 : 377.)

Tripathi, L.K.1988, (ed), *Position and Status of Women in Ancient India*. Varanasi, Benaras Hindu University.

Tripathi, Ram Nath, 1963, *Krttivasi Bangla Rāmāyana aur Rāmacarita Manas*. Aligarh, Bharat Prakashan Mandir.

Tulsidas, *Rāmacarita Mānas,* Prasad, R.C.(ed.), 1990. 2nd ed. Delhi, Motilal Banarasidass.

Tulsidas, *Rāmacarita Mānas,* Hanuman Prasad Poddar,(ed.), 2016 (Smvt), Gorakhpur, Geeta Press.

Udāra Rāghava, Quoted by Bulcke, C.1962 : 196.

Upadhyaya, K.D. 1993, Story of Rama in the folk tradition of Hindi region, see Singh, K.S. 1993: 67-78. *Rāmakathā in Tribal and Folk Tradition in India*. Calcutta, Seagull Books.

Uttararāmacarita of Bhavabhuti, see, Belvalkar, S.K.1915.

Vaidya, C.V. 1906, *Riddle of the Rāmāyana*. Delhi, Oriental Publishers.

Vaidya, C.V. 1966, *The Mahābhārata: A Criticism*. Delhi, Meherchand Lachmandas.

Valmiki Rāmāyana, 1969, Hari Prasad Sastri (English tr.) 2 vols. London.

Valmiki Rāmāyana, 1969-92, (English text and tr.) Pt L *Bāla, Ayodhyā Kāṇḍas;* Pt. II *Araṇya, Kiṣkindhā* and *Sundar Kāṇḍas;* Pt. III *Yuddha* and *Uttara Kandas*. 4th ed. 1995. Gorakhpur, Geeta Press.

*Valmiki Rāmāyana,*1981-82. Raghunathan, N (tr.) 3 vols. Madras, Vighneswara Publishing.

Valmiki Rāmāyana, North Western Recension, 1923, Dayananda Mahavidyalaya Edition, Lahore.

Varma, D. 1937, Evolution of the myth of Ahalya Maitreyi, see, *G.N. Jha Commemorative Volume. 427*- 33. Poona.

Vāyu Purāṇa,(tr. and annotated) Tagare,G.V. Ancient Indian Tradition and Mythology Series, 37, 38. (see. Bulcke, C. 1962 :295)

Vāsudevahaṇḍi, Sanghadasa, II, Bhavnagar, Jain Atmananda Sabha. (see, Bulcke, 1962 : para. 253 and p. 294.)

Vatsyayana, *Kamasutra.* (ed. and Hindi tr.) Sastri, Devdatta,1964, Varanasi.

Vicitra Rāmāyana (Odisi) of Visvanath Khuntiya (tr.) Yogeswar Tripathi, 'Yogi', 1986-87. Bhuvan Vani Trust, Lucknow.

Vishnoi, Savita 1987, *Economic Status of Women in Ancient India.* Meerut, Kusumanjali Prakashan.

Viṣṇu Dharmasūtra; Julius Jolly tr. *Institute of Vishnu.* Sacred Book of the East. Max Muller (ed.), Vol. III. Delhi, Motilal Banarsidass.

Viplu Purāṇa, (see.) Wilson, H.H. 2007. *Visnu Purāṇa : A System of Hindu Mythology and Tradition,* Ganesh Publishing. (Synopsis, *European Discovery of India,* Vol. V. 2007 :390)

Vivekananda, Sw.1948, Women as chattel in the *Rāmāyana. Poona Orientalists,* Vol. XIII, 3-4.

Vivekananda, Sw. 1949, Treatment of abducted women *in Rāmāyana* age. *Poona Orientalists,* Vol. XIV: 85-88.

Vivekananda, Sw.1950, Ascetic attitude towards women in *Rāmāyana. Poona Orientalists,* Vol. XV- XVI : 77- 85.

Vivekananda, Sw. 1956-57, Widows in the Rāmāyana. *Journal of the Oriental Institute,* Vol. VI : 2-3.

Vyas, L.P.(ed.), 1992, *Rāmāyana its Universal Appeal and Global Role.* Calcutta, Ananda Publications.

Vyas, M. N. 1993, Tribal view of the *Rāmāyana* : An exercise in the anthropology of knowledge, see Singh, K.S. 1993: 10ff.. *Rāmakathā in Tribal and Folk Tradition in India.* Calcutta: Seagull Books.

Vyas, S.N, 1967, *India in the Rāmāyana Age: a Study of the Social and Cultural Conditions in Ancient India as Described in Valmiki's Rāmāyana.* Delhi, Atma Ram and Sons.

Waardenburg, Jacques 1973, *Classical Approaches to the Study of Religion.* Paris, Mouton.

Wadia, A.R. 1977, *Ethics of Feminism (a study of the revolt of women).* New Delhi, Asian Publications Services.

Wadley, Susan 1988, Women and the Hindu tradition, see, Ghadially, Rehana (ed.), 1988: 23-44 *Women in Indian Society.* Delhi, Sage Publications.

Walthall, Anne 2000, *Servants of the Dynasty (Palace Women in World History).* Berkley, University of California Press.

Wangu, Madhu Bajaj, 2003. *Images of Indian Goddesses; Myths. Meanings and Models.* 99-103, Delhi, Abhinav Publications.

Wantanebe, K 1907. The oldest record of the *Rāmāyana* in a Chinese Buddhist writing. *JRAS,* 1907: 99-103. London.

Weber, A.1870 : 1-70. *Ueber des Rāmāyana.* Abhandlungen der Koenigl Akademie der Wissensen zu Berlin (English tr. by Boyd, D.C. 1973. Bombay).

Weber, Max 1921, *Hinduismus und Buddhismus, Gerammeite Aufsatze zur Religions Sociologie.* Vol.2, 9-15. Tubingen.

Whaling, F. 1980, *Rise of the Religious Significance of Rama.* New Delhi, Motilal Banarasidass.

Whaling, Frank 1983, *Contemporary Approaches to the Study of Religion.* 2 vols. New York, Mouton.

Whitehead, George, 1930, *Unfair Sex (Truth about Women).* London, Herbert Jenkins.

Whitney, W.D. 1905. *Atharvaveda Saṁhitā.* Harvard Oriental Series, VII, VIII. Cambridge Mass.

Wilson, H.H.1854. *Ṛgveda Saṁhitā* London. Trubner.

Winternitz, M. 1927, *History of Indian literature.(tr.* from German). 2 Vols., Calcutta, University of Calcutta (reprinted by Motilal Banarasidass, 1985-88).

Wurm, Alois, 1976, *Character portrayals in the Rāmāyana of Valmiki: Systematic Representation.* Delhi, Ajanta Publications.

Yajñavalkya Smriti, (tr.) Gharpure, J.R. 1937-38. Collection of Hindu Law Texts. 2 vols.

Young, F.W. and Bacadayan, A.A., 1965, Menstrual taboos and social rigidity. *Ethnology* Issue, Vol. 4. 92.

Yousuf, Ghulam Sarwar, 1992, Sita *devi* in Malay *Wayang Kulit Siam,* see Vyas, L.P.(ed.), 1992, 31-40. *Rāmāyana its Universal Appeal and Global Role.* Calcutta, Anand Publications.

Zaheer, M. 1981, *Temples ofBhitargaon,* fig. 74, 75. Delhi. Agam Kala Prakasan.

Zieseniss, A. 1928, *Die Rama Saga bei den Malaien Ihre.* Hamburg.

Index